Reshaping France

Reshaping France

Town, country and region during the French Revolution

edited by

Alan Forrest

Professor of Modern History, University of York

and

Peter Jones

Reader in French History, University of Birmingham

Manchester University Press

Manchester and New York

Distributed exclusively in the USA and Canada by St. Martin's Press

Published by Manchester University Press
Oxford Road, Manchester M13 9PL, UK
and Room 400, 175 Fifth Avenue,
New York, NY 10010, USA

Distributed exclusively in the USA and Canada
by St. Martin's Press, Inc.,
175 Fifth Avenue, New York, NY 10010, USA

British Library cataloguing in publication data
Reshaping France: town, country and region during the
    French Revolution.
    1. Social change. Influence of French Revolution, 1789–
    1799
    I. Forrest, Alan II. Jones, Peter *1948–*
    303.48

Library of Congress cataloging in publication data
Reshaping France : town, country, and region during the French
    Revolution / edited by Alan Forrest and Peter Jones.
        p. cm.
        "The present volume is the product of a conference held in
    Manchester in March of 1989 to mark the bicentenary of the French
    Revolution" — Introd.
        Includes index.
        ISBN 0–7190–2995–3
        1. France — Politics and government — Revolution, 1789–1799–
    Congresses.   2. France — Social conditions — 18th century–
    –Congresses.   3. France — Economic conditions — 18th century–
    –Congresses.   I. Forrest. Alan I.   II. Jones, Peter. 1949–
    DC148,R47   1991
    944.04 — dc20   90–19674

ISBN 0 7190 2995 3 *hardback*

Photoset in Linotron Janson
by Northern Phototypesetting Company Limited
Printed in Great Britain
by Bell & Bain Limited, Glasgow

Contents

Acknowledgements

As editors of a volume which grew out of a series of conference papers, we should like to acknowledge the help of those who made that conference possible. In particular, we are indebted to the two bodies under whose patronage our discussions were held – the Society for the Study of French History and the Eugene Vinaver Memorial Fund – whose enthusiasm guaranteed the success of the entire enterprise. The French government, through its Conseiller Culturel in London, Philippe Guillemin, was generous in its support, and contributions towards the cost of bringing speakers to Manchester were made by the British Academy, the British Council and the Research Support Fund of the University of Manchester. We should also like to thank those who offered help with the organisation of the conference, most especially Joe Bergin, Malcolm Crook and Marianne Elliott; the Centre Départemental de Documentation Pédagogique of the Hautes-Pyrénées, in Tarbes, who gave permission for the use of the cover illustration; and Sarah Blowen, who translated those chapters which were originally submitted in French.

A.I.F.
P.M.J.

ALAN FORREST *and* PETER JONES

Introduction

The present volume is the product of a conference held in Manchester in March 1989 to mark the Bicentenary of the French Revolution. In a year that has seen a plethora of discussion and commemoration such a statement will cause little surprise; but it should not act as a deterrent to the potential reader. For the Manchester conference, organised round the precise theme of 'The French Revolution: Town, Country and Region', proved unusually cohesive, focusing on the interrelationships between town and country, nation and province during the period of administrative and political restructuring that was the French Revolution. Besides many of the leading English specialists in the field, the occasion attracted scholars from France and from many parts of the English-speaking world, from Ireland, Canada, the United States and Australia. Three distinct generations of researchers took part, and they brought to the subject a range of interests, disciplines and expertise of corresponding breadth. Their papers, revised in the light of the often animated discussion, form the subject-matter of the present book.

The emphasis which this volume places on the social history of the Revolution may seen rather perverse, and more than a little unfashionable, in a decade where Revolutionary research has come increasingly to be dominated by political and ideological pre-occupations. Yet in the pursuit of intellectual and philosophical explanation there is perhaps a danger that the local context becomes obscured. Montesquieu and Rousseau played only a very limited part in the Revolution as it was experienced in Châteauneuf-du-Pape or Jouy-en-Josas. And, in any case, the chapters presented here do not fall easily into the category of conventional social history. The intellectual pivot of 'town, country and region' is a broad one, which covers questions of institutional reform and local politics as much as the social issues of class and hierarchy. It is central to the ways in which historians have looked at the history of the French provinces during the Revolutionary years, years when local communities were forced to redefine their identities in the face of creeping centralism and the rhetoric of the nation. Indeed, it may be said to form an essential part of the cultural history of Revolutionary France and offers a panoramic approach to contemporary perceptions and mentalities. In this sense, the theme of 'town country and region' may be felt to capture, in a pleasingly spatial way, the range of research currently in progress. The very format of the conference encouraged diversity of interpretation, and it has enabled the editors to publish a volume in which the contributors address a common set of themes, but do so from widely differing angles of vision.

'La question ville-campagne' has, of course, a long and honourable pedigree in the historiography of the French Revolution. It has been invoked by historians since the time of Michelet, principally as a tool to aid in the decoding of counter-revolution. In our own century it was reintroduced into historical analysis by such historians as Paul Bois and Marcel Reinhard in France, Alfred Cobban in England and Charles Tilly in the United States, and it has since become subsumed into general histories of the French Revolution. But, however subtly the relationship between town and country is analysed, it is nearly always expressed in confrontational terms – as the conflicts of interest between townsmen and country dwellers, between consumers and producers of food, or as the reaction of the countryside to the intrusion of urban values into a traditional and partly autarchic world. Tilly, in particular, sees the root of conflict in structural economic change. To understand rural counter-revolution in the West, he invokes the 'general conceptions of urbanization and of its relationship to community organisation', arguing that these are major indicators of political behaviour in the strife-torn region of southern Anjou. For 'the most urbanised sectors of the West gave the most uniform support to the Revolution. The intensest conflicts arose at the junctions of rural and urban life. And, most concretely, the struggle of city and country informed the whole development of the counter-revolution.'[1]

Where Tilly offers a sociological model to explain rural counter-revolution, Cobban goes further. In his influential but often infuriating *Social Interpretation of the French Revolution*, he broadened the applicability of the town-country hypothesis, positing it as one of the principal motor forces of the Revolution itself. Cobban's aim, of course, was to counter the current Marxist hegemony in French Revolutionary studies, to negate the claim of Georges Lefebvre, Albert Soboul and others that (in Soboul's words) 'the Revolution is explained in the last analysis by a contradiction between the relations of production and the character of the productive forces'.[2] That this interpretive hegemony has now been shattered is, at least in part, a reflection of the power of Cobban's onslaught. But what did he suggest to put in its place? It is a valid criticism of Cobban that his positive contribution to a 'social interpretation' seems rather thin, and that a large slice of it is based, precisely, upon the issue of town-country relations. Peasants and townsmen, both in the last years of the *ancien régime* and during the Revolution itself, are shown to be in almost perpetual conflict. 'In the years before 1789', he writes, 'the antagonism of the villagers for the towns, the refuge of "the cowards and the idle", home of the "capitalists" and their servants, was coming out into the open.'[3] According to this formulation, the *cahiers de doléances*, the *bailliage* elections and the Great Fear become symptoms of the town-country conflict; and likewise the religious schism, counter-revolution and the enforcement of the Maximum. In broadening the applicability of the model he, too, placed primary emphasis on the opposition, even the necessary opposition, between town and country. At times his use of the concept becomes so mechanistic that he risks preaching a rival form of social determinism.

But do the relations between townsmen and country dwellers have to be viewed in this deterministic way? Georges Lefebvre himself saw the grievances of the lower classes of society – whether the poor of the towns or those of the villages – being directed against a common enemy in the later eighteenth century: the inexorable expansion of the market economy, of trade and capitalism. Such groups were not of necessity condemned to a posture of mutual antagonism. More recent work has added new dimensions to the study of town and country. In his sensitive essays about the relationships between Parisians and the villagers of the Ile-de-France, Richard Cobb underlines the complexity of town-country contacts within the catchment of France's most demanding and intrusive urban community. The Revolution, he rightly notes, made for greater ambiguity and, hence, greater scope for dispute, and this was not confined to matters of provisioning. 'Was it right for the sections on the edge of the city to interfere in the internal affairs of the villagers almost within sight of the gates?', he asks. 'Were the villagers to be their own masters in such important matters as the decision to keep their churches open and to allow the celebration of the old feast days? Was the local *garde nationale* the sole repository of armed force, or could Parisian soldiers be sent in to impose the will of the city?'[4] In one sense Paris was unique: it was not only a city and a market but also the centre of a highly centralised government machine. In another sense, however, it symbolised the relationship between the Revolution's *cadres* – almost always to be found in urban centres – and the people whom they sought to administer. Disputes between townsmen and countrymen could often conceal other conflicts: between the law and the citizen, the government and the governed.

Recent research on French provincial history has emphasised the huge variety of local conflicts which often dominated political life at departmental and district level. Long-running quarrels can seem ubiquitous – between town and town, village and village, over market zones and grazing rights, traditional privileges and long-nourished slights. Among others, Alison Patrick has discussed the workings of local government in departments far removed from Paris; D. M. G. Sutherland has examined the differences of interest between those peasants who owned some land and those who rented from landlords; and Ted Margadant has analysed what he terms the 'rhetoric of contention' between towns eager to profit from the redistribution of administrative dignities.[5] Disputes between town and country are part of a much wider pattern of social relationships. Contemporaries were keenly aware of this, and the eighteenth-century *maréchaussée* knew better than any modern-day historian just where tensions were likely to reach flashpoint. Yet such considerations tend to be overlooked in the more general histories of the French Revolution: except in the single case of the Vendée they rarely earn more than a desultory footnote. It is this imbalance which the present volume sets out to redress. It seeks to re-examine the difficult and often shifting relationships between town, country and region in Revolutionary France. In the process, it is hoped that it will update the rather mechanical approach so reminiscent of the 1960s and draw attention to the complementarities as well as the polarities which informed that relationship.

The chapters presented here deal with very different aspects of the topic under discussion. They examine such diffuse questions as the state of the economy, popular perceptions, tradition and folk memory. It is not the intention of the contributors, any more than it was the intention of the original conference, to rewrite Alfred Cobban or to offer some new 'social interpretation' of the French Revolution. Any such claim would be wholly pretentious and would lie beyond the brief which we gave ourselves. The aim of the book is at once more diffuse and more modest. By examining the diversity of France's urban, rural and regional history during the Revolutionary period, it seeks to place local aspirations within their geographical as well as their social context, and to help explain the psychology of Revolutionary politics at a local and regional level. It is intended as a contribution to our understanding of the spatial dimension of the Revolutionary process.

Certain themes recur under different guises. One is the insistence of the Revolutionaries on the primacy of the nation, which was fraught with implications for traditional local sensibilities. As Norman Hampson demonstrates, the classic concept of the 'nation' emerged only gradually, evolving from the provincialism of the last years of the monarchy to the exclusive and intolerant republicanism of 1793. Local and regional loyalties came to be condemned as unpatriotic or even counter-revolutionary; town and country, like province and parish, were all subsumed into the nation, and it was expected that the loyalties of all Frenchmen would be fused in the process. As Jean-Paul Bertaud shows, it was this new concept of the nation that was taught to the volunteers of 1792, not merely by incorporation in the armies, but by parents, local authorities, political clubs and constitutional priests as well. The result was 'an army expressing solidarity with the nation' which 'was ready to assume its rights and its independence'. The idea of the nation had, of course, a highly propagandist value in motivating the young soldiers. In Bertaud's words, it was 'more than the simple sum total of all the citizens; it was a superior entity which was henceforth sovereign in the land'.

Various of the domestic reforms of the Revolution also helped to forge the nation through the creation of a national civic order. The significance of elections and the frequent recourse to this form of consultation in the early years of the Revolution are discussed by Malcolm Crook. The administrative reforms of 1790, involving the unpicking of the old territorial institutions and the reshaping of France according to a new administrative logic, are analysed by Isser Woloch. And Ceri Crossley, through the intermediary of Michelet, reminds us of the value of the *fédérations* in building bridges between town and country. Yet there were limits to the power and influence of the nation. Paul Butel shows how very differently trade and industry responded in different parts of the country: in fact it is difficult to talk of a national urban economy. In cities like Bordeaux a very clear consciousness of the city's identity, even of its apartness from the nation, was still evident. And very soon the old polarities re-emerged. The history of the Revolutionary Vaucluse, as Jonathan Skinner notes, was dominated by a recurring conflict between Avignon and Carpentras which plunged the former Comtat into virtual civil war. Even elections and administrative renewal could be two-edged weapons, reminding local people of their grievances and jealousies in spite of the ubiquitous rhetoric of common purpose.

National unity, in other words, could be wafer-thin, concealing a host of hatreds and disagreements. Repeated invocation of the French nation and the indivisibility of the Republic could not rid France of the images and mentalities of previous centuries, a point graphically brought out in iconography and literature. In this regard Michel Vovelle's chapter on the representation of the countryside in the iconography of the period is especially illuminating. He is concerned not with the depiction of peasants by country people – for there is practically no iconography of rural origin – but rather with the ways in which the urban bourgeoisie reinterpreted the countryside as a function of its own political and social priorities. Where the peasant does appear, he is presented, says Vovelle, as 'a partner, sometimes cajoled, sometimes feared, but always distant'. But at various key moments of the peasant Revolution – most notably during the Great Fear of the summer of 1789 – he is almost completely absent. Similarly, in the Year II and after the fall of Robespierre, the peasant vanishes from the pictorial record – a fact which demonstrates his lack of usefulness for this exercise in urban pedagogy. Verbal images, of course, could be equally distorting, as Colin Lucas demonstrates in his eloquent presentation of the language used to discuss the urban violence in Paris during 1789. Like the countryside, the popular districts of the capital could seem something of a foreign country when viewed by the bourgeoisie. Even at the outset it is clear that contemporaries were keenly aware of town-country dichotomies, and their awareness would soon be translated into distinct town and country discourses on the French Revolution, by Michelet in particular. He talked of the all-embracing nation of the 1790s, at once urban and rural. Both had an important part to play: 'Revolutionary energy', in Ceri Crossley's words, 'circulated through the body of France, urban and rural, but that energy was above all relayed and transformed by Paris'. It is a memorable image, but the image of an highly idealised Revolution. Patriotism notwithstanding, even Michelet was forced to acknowledge a recrudescence of the town-country polarity as events proceeded and the early innocence was lost.

In part this polarity may reflect basic economic realities. But the question must then be asked: were urban and rural economies at the end of the eighteenth century independent or interdependent? Is the image of conflict conveyed by historians like Cobban, Bois and Tilly sufficiently well rooted to provide a general explanation of the Revolutionary process? Or should we look to the example of the Pays de Caux, as described recently by Guy Lemarchand, where cottage industry played a highly integrative role and town and country blurred into a single monetarised and commercialised economy?[6] Regional contrasts between, say, Normandy and the Massif Central, might seem sufficiently great to make any generalisation on a national scale well-nigh impossible. In their chapter T. J. A. Le Goff and D. M. G. Sutherland focus with exceptional clarity the consequences of the Revolution for the rural economy. The argument is fairly pessimistic, concluding that only viticulture showed any signs of dynamism in an otherwise depressed economy, whereas both grain and animal husbandry slumped badly. Reforms of property rights and the tax structure might have benefited the peasantry, but any advantages gleaned from these changes were sacrificed through the financing of the foreign war and the costs of centralised administration. And, in any case, the authors continue, much depended on the status of the individual, on whether he was a property holder or a tenant. Yet there is little reason to suppose that rural misery was counterbalanced by urban prosperity, or that the decline in urban markets did not have an adverse effect on countrymen's income. In his turn, Paul Butel offers an acute analysis of the economic effects of Revolution – and especially of the Revolutionary Wars – on the urban economy. Decline was especially serious in those areas dependent on the Atlantic economy, but once again it is the interaction between towns and their hinterland that is most striking. The merchant-millers of Montauban and the ropemakers of Tonneins were badly affected by the loss of Santo Domingo, and local credit networks were seriously disrupted by the slump in overseas trade. The Revolution, in short, produced shifts within the economy, both urban and rural, shifts that were aggravated by administrative reforms which, as Isser Woloch shows, often split up market networks and cut off towns from their rural hinterland.

This in turn raises another theme, that of administrative reform and the birth of a civic tradition. The most important measures here all date from the 1789–91 period – like the abolition of provincial immunities as part of the legislation of 4 August 1789 or as a consequence of the division of France into its eighty-three departments. But are such measures to be seen as the extension of urban influence, as a victory for urban penetration of the countryside? The unedifying brawling that took place between rival administrative centres might suggest that it was. But Isser Woloch's chapter is a timely antidote to those who would see the new civic order as a mechanism to concentrate decision-making in the towns. Or at least the definition of such 'towns' would have to be quite extraordinarily elastic, since the municipal reform of 1789 conferred administrative status, elective bodies and a considerable degree of autonomy on the very lowest common denominator, the rural commune. This was in no sense accidental: before the Committee on the Constitution intervened, the Assembly was intent on granting the same form of elective local government to every 'town, bourg, parish, or rural community' in the land. The protection of rural interests, in other words, was deliberate, just as much of the rhetoric that accompanied these reforms was directed against the concentration of power in urban centres. 'From the beginning', says Woloch, 'the revolutionaries in France set out to create uniform administrative mechanisms in the most basic units or cells of their society.'

There were, of course, considerable dangers in such root-and-branch territorial reform. Economic links and judicial networks were sometimes disrupted and rural communities cut off from traditional points of contact. And if small- to medium-sized towns certainly profited from their increased administrative responsibilities – towns like Foix and Digne, Tarbes and Privas, whose prosperity in the nineteenth century would be closely linked to their place in the state administration – large provincial centres like Grenoble and Bordeaux lost much of their regional importance. Besides, many urban centres were weakened by serious population loss during the Revolutionary years, the result of repeated body-blows to their local economy. It is therefore difficult to claim that the cities were the overall winners in the administrative lottery over which the Revolution presided. But what of rural areas? Did territorial reform regenerate the countryside or trigger widespread alienation? Though, again, the local picture could be very mixed, many village communities were satisfied to see justice, administration and tax assessment devolved and made more accessible; and the village mayor was now a *notable* in his own right, even if many of the tasks he was called upon to perform (like requisitioning and conscription) served the interests of the state more than those of his fellow-villagers. Moreover, the new administrative structures helped to forge a civic tradition at grass-roots level which had not existed under the *ancien régime*. This underpinned both the agrarian radicalism analysed by Peter Jones and the village political culture explored by Jonathan Skinner. The potential had already been created for village republicanism in large areas of rural France.

Two of the chapters in this collection offer studies of the anatomy of urban elites, though elites of a very different kind. William Scott's study of a powerful, but unsure, Marseille bourgeoisie invites comparison with the merchant communities of other eighteenth-century port cities, such as Paul Butel's Bordeaux. What Scott succeeds in portraying is the ambivalence of the position of the *ancien régime* merchant, at once an exploiter and the victim of exploitation. He looks at merchant perceptions of their own position and compares them with the perceptions of them held by others; and he suggests that with the coming of the Revolution these perceptions necessarily changed. Attributes which had previously been seen as weaknesses could often be turned to advantage in the new political climate, while many of the perceived strengths of the merchant community gave rise to suspicion and political obloquy. It is a fascinating instance of a social elite forced to justify itself to a society where its values were suddenly under attack. Scott accepts that in a city like Marseille the urban bourgeoisie did form a social class and that they constituted a substantial part of the Revolutionary elite. That they felt insecure and unloved is, he argues, part of their collective psychology. In contrast, the Paris *sans-culottes* were a political elite, and a proudly self-acknowledged one at that. It is their social identity that is in doubt: as Michael Sonenscher explains, their rhetoric and their socio-economic reality were often some distance apart. He shows that the now conventional stereotype of the *sans-culotte*, that beloved of George Rudé, Albert Soboul and others, cannot easily be sustained, since 'it has become increasingly difficult to explain the emergence of the *sans-culottes* in terms of the interaction between artisanal workshops, the market for corn and the membership of Parisian sectional assemblies and popular societies'. Rather, he sees the phenomenon in political terms, seeking their origins in the Paris sectional debates of 1791 and analysing the multiple factors which contributed to their influence.

Channels and patterns of politicisation are another major theme in these chapters, and one that is discussed from a variety of different angles. Malcolm Crook, Hugh Gough, Peter Jones, Michael Sonenscher, Martyn Lyons, Jonathan Skinner and Ceri Crossley are all concerned with the question of political education and with the dispersal and diffusion of information, and their contributions are far too rich to be adequately summarised in a few cursory lines. All are in loose agreement that new ideas emanated primarily from the towns, with their literate elites and their established role in regional administration. Several of the contributors talk of the town as a *relais* of revolutionary energy to the surrounding countryside, of a 'seepage' of political awareness from town to country, or of the 'democratic patronage' of urban activists in the affairs of country dwellers. For it is generally accepted that there was a considerable *décalage*, both in ideas and in political practice, between town and country, with rural militants deriving inspiration and organisation from urban models. Peter Jones, discussing the growth of rural radicalism in the Paris *pourtour*, notes the important part played by deputies-on-mission in bridging these differences and in raising levels of political consciousness. Malcolm Crook suggests that elections, too, can be seen as a channel of politicisation, though it is unclear whether they enlisted the countryside behind the leadership of the town or helped to articulate a growing urban–rural dysfunction. And Hugh Gough points to the forging role of the provincial press in the emergence of Revolutionary consciousness. Significantly, he finds that the incidence of newspapers followed closely upon patterns of urbanisation. Those departments with several papers were all endowed with a strong urban base, with printshops, postal services and an active political infrastructure; in contrast, those which did not have a single newspaper, like the Aude and the Lozère, tended to be sparsely populated, with low levels of urbanisation. Communications were clearly important here, with poor transport links cutting off rural communities from urban influences.

On the other hand, there is little evidence that popular culture acted as an impervious barrier to politicisation, or that *patois* prevented rural Frenchmen from participating in a national Revolutionary consciousness. Whatever the *abbé* Grégoire might have supposed, rural communities were quite capable of gaining access to Revolutionary ideas without a mastery of written French or an understanding of the national language. The villagers in the Vaucluse discussed by Jonathan Skinner were certainly not protected by their patois from taking part in the national political debate, even if their plight during the federalist revolt in the South-east stemmed largely from their reliance on Marseille, rather than on Paris, for inspiration. In a chapter discussing the whole question of linguistic conformity during the Revolution, Martyn Lyons rejects any blanket idea of 'linguistic terrorism' to plead for a more nuanced picture of the republicanism of non-French-speakers. French, he admits, might be essential to the Revolution of the elites, that of political clubs and provincial office-holding; but popular republicanism could be just as powerfully expressed in the spoken tongue, and there is little reason to suspect, as Barère so memorably did, that it was their separate language – be it Breton or Flemish, Basque or Catalan – which made the people of the periphery disaffected from Jacobin centralism. If Jacobinism were to become widely implanted, indeed, it needed to harness popular culture to the Revolutionary cause, and that required a tolerance of cultural pluralism which the Jacobins seldom showed.

In its turn, of course, the experience of the Revolutionary decade would come to shape popular culture as attitudes embraced during the 1790s became entrenched and exacerbated in the political battles of the following century. Jonathan Skinner's chapter shows how the Revolution would form a central part of the political tradition of Comtadin villagers, and his view is supported by others, particularly by Peter Jones. This insight is not without precedent: its origins lie in the work of André Siegfried and Paul Bois. But Skinner adds depth and detail to our understanding of the process of politicisation in the rural South-east, demonstrating that the villagers were, by the 1840s, imbued with a clear political tradition of their own, one that found its images and role models in the Republic of the Year II and whose political geography was still largely that of fifty years before. Peasants in their part of France had become permanently involved in the political process: they were not to be 'manipulated by the politics of the highest urban bidder'. His conclusion is not only of interest for its own sake. It also fills a gap in the interpretation of rural politicisation offered by Maurice Agulhon, who rather implausibly denied the significance of traditions descending from the 1790s. For, as Isser Woloch shows, the Revolution also marked the beginning of a new civic culture in France, one which penetrated the canton, the commune, even the smallest village community. Seen in this light, 1789 can no longer be dismissed as 'a magnificent irrelevance' in explaining the transformation of rural France. Rather, it becomes a touchstone for nineteenth-century politics, in the cities as in the countryside. No matter what regime came after, the political loyalties created during the 1790s would subsist as part of the culture of France. For tradition, too, had been recast during the 1790s. The impression made by this bold experiment in politicisation – by this first 'république au village' – would never be completely eradicated.

Notes

1 C. Tilly, *The Vendée*, London, 1964, p. 340.
2 A. Soboul, *Précis d'histoire de la Révolution Française*, Paris, 1962, quoted in A. Cobban, *The Social Interpretation of the French Revolution*, Cambridge, 1964, p. 8.
3 Cobban, *Social Interpretation*, p. 93.
4 R. C. Cobb, *Paris and its Provinces*, Oxford, 1975, p. 89.
5 A. Patrick, 'French Revolutionary local government, 1789–92', in C. Lucas (ed)., *The Political Culture of the French Revolution*, Oxford, 1988; D. Sutherland, *The Chouans*, Oxford, 1982; T. Margadant, 'The rhetoric of contention: conflicts between towns during the French Revolution', *French Historical Studies*, 16 (1989), pp. 284–308.
6 G. Lemarchand, *La fin du féodalisme dans le Pays de Caux*, Paris, 1989, pp. 276–91.

The idea of the nation in Revolutionary France

Towards the end of the *ancien régime* the word 'nation' existed in people's vocabulary rather than in their consciousness. Parlementaires tended to prefer it to 'kingdom' as a matter of tactics: it was more Roman and it had republican overtones that hinted, without any embarrassing precision, at the existence of political rights that were not derived from a gift of the crown. This did not prevent most Frenchmen, especially those who lived in the *pays d'états*, from thinking of themselves as belonging to a province rather than to some abstraction known as France.

These attitudes were much in evidence in the political crisis that preceded the actual Revolution. The Breton Parlement, preparing itself for Lamoignon's judicial *coup d'état* of 8 May 1788, proclaimed that it could accept only measures that were both voted by the Estates General and endorsed by the Estates of Brittany.[1] Three months later the Rennes bar was a good deal more emphatic:

> Il n'y a aucune loi qui ne devienne particulière à la Bretagne dès qu'on veut l'exécuter dans cette province ... les états-généraux même ne peuvent rien sur l'administration de la Bretagne, parce qu'elle se réunit en corps de nation, parce qu'elle a tous les deux ans ses états-généraux, parce que c'est là, et nulle part ailleurs, c'est dans cette assemblée et dans le parlement qu'elle est représentée et défendue.[2]

A pamphlet attributed to Portalis made the same claim for the 'nation provençale'.[3] Going one better, a 'Toulousain patriot' appealed to the 'droits naturels des municipalités'.[4]

In June 1789 in Artois the *noblesse entrante* – those who had the right to attend the local estates in person – declared that even if the kingdom should decide to adopt a new constitution, the estates of Artois should ensure that their own constitution was not changed. They repeated this more emphatically in April, at the meeting where deputies were elected to the Estates General: 'La province d'Artois, quant à sa constitution, est absolument étrangère et indépendante des états-généraux. C'est à la nation artésienne à prononcer sur ce point.'[5]

Such views were not confined to the nobility. The Rennes proclamation included amongst its signatories Lanjuinais and Le Chapelier, who were soon to be singing a very different tune. The Third Estate of St Malo, threatening to boycott the meeting of the estates of Brittany, said that they would have been tempted to follow 'the new form of representation of the restored estates of Dauphiné' if they had not been deterred by their respect for 'la forme antique' of their own constitution.[6] Robespierre and Mirabeau referred to their 'nations' as Artois and Provence. If Riom, where he was virtually unknown, elected Malouet to the Estates-General by acclamation, this was not out of respect for his qualities as a naval administrator. The Riomois calculated that, as a friend of Necker, he was the man they needed to defend them in their running war with Clermont-Ferrand.[7] Men sometimes talked in abstract categories, but their actions were usually calculated in terms of local interest.

There was, as the Malouins reminded themselves and us, one discordant note in this chorus of provincialism: Dauphiné. Even the Dauphinois claimed that their local privileges could be withdrawn only with their own consent, but they insisted that when they became part of a free nation 'les Cours du Royaume déposeront sans regret le mandat qu'elles ont reçu, pour voir établir un corps vraiment constitutionnel.' A pamphlet attributed to Barnave put forward the view that 'la patrie d'un Français doit être dans toute la France'. When asked by the Béarnais if they were not afraid of losing their right to decide on local taxation, the Dauphinois replied rather patronisingly, 'Ne songeons plus à ce que nous avons été mais à ce que nous voulons être: des Français libres sous un Roi.'[8]

With the meeting of the Estates General the outlook of Dauphiné soon became that of France as a whole and no more was heard of provincial sovereignty – which did not prevent rival towns from engaging in ferocious struggles over the location of *chefs-lieux* when the provinces themselves were sacrificed on the altar of the nation. The summoning of the Estates General, however, opened up a new area of disunity by giving a new importance to the division of French society into orders. There was virtually unanimous agreement, at least amongst the laity, that in the new France sovereignty was derived not from God but from the people. Rousseau had argued that the general will could emerge only from the deliberations of the entire body of citizens. This could point in one of two conflicting directions. One could argue that national sovereignty was compatible with the separate representation of the three orders of the state within a single parliament. No one could claim that the distinction between Lords and Commons in England prevented the British from seeing themselves as one nation. Rousseau was no guide here since he denied that sovereignty could ever be expressed through representatives, something that was conveniently ignored by most of those who invoked his authority. Alternatively, one could maintain, as Sieyès did in his famous pamphlet, that the Third Estate *was* the nation. Anyone who claimed a particular status that was conferred on him by birth – and presumably by ordination – automatically excluded himself from the sovereign people. How this affected the status of the king was a question that Sieyès preferred not to ask, or at least not to answer, apart from one reference to the executive as an *ad hoc* product of the representative will.

The long stalemate that followed the opening of the Estates General was therefore, from one point of view, a tug of war between two concepts of the nation, which became an explicit trial of strength when the Third Estate assumed the title of *Assemblée Nationale*. Eventually they won. The king commanded the other two orders to join them, on 26 June; the night of 4 August swept away parlements and provinces, reducing local particularism to a matter of sentiment; noble status itself was abolished – on the proposal of nationally minded nobles – on 19 June 1790. The Fête de la Fédération in the following month was experienced as a great national event: the French family gathered round its head in a demonstration of fraternal unity.

This bright picture contained its inevitable shadows. The *émigrés* had physically separated themselves from a nation that they refused to accept. Within France there were nobles who wanted nothing to do with the new regime and considered themselves spiritual exiles in their own country. Perhaps more important was the tendency of some of the revolutionaries to exploit popular belief in the existence of an aristocratic plot for their own purposes.[9] The difficulties of the new order were more or less plausibly attributed to the machinations of the Enemy, an undefined 'aristocracy' that refused to integrate itself within the nation and would stop at nothing to restore the old habits and attitudes. With time and luck, if the Revolution had settled down, the *émigrés* and their allies in France might have come to terms with the inevitable and the aristocratic plot lost its plausibility and usefulness.

In the meantime there were two outsiders to be accommodated: the king and the clergy. Louis XVI, at the Séance Royale of 23 June 1789, had proclaimed his willingness to become a constitutional monarch and the revolutionaries were agreed that a country the size of France needed a king. This apparent consensus concealed a fundamental disagreement over both practice – what effective power the king was to retain – and principle. For most of the deputies the king was the man chosen by the nation to be its chief executive, on such terms as it should think fit to ordain. The 1791 constitution admittedly defined the monarch as one of the agents of the general will, but the Assembly claimed to be the actual embodiment of that will. From Louis's point of view, the constitution was something that he had chosen to bestow on his people. In a sense, the nation belonged to him rather than he to it. He was prepared, indeed morally obliged, to dedicate his life to its service, but as someone outside and above it. This divergence of views was at the root of most of the constitutional debates in the Assembly, which concerned the status of the king rather than that of the nobility, even if most of the monarchists were noble.

The second outsider was the Church. From the viewpoint of most of the deputies, religion was a necessary aspect of the life of the nation, something that existed for the good of society. Religious policy was therefore on a par with economic or foreign policy and the more radical deputies, like Robespierre, were fond of referring to priests as *officiers de morale*. The clergy were, on the whole, prepared to accept the idea of popular sovereignty in secular matters, but where the spiritual world was concerned many considered themselves to be bound by their overriding allegiance to canon law. It was this theoretical impasse, rather than disagreement over the terms of the Civil Constitution of the Clergy, that produced the catastrophic breach between the revolutionaries and a substantial part of the Church. The non-juring clergy believed that they were not free to take an oath to a nation that insisted that they should render unto Caesar the things that were God's. To the incredulous dismay of the deputies, raised in the secular culture of the Enlightenment, almost half of the clergy broke away, taking with them the allegiance of a substantial proportion of French Catholics who could no longer identify themselves with a nation that seemed to them to be denying their faith.

Once the Revolutionary order appeared to be striking root, it raised the question of the kind of relationship that should exist between regenerated France and states which their rulers were said to regard as a kind of dynastic real estate. Great Britain was in a class apart; it was a nation rather than the possession of its king, but a natural – and national – rival whose activities were viewed with understandable suspicion. Foreign policy was a subject on which the Enlightenment spoke with two voices. Most of the *philosophes* had been both pacific and cosmopolitan, echoing Montesquieu's remark that he was human by nature and French by accident. Rousseau had thought along different lines, sighing, as usual, for the bracing air of Sparta. At the beginning of *Emile* he argued that 'Toute société partielle, quand elle est étroite et bien unie, s'aliène de la grande. Tout patriote est dur aux étrangers; ils ne sont qu'hommes, ils ne sont rien à ses yeux.' And he continued: 'Aussi les guerres des républiques sont-elles plus cruelles que celles des monarchies.' Rousseau always insisted that to exercise an effective influence on conduct, a sense of national identity must be localised and that the tight bonds that linked an individual to his fellow citizens implied a suspicious attitude towards everyone else.

On this question, as on so many others, the revolutionaries fluctuated uneasily between Montesquieu and Rousseau. The issue took practical form in 1790 when 'despotic' Spain called for French support, under the terms of the Family Compact, against 'free' England, in a colonial quarrel that it defied human ingenuity to present as any kind of a liberation struggle. The ambivalent Constituent Assembly applauded both tributes to British freedom and threats to invade the British Isles. In the end cosmopolitanism won, helped by the fact that Spain backed down, and the deputies issued a remarkable proclamation that France had no territorial ambitions anywhere in the world and renounced aggressive war. They were still struggling to preserve their pride in what the French nation had achieved by its Revolution from contamination by a sense of national superiority, although they could scarcely help feeling that the new France was a cut above the old Europe. As late as the summer of 1792, after war had already broken out, the Legislative Assembly conferred French citizenship on a number of distinguished foreigners who were held to be a credit to humanity at large. It was this that allowed Paine to take his seat in the Convention.

Towards the end of 1791 the pacific attitude gave way before propaganda for a war against 'despots', thanks in great measure to the campaign of Brissot, who hoped to exploit a limited war for tactical purposes but who also commended war itself as a source of moral purification. Prussia and Austria had been making threatening noises and the minor German princes had allowed an *émigré* army of liberation to parade its insignificance on their soil, but the war did not begin as a counter-revolutionary crusade. The French nation, which had not yet learned to personify itself as Hercules, was flexing its infant muscles.

The way in which the conduct of the war passed from eighteenth-century ritual to something very different was in part the responsibility of the allies, who showed that they felt under no obligation to observe the customary civilities when dealing with Revolutionary France. Brunswick's ferocious Manifesto threatened Paris with destruction and declared that National Guards who joined in the fighting would be treated as *francs-tireurs*. The British were the first to nationalise the war by forging French currency and intercepting imports of food. George III would never have resorted to such measures in a war against one of his foreign 'cousins'. If republican France was eventually to go much further in the direction of total war, the revolutionaries could claim with justice that they had been provoked.

The whole conception of the nation and the relationship between this abstraction and the actual people of France was transformed by the proclamation of the Republic in September 1792. As readers of *De l'Esprit des Lois* were well aware, republics were qualitatively different from monarchies, since they depended on a citizen body living in a state of rough equality and activated by *vertu*, in other words, a readiness to seek its personal fulfilment in the service of the community. To be a republican therefore implied complying with certain standards of behaviour as well as holding particular views about politics. As Robespierre insisted, within a republic the only citizens were the republicans. The nation, which was naturally synonymous with the Republic, had initially been seen as a unifying concept even if, from the start, some people had opted out and others had been branded as enemies. Henceforth, it was to become more and more exclusive, a civic elite – which might even be a minority – within a population that inhabited the same territory but did not form a single community. In this sense the nation had become a kingdom – or rather a republic – of the saints.

Saint-Just, in the maiden speech to the Convention that established his reputation overnight, spelled out some of the consequences of this way of thinking.[10] One did not have to exclude one's self from the nation by deliberate choice. Louis XVI, by virtue of his office, had never been a part of it: 'On ne peut régner innocemment.' The nation consisted only of those who had subscribed to its social contract, which united them in a community of rights and obligations. Relations between this community and anyone outside it were those of a state of nature, involving no legal or moral obligation. The king should therefore be treated as a prisoner of war. Since he was more dangerous alive than dead, he should be killed – which suggested a rather alarming attitude towards prisoners of war. The Convention as yet was unconvinced, even when Saint-Just's argument was taken up by Robespierre, and it opted for a trial. Some of the deputies may have realised that the logic of Saint-Just's argument meant that it would be possible to proscribe any section of the population which the government or the Assembly decided to identify as not belonging to the nation.

When power had passed first to the Montagnards and then increasingly to the Committee of Public Safety, the point of view that the deputies had rejected in the autumn of 1792 became official doctrine. Speaking in the name of his colleagues on the Committee, Saint-Just told the Convention, on 10 October 1793,

> Vous avez à punir non seulement les traîtres mais les indifférents mêmes; vous avez à punir quiconque est passif dans la République et ne fait rien pour elle; car, depuis que le peuple français a manifesté sa volonté, tout ce qui lui est opposé est hors le souverain; tout ce qui est hors le souverain est ennemi.[11]

This was the same argument that he had employed against the king. Whatever had happened during the Revolution had been an assertion of the sovereign will of the nation. Anyone who challenged it or pursued his own personal interests instead of devoting himself exclusively to the public good, as defined by the government, excluded himself from the nation and became an outlaw, to be treated as a known enemy rather than a man whom one might decide to put on trial but had to treat as innocent until his conviction.

This was the mental attitude behind the law of 22 prairial II or 10 June 1794. The kind of behaviour that had previously led to people being classified as suspect was now defined as criminal. This stretched from royalism, through food hoarding, to include dishonest government contractors, vexatious officials or those who compromised the safety of the republic in any way. This was a matter of judgement rather than of fact. Such crimes were offences against the nation; anyone who committed them was an *ennemi de la patrie* and the objective, when dealing with such people, was 'moins de les punir que de les anéantir'. Revolutionary justice, in other words, was more concerned with defining what sort of person a man was than with establishing what he had actually done. If he belonged to the nation, he was entitled to be treated as a citizen. If not, as an enemy, he had no right to employ counsel, call witnesses and so on. It was unfortunate that the distinction had to be made before the trial began, but no one would have been accused of conduct unworthy of a republican unless there had been reason to presuppose his guilt in the first place. The trial itself was a matter of conviction in more ways than one: what the jury was doing was deciding whether the accused looked like a member of the nation or not. In the latter case, it was logical to ordain that the only penalty available to the court should be death, irrespective of the seriousness of the offence, since it involved a breach of the social contract.

Where relations between the republic and foreigners were concerned, military victory inclined the nation in the direction of nationalism. Robespierre's admirers are prone – with good reason – to commend his level-headed advice on the dangers of going to war, and his famous observation that no one liked being liberated by armed missionaries. They are rather less vocal about his attitude a year later when he called France 'une grande Nation destinée à punir tous les tyrans du monde' and declared his belief that 'Personne n'ose douter qu'une armée française, toujours bien conduite contre les tyrans, ne soit invincible.'[12] This chauvinistic nonsense, where the emphasis was less on the regeneration of Frenchmen by the Revolution than on their inherent national qualities, still postulated a world in which the French nation was fighting to liberate oppressed people from their 'tyrants'. Whatever plausibility this might have in the case of the Austrians and the Prussians, Great Britain seemed to pose particular problems.

On 8 October 1793 the Committee of Public Safety persuaded the Convention to extend the embargo of British shipping to include British cargoes carried under other flags. Robespierre then secured the passage of Fabre d'Eglantine's amendment that all British civilians should be interned. On the following day he complained that, six weeks before, someone had said that France was not at war with the British people. 'Ce discours m'a fait frémir': the French republic could be founded only on the ruin of British merchants. A week later, when the proposal had been made to extend internment to all enemy aliens, someone accused the Committee of Public Safety of wanting to 'nationalise' the war. Saint-Just denied this, insisting that the British constituted a special case since 'ils ont violé le droit des gens envers nous avec une barbarie auparavant inconnue'. This was near enough to the truth to pass muster, but it scarcely explained what followed:

> On peut vouloir le bien à tous les peuples de la terre; mais on ne peut en effet faire du bien qu'à son pays. Votre Comité, convaincu de cette vérité, n'a vu dans l'univers que le peuple français . . . Votre Comité de Salut Public a pensé que, dans nos rapports étrangers, aucune considération ne devait approcher de nous, qui fût indigne de la fierté de la République et du courage des Français.[13]

Little by little the concept of the nation was shifting from the ideological to the geographical in foreign policy, while the opposite process was taking place on the domestic front. Internally, the nation was purging itself of all those Frenchmen who were unworthy to belong to it; where foreigners were concerned, 'fierté' and 'courage', were identified not merely with Revolutionary regeneration but with the abiding qualities of Frenchness. Saint-Just then resorted to some rather tortuous logic: both the ban on British exports and the arrest of British civilians were really directed against the government, rather than against individuals, since some civilians were spies. England was a second Carthage, but what had made the first one so objectionable had been its government rather than its people. Once the British had had their revolution, the French would welcome them as friends. That was the real point of the embargo: since British merchants were the enemies and oppressors of the people, their ruin would be welcomed by the majority of the British population. He then went off in an entirely contrary direction: 'Quelle que soit la raison qui ait banni un homme du sol où il est né, son coeur y tient comme l'arbre tient à la terre, ou il est dépravé.' Robespierre spelled out the implications of this for all those radicals, like Paine, who had sought asylum in Revolutionary France. 'Je me méfie indistinctement de tous ces étrangers dont le visage est couvert du masque du patriotisme.' Before the end of the year the Convention had expelled all its foreign deputies. It was not enough to be French to be accepted as part of the nation, but it had become an indispensable preliminary. Foreigners were suspect and suspects were not entitled to the protection of the law. These xenophobic conclusions were not entirely the product of ideology. The political arena had been invaded by a handful of dubious foreigners who made up in activity for what they lacked in numbers. It is still impossible to be sure whether they were merely ambitious busybodies or foreign agents. A letter from the British Foreign Office to the Swiss banker Perregaux, at present reposing – for reasons that one can only guess – with Danton's papers, shows that the British government was paying agents who posed as extremists in the Jacobin Club.[14] The republicans were not alone in failing to observe the conventions of eighteenth-century warfare. This scarcely accounts, however, for the barbaric decree of 27 May 1794 that no British or Hanoverian prisoners were to be taken. This was more honoured in the breach than the observance – which does not make it any the less abominable – but it was not entirely disregarded.[15]

The collapse of the dictatorship of the Committee of Public Safety on 9 thermidor put an end to a conception of the French nation that denied any rights to those whom the government chose to define as outside the magic circle. Henceforth, both domestic and foreign policy were conducted with more regard to the customary norms. The Revolution, however, had destroyed national unity as a fact, whatever politicians might say about the nation. A concept that in other countries was a call to unity was a reminder of division in a republic that was rejected by a substantial part of its population. Those who appealed to the nation had in mind what the revolutionaries had aspired to create from the beginning, a country unified, democratic, egalitarian and republican in essence if not in name. Their opponents were more concerned with the sort of society that had actually emerged, to which they had no desire to belong. Each side claimed a kind of legitimacy that it denied to the other. Each believed itself to be the custodian of the true national heritage, to be quintessentially French. It still does.

Perhaps in compensation for this lack of unity at home, a Revolution that had initially been essentially concerned with the regeneration of France increasingly assumed the shape of a commodity for export. At one level this was a matter of military conquest and the creation of satellite republics more or less shaped in the image of France. *La Grande Nation*, the heir to the cultural ascendency of eighteenth-century France, imposed itself through its armies rather more than through its ideology. That, however, was not the end of the story. After the defeat of Napoleon, the gospel of nationalism, as it had emerged out of the French Revolution, proved to have an extraordinary potency. The Revolution that had destroyed France as a nation served as an inspiration to nationalists all over the world.

The way in which the concepts of nation and nationalism evolved and blended with each other can be seen in microcosm in the works of Mercier, a man personally involved in the Revolution and a writer whose real if limited talent made him a sensitive barometer as he registered changes in the mental climate. In the years before 1789 he was both cosmopolitan and Anglophile. He wrote in 1766, 'De tous les patriotismes, le plus noble, le plus juste, le plus vrai est l'amour de l'humanité.'[16] In his utopia, *l'An 2440*, six years later, he described patriotism as 'un fanatisme inventé par les rois et funeste à l'univers'. In the year 2440 'L'Anglais est toujours le premier peuple de l'Europe.'[17] His rather optimistically entitled *Notions claires sur les Gouvernements*, which was full of praise for Montesquieu and oblique criticism of Rousseau, maintained the same attitude, condemning political fanaticism, advocating the creation of a single European community and ridiculing those who chose the Greek city states as their models. He hoped that France would progressively align herself on England: 'Plus nous entrerons en communication avec les pensées et les raisonnements du peuple Anglais, plus nous perfectionnerons notre Gouvernement comme il doit être perfectionné, d'une manière lente, insensible mais plus sûre qu'une refonte subite.' Revolutionary movements were always the source of extreme oppression: 'La politique qui tyrannise les contemporains pour fonder dans l'avenir des jours plus prospères est évidemment fausse.' And 'L'autorité originelle de la nation est incontestable mais elle se perd et devient nulle par le fait. Le peuple est lié en quelque sorte envers ceux qu'il a chargés de l'exercice de sa suprême puissance.' It retained the theoretical right to resume its sovereignty, but 'l'exercice de ce droit est si difficile que l'Histoire en donne très peu d'exemples'.[18]

History surprised him by providing another one in 1789 and Mercier responded to the new situation by a sharp about turn. The title of the book that he brought out in 1791 was a programme in itself: *De Jean-Jacques Rousseau considéré comme l'un des premiers Auteurs de la Révolution*. The Revolution had elevated 'la nation française au-dessus de toutes les nations du monde.' It was France and America that were now going to regenerate the world, and 'les riches et cruels habitants de Londres' were 'les plus pâles adorateurs de l'or, les plus durs, les plus inhumains, les plus froidement vicieux de tous les mortels.'[19]

During the next few years Mercier was too busy as a journalist and as a member of the Convention – he spent some months in gaol as a Girondin – to have time to write books. When he produced his *Nouveau Paris*, towards the end of the Directory, his views about the recent activities of the French nation were extremely confused. On the whole he was inclined to denounce the *terribles innovateurs* whose objective had been to 'substituer l'amour de la patrie à tout le reste'. 'On a voulu faire de nous des hommes entièrement nouveaux, et l'on n'en a presque fait que des sauvages.'[20] In the shipwreck of all his old ideals, he clung to three planks for salvation. The first was pride in the achievement of the *Grande Nation*. 'Les Français ont plus fait en trois années que ce peuple justement célèbre [Athens] n'en a fait en trois siècles.' 'Des langues étrangères! Je croyais qu'il n'y avait qu'une langue en Europe, celle des républicains français. Même avant la révolution notre langue était celle de l'Europe.'[21] The second was the Machiavellianism of the British. 'Tous les hommes atroces qui poursuivirent tous les républicains furent les agents ou les instruments des puissances étrangères, mus par le Cabinet britannique.' They made up a curious bunch: Robespierre, Louis XVI, Orléans, Babeuf and Puisaye! 'Guerre, guerre éternelle aux Anglais!'[22] The third might be described as the *tricolore* man's burden. However unfortunate the results of the Revolution might have been in France, it was still a national duty to spread the Gospel to the lesser breeds outside the law. 'Nos armées victorieuses resuscitent la république romaine ... ce sont les Français qui rétablissent les consuls, ils régénèrent les peuples qui veulent être leurs amis.'[23]

One Mercier does not make a Revolutionary summer, but his migrations may still tell us something about the changes in the climate. The Revolution had transformed the nation from a cliché to a programme. The attempt to implement that programme had created a kind of Procrustean abstraction that destroyed the thing that it aspired to create. What survived was both a fractured nation and a concept of national purpose that gave the Revolution, whether one thinks of its armies or its ideology, its extraordinary resonance throughout the rest of the world.

Notes

1   *Recueil de pièces pour servir à l'histoire de la Révolution en France*, II, n.p., n.d., John Rylands Library.

2   *Recueil de diverses pièces concernant la Révolution du 8 mai 1788*, n.p., n.d., John Rylands Library.

3   *Recueil de pièces . . .*, VII.

4   *Ibid.*, V.

5   Archives Nationales, C14, Procès verbaux de la noblesse.

6   *Suite au nouveau Recueil ou choix de pièces et d'ecrits divers*, n.p., 1789, John Rylands Library.

7   Robert Griffiths, *Le Centre perdu: Malouet et les ·'monarchiens' dans la Révolution française*, Grenoble, 1988, Ch. 2.

8   *Recueil de pièces . . .*, II, III, VI.

9   See P. Higonnet, *Class, Ideology and the Rights of Nobles during the French Revolution*, Oxford, 1981, *passim*.

10   Speech of 13 November 1792.

11   C. Vellay, *Oeuvres complètes de Saint-Just*, Paris, 1908, 2 vols, II, p. 76.

12   Speeches of 8 and 10 March 1793.

13   Vellay, *Oeuvres complétes de Saint-Just*, II, pp. 96–7.

14   N. Hampson, *The Life and Opinions of Maximilien Robespierre*, London, 1974, p. 214.

15   When the frigate *La Boudeuse* captured an English merchantman, her captain reported, 'Je fis venir l'équipage à bord, que je fis fusiller d'après le décret.' Archives Nationales BB[4] 42 (marine) fo. 218.

16   *Des Malheurs de la Guerre*, Paris, 1766, p. 52.

17   *L'An 2440*, London, 1772, pp. 267[b], 405.

18   *Notions claires sur les Gouvernements*, Amsterdam, 1788, 2 vols, I, pp. 40, iv, 45, 76, II p. 407.

19   *De Jean-Jacques Rousseau considéré comme l'un des premiers Auteurs de la Révolution*, Paris, 1791. 2 vols, II, pp. 185–5, 91[n].

20   *Le Nouveau Paris*, Paris, n.d. 6 vols, I, pp. 20–1.

21   *Ibid.*, I, p. 119, vi, p. 31.

22   *Ibid.*, II, pp. 231, 235.

23   *Ibid.*, III, p. 24.

B

The countryside and the peasantry in Revolutionary iconography

In the context of a conference devoted to town, country and region, I have chosen to concentrate on the countryside and the peasantry using as my starting point the iconography of the period. This choice is expedient since any attempt at describing the urban world would probably prove to be a never-ending task. This does not apply to the rural world, which has a far less perceptible presence. And yet, the links between town and country cannot be overlooked: the image conveyed by pictorial evidence is, in effect, that of the peasant seen from the urban viewpoint, rather than that of rural society seen through its own eyes. Of course, such a definitive statement raises a number of objections from the outset. What about pottery, for instance? Does that not give the true flavour of the French countryside? Yet even Nivernais earthenware is far from being specifically rural, even if it was destined for a clientele residing predominantly in small country towns and villages. It is with this often paradoxical history of an illustration, an image or a representation that we shall concern ourselves. To what extent was the Revolution, as it was played out in the countryside, given pictorial expression? And how exactly was it portrayed? The rhetoric of the Revolutionary image is divided in this respect – on the one hand we find total silence; on the other, grandiloquence, both of which are revealing. Through these sequences of images, a complete and instructive portrait of the peasant emerges — showing how he was both present in and absent from representations of the Revolution — even if this portrait was a consistently biased one. He was a partner, sometimes cajoled, sometimes feared, but always distant.

In this analysis we shall not attempt to build up a comprehensive picture of the peasant as he was depicted in the graphic art of the final years of the *ancien régime*: that alone could provide the subject for another study. It is sufficient to draw attention to the image of the shepherd in pastoral setting, as shown by, for example, the romantic paintings of Boucher, the tapestries of Leprince or the shift towards a Rousseauesque populism as found in the mannered works of Greuze. We should not forget, either, the presence of the rural landscape in the drawings and engravings of those artists who were at that time rediscovering the countryside (one thinks of the views of the country around Aix by Constantin) or the more precise vision of the technicians expressed in the plates illustrating the *Encyclopédie*. But the France of Louis XVI had no equivalent of Goya, who, in his sketches for tapestries for the Escorial Palace, was anxious to reflect a vision of that other world stretching beyond the gates of the city which was at once real yet highly stylised.

In this context, the turning point that was 1789 was to be truly revolutionary, giving access to new means of expression through the use of prints, engravings and pottery, all elements of an art form which, if not popular in itself, was destined for a mass public. It is true that the traditional print-makers – in Chartres, Orléans and elsewhere – had diversified their production throughout the eighteenth century, introducing alongside devotional images a secular vein which often used country scenes for its setting: 'I've broken my clog', sings the shepherdess in the couplets which accompany a Chartres print, much to the confusion of the clumsy shepherd who was trying to stick his foot in it. But all this does not take us very far: quite a different discourse would shortly replace these innocent naiveties.

The symbolic hero of the Third Estate

An initial sequence of images, corresponding to the crisis of 1789 itself, confronts us with the presence–absence paradox to which I have already alluded. For one is amazed to discover that the peasant movement, linked to food shortages and high prices, does not receive any pictorial expression. This is most evident in the illustrated histories of the period. The customary, rather facile leitmotif is the reproduction of pictures by Hersent, engraved by Pierre Adam, on the theme of 'Louis XVI distributing charity to poor peasants' . . . and yet we know that we are dealing with one of the successes of the salon of 1817. This is a significant temporal discrepancy for a picture carrying an unambiguous message – that of the return of the father-king and of his benevolence – which rings out as a reproach to the ungrateful French. The revolt of 1789 appears to have been conjured away, at least in the countryside, for it is true that the prints do convey some traces of the unrest in urban areas, from Strasbourg to Rennes or to Aix. The rural mobilisations were not thought worthy of inclusion in the pictorial record. On the other hand, the elections to the Estates General did give rise to some interesting works, notably the series of prints on the theme of 'Deliver us, Lords' which list the burdens and the scourges which fell upon the peasant: the gamekeeper, the *octroi* tax collector, the *gabelou* and the lawyer. But this series of prints is a fairly isolated case.

Even more striking is the absence of images relating to the *Grande Peur*. Turning again to the standard iconographical evidence, one always finds reproduced the same anonymous image: a castle is stormed by a group of peasants, the noble occupants are fleeing by coach, even a church is in flames which hardly reflects the facts of the situation. Does this really represent the *Grande Peur* or a subsequent episode? In any case, one cannot but be struck by the isolation of this ambiguous testimony.

The skilled engraver Janinet illustrated a similar scene. At about this time he was introducing the English technique of aquatint on coloured plates which he used to chronicle the day-by-day events of the hot summer of 1789. The scene takes place in August: a lord, Monsieur Walsh, disarms the aggressive actions of his tenants by offering them a banquet in front of his castle. What a good way, one might suppose, to deflect the fury of the populace.

In contrast to this deafening silence, it is worth pointing to the presence of the peasant in a different category of graphic production which burst upon the scene at this time: the series depicting the symbolic representation of the three orders. Only by the use of allegory was Revolutionary society able to allude to a situation which it refused to evoke in its daily reality. Indeed, the analysis of these prints holds some surprises, for the bourgeois hides behind the peasant in order to make him the symbolic figure of the Third Estate.

The bourgeois, depicted as a merchant or urban tradesman, is not entirely absent from the allegories of the three orders; he can be found in propagandist guise linked with the nobleman and the prelate on the new ship of state navigated by the firm hand of Necker. In more modest vein, a merchant haberdasher's shop sign, now on display in the Musée Carnavalet, depicts a cleric, a nobleman and a Parisian tradesman dividing between them a tricolour ribbon in order to make cockades. But these illustrations are relatively rare examples.

It is the peasant who represents the collective image of the Third Estate in the majority of cases. The model most commonly used was a painting which hung in the town hall at Aix, popularised by engravings. It shows a peasant, heavily burdened by the whole weight of the kingdom which is depicted by a globe, while the nobleman and the prelate look on without helping him. This original version, whether dressed in sixteenth-century attire or modernised, inspired many variations on the theme of the peasant crushed by a heavy load, defined as work, misery and humiliation but also as production – for it was he who was the provider of all riches. But on the theme 'I am weary of carrying the load', a change becomes apparent inasmuch as the villager becomes more active: 'This will not last for ever.'

Then we see the world turned upside-down: the peasant who, until then, had been the mount of the nobleman and the priest, takes his revenge by now riding astride his partners. From the end of his sword hangs a hare which he has just killed. The stress on the victory over hunting rights is much more than purely anecdotal, if one considers the importance of the demands made in the *cahiers* which included these symbolic satisfactions as well as those of a more material nature. This manifestly popular theme was much elaborated upon, and the double image of times past and times present can also be found employing female characters.

However, lest we should suppose that this is a true portrayal of the peasant, other prints unmask the hidden intention. In a series covering the theme of the union of the three orders and the return to calm and unanimity, the peasant finds himself once again carrying the burden of the kindom with the caption: 'Now everyone must help carry the heavy burden'. This is the language and reasoning of the bourgeois in peasant's clothing. At times it is not without a note of derision that the peasant is made to play this role. We observe, in a good quality drawing entitled the 'Ballet of the three orders', a rustic, self-conscious and clumsy in his rags and tatters, trying to ape the steps of the gracious minuet of the privileged classes. Nevertheless, this peasant has a useful role to play when it is his turn to speak, often in the guise of

Père Gérard (the only real peasant *député* in the Estates General who retained his rustic attire): he is pictured at the door of his cottage or even out in the fields offering the peace of honest folk to his former enemies. 'Shake on it, I knew that you would become like us'. In one version he is addressing a nobleman and a priest; in a second version the nobleman has disappeared. Perhaps he has already emigrated.

Was a compromise possible? The ambiguities of the 'Année Heureuse'

We might say that these are images of biddable peasants in the service of the party of order. And initially, such is indeed the message. It emerges from Nevers pottery, which, in taking up Revolutionary themes, became highly popular. On wedding plates the effigy of the patronymic saint was sometimes replaced by a likeness of the bridegroom himself: 'Jean Duc, good citizen'. More often than not, though, the earthenware took up the same interlocking themes as the prints we have just described, even if this meant simplifying them in the form of trophies or talking symbols: 'I am weary of carrying the load, let the strongest bear it', and concluding 'Long live prosperity'.

The year 1790 began with what one might call the theme of the pastoral symphony. In the print 'New Year's gifts for the king', good peasants and gardeners from the countryside around Paris bring the king samples of their produce, even a lamb. But when the Dauphin asks 'Does he bite?', a young peasant girl replies with malice: 'No, sire, he's not an aristocrat'.

In this sometimes rather ambiguous bucolic vein, a newspaper engraving (from the *Révolutions de France et de Brabant*) shows the king as a good shepherd watching over his flock. But the real world is already on the scene in the guise of the *abbé* Maury and malevolent aristocratic advisers.

Yet, we know that much is veiled by this myth of the 'année heureuse' and that a strong popular movement continued in certain rural areas such as the South-west (from the Limousin to the Quercy and to Périgord.) Ought we then to reconsider and admit that our theme is quite plainly overshadowed by another? Not entirely, for there is still evidence to be found. A book dating from the end of the last century contains some very poor photographs of the home of Brissot's father who was a *traiteur* in Chartres and who owned a number of paintings.

These compositions show rare examples of a very different subject-matter: in one a convoy of wheat travelling under armed guard; in another a riot in a market square. At least this is what they appear to portray – for mercenary reasons the present owner refused to let me view the paintings. Perhaps one day we shall see them on display at Sotheby's in London.

Fortunately however, we do have access to engravings which bear witness to a fresh way of thinking. One of these which is executed in a truly popular style shows a plebeian hero sporting hat, moustache and cutlass (rather in the mould of the bandit or righter of wrongs found in popular folklore). In true fairy-tale fashion, he is attacking a beast with two heads (the aristocracy and the clergy), which he overcomes ('I think it's still alive') and then rips open ('I can't find the heart'). In other engravings a different monster terrorises the countryside; a kind of weird combination of dummies representing the nobleman, the priest, the lawyer . . . the trio hated by the peasantry. But in the background, a posse of peasants armed with pitchforks and flails is on its trail.

A very beautiful aquatint in a less popular style shows 'The night-time travellers'. In a nocturnal landscape, a nobleman and a priest are taking flight . . . but close by stands a peasant with a pitchfork who is shining his lantern on them. Not all works developing the theme of the chase are so restrained. The majority are far removed from repre-sentations of the jubilant peasant, happy that he is at least free to shoot rabbits . . . now is the season for hunting aristocrats. In one print a group of huntsmen fire on Capuchin monks who have taken refuge in a tree. In another, the ever-present huntsmen are taking potshots at nobles and priests from the court who are depicted as fleeing game birds. Soon, the escalating violence would break all bounds.

Yet efforts were still being made to contain it and the most striking example of the attempt to harness the peasant to the bourgeois com-promise was the *Almanach du Père Gérard*. This publication, which, in the autumn of 1791 first brought its author Collot d'Herbois to public notice, might be described as both a layman's guide to the constitution and a self-instruction manual for country dwellers. The many carefully prepared engravings which it contained have a deliberately simplified subject-matter that illustrates a message more complex than is at first apparent: it can be interpreted on at least two, even three levels. Some sections use the good peasant to put across a message to townsfolk, other pages dealing with property and the respect for order are aimed directly at the peasants themselves, and there are sequences in which a Rousseauesque patriarch delivers a lesson which could even be destined for the king and his entourage.

This compromise was short-lived, however. In 1792 the rustic leitmotif was still linked to the king, at a time when the royal image was being systematically debased. But after the fall of the monarchy the previously restrained approach was no longer in fashion. The royal personage became bestialised – we now see the king out in the fields in the form of a pig and, even worse, a poor quality pig unfit for consumption. 'Oh the accursed animal', cries out the peasant farmer who is about to slaughter this pig with royal features, 'it's cost me a fortune to fatten him up.' Once again, the fury of the peasantry was invoked to serve the Revolution as it entered a new phase. However some of the former reticence remained; the peasant was still a disturbing and distant partner. Even in the illustrated plates of the *Tableaux Historiques de la Révolution Française* which had followed events since 1789, the rural world is almost entirely absent. Trees and landscapes appear only in the pictures of military campaigns. An exception confirms the rule: right from the outset of the Revolution the camp at Jalès is depicted as a desolate, lonely place situated on the edge of the world. Later, in the depictions of the siege of Nantes, or of the scene beneath the cliffs at Granville, we discover a different peasantry bearing arms – that of the counter-revolution. The time had come for a segment of the country-side to set itself against the town.

A world to reconquer

It is tempting to suggest that the peasant disappeared from the scene in Year II. For at the time of the Maximum the countryside was hardly visible in Revolutionary iconography. Yet the one or two exceptions to this rule are not without significance. An anonymous print shows a group of patrolmen in a village, but are they part of the rural National Guard or a detachment of the *armée révolutionnaire*? In another illustration, a *représentant-en-mission* or one of his delegates is reasoning with a group of peasants at the foot of a hay waggon . . . a modest level of instruction in view of the difficult combat ahead.

There are, however, some significant exceptions to this silence and generally they are linked to two themes: the peasant counter-revolution and the Vendée, on the one hand; and dechristianisation, on the other.

The insurgent Vendée appears not to have been able to find a graphic mode of expression for its struggle, which leads one to conclude that the Vendeans had hardly any technical means of producing prints. Yet the rarity of these graphic reproductions remains significant. One of the few royalist engravings available to us shows the Vendée giving birth to thousands of royalist soldiers. The paradox of this unrealised dream has been remarked upon: the image personifying the Vendée bringing forth armed and well-disciplined cohorts conveys exactly that which could never be achieved. The very real anger of the peasantry is never depicted. In opposition to this, we find the republican dream (not less mythical, if better organised): that of a patriotic Vendée. It begins by denouncing the crimes of the Vendean bandits and explaining what the appropriate reaction to them should be. In their series of watercolours, the Lesueur brothers evoke a scene which may or may not have taken place, but which was certainly exceptional: a group of women is seen protecting a tree of Liberty from the axes of royalist brigands. Then the example of a mythical hero figure is blown out of all proportion: we find Vilvier *mère*, surrounded by her children, defending her cottage from invading Vendeans by threatening to set light to the barrel of gunpowder at her side. This is the heroic posture of antiquity. In the same vein, we come across the 'blacksmith of the Vendée' who, curiously enough, has been transmuted to an alpine landscape. He carries on his shoulder his mighty hammer: he has learned that royalist bandits are blazing a trail of destruction and so the popular hero sets out to meet them.

The campaign of dechristianisation in the Year II was also a good occasion to begin a cultural offensive directed against the rural population. It elaborated on the theme of the *fête*: typical images would show celebrations of the Cult of Reason or a village masquerade. Hubert Robert himself, hardly a stern revolutionary and one who was soon to end up in prison, depicted 'Liberty in the fields'. One of the most curious of these works is the engraving by Mathieu in the style of Delaunay on the theme 'Girls of a marriageable age at Saint Nicolas de la Chesnay'. This is placed in a pastoral setting not unlike those which were popular in the 1780s, and the original version showed the girls on a pilgrimage through the forest to the shrine of a bearded and mitred Saint Nicholas. The updated version of Year II keeps the girls, but the former 'idol' is replaced by an antique warrior, possibly representing the people of France.

No doubt these engravings form part of a pedagogy which could take other forms: theatrical scenes which transfer the festive aspect of dechristianisation to a rural setting, or which borrow from Grétry's 'republican rosary' or perhaps even the 'Homage to Liberty'. The Festival of the Supreme Being and the vast iconographic production which accompanied it illustrate this theme. We have some representations of village celebrations of the Supreme Being in popular art. But above all we should remember that David's scenario for the Parisian ceremony brought the countryside right into the heart of the city in the shape of the float symbolising agriculture which played a central role in the procession. Paintings and allegories embroider the central motif. A beautiful poster proclaiming that 'the people of France recognise the immortality of the soul and the existence of the Supreme Being' is decorated with the image of a rural *sans-culotte* sowing this essential truth to the four winds. Similarly, another allegorical representation shows a family coming to pay homage to the Supreme Being at the foot of the agriculture float.

Why did the symbolism of the Supreme Being exploit rural themes? It was without doubt an appeal to the man of the fields who was close to nature, but a nature no longer divinised in the Egyptian mode venerated by Hérault de Séchelles and the members of the Convention on the occasion of the Festival of Regeneration of August 1793. This nature which was so familiar to the heirs of the eighteenth century materialists had been harnessed by the Supreme Being, and who better than the peasant living in everyday proximity to nature to offer up worship.

A fine engraving entitled 'Homage to the Divinity' may be taken to sum up the Robespierrist ideal: in a mountainous landscape a man of the people – a peasant – is kneeling in adoration; he is worshipping the universe about him, the great being as worshipped by Jean-Jacques and the Incorruptible. It was all a dream, of course. On the eve of 9 Thermidor, never had the countryside been so near and yet so far.

The revolution is over

Images of the town figure overwhelmingly in the iconography of the Directory. The countryside puts in a few appearances, it is true, in a round-about way, but no longer as part of an organised discourse. And yet the round of civic festivals still found a place for the Festival of Agriculture. We know this from the work of artists like Lesueur, who faithfully chronicles day-to-day events. Otherwise the countryside became the place where bandits, as depicted by the watercolour artist Bericourt, surrounded farms, intent on pillage, raped girls and burned the farmer's feet in an effort to make him reveal where he had hidden his savings.

The rustic *védutistes* also reappeared at about this time, having hardly had the chance to express themselves earlier. They set off in pursuit of ruins and monuments: witness the contemporary view of Cluny abbey, as yet undamaged. During this period when François de Neufchâteau was pioneering economic statistics, it is also interesting to look at the illustrative plates of the many engravers who took up this development and who used the style of the *Encyclopédie* to portray technical innovations in the countryside. But these were short-lived touches and to my mind it is Lafitte, with his very beautiful series of engravings illustrating the republican calendar, who best characterises the art of the period. In the years preceding the Directory, Lafitte had been a committed, not to say dedicated, illustrator of the great moments of the Revolution, from the Champ de Mars massacre onwards. But now his heroes appear lacklustre, his goddesses ungodly, content to be ordinary languid beauties or to reveal their charms to the rhythm of the changing seasons. It is on this bucolic note that our Revolutionary itinerary comes to an end.

The history of a misapprehension

Must we conclude on a note of misapprehension? It would be naive to blame the Revolution for not throwing up a latter day Le Nain or a precocious Van Gogh to paint its potato-eaters.

Throughout this analysis, a constantly renewing dialectic has emerged. We could say that the peasant's role in this has been as a pretext, or as an object for manipulation. Sometimes he was used as an example, albeit an allegorical one, and sometimes as an image of the kind of purity that was in such great demand – the exemplary life in the field – as popularised by Rousseau. And yet, in contrast, he was sometimes depicted as an instrument of savagery which was occasionally exploited, but more often hidden from view. At any event, the peasant remained from the very beginning the object of a civic pedagogy which sought to fashion him so that he absorbed and reiterated its ideals or, at the very least, its rhetorical postures.

In the almost total absence of graphic representations generated from within the peasantry itself (save for the artefacts and residues of popular culture), this iconography is above all a reflection of the successive political stances of the Revolutionary bourgeoisie – not that these should necessarily be judged in Machiavellian terms. For this iconography also expressed fear of a world which remained profoundly foreign to that bourgeoisie.

It would be an interesting exercise to examine these ambiguities in the light of other forms of Revolutionary discourse – the written record, of course, but also the festival. Here, too, we would find the same mixture of exclusion and inclusion of the peasantry. In the cycle of festivals organised under the Directory, the Festival of Agriculture was the only one dedicated to honouring a professional group: it was also the most frequently deserted – the expression of an appointment that was never kept.

Figure 1 Misery of the French Peasant in 1789.

Figure 2 An appointed representative requisitions the harvest.

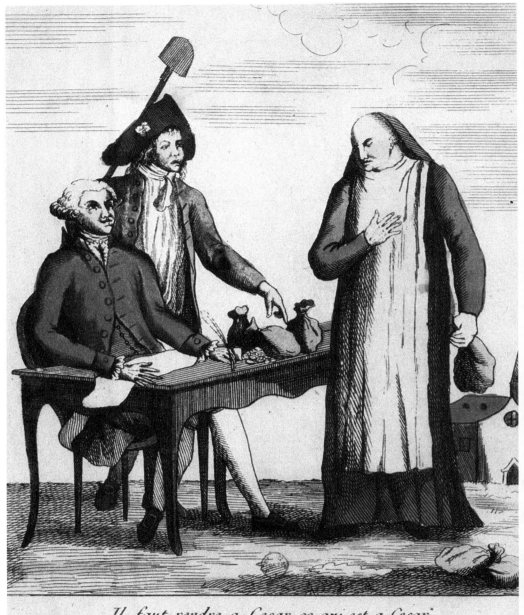

Il faut rendre a Cesar ce qui est a Cesar
Et a la Nation ce qui est a la Nation

Figure 3 The parasitic Church at last having to restitute its ill-gotten gains.

Figures 4 and 5 The peasants bearing the full weight of the privileged classes.

Figure 6 The rights of the landowning classes now abolished, the Nation dreams of reconciliation.

Figure 7 Patriotic dance under the Tree of Liberty.

FÊTE CÉLÉBRÉE EN L'HONNEUR DE L'ÊTRE SUPRÊME

Le 20 Prairiale l'an 2me de la Rep

La véritable Prêtre de l'Être suprême, c'est la Nature, son temple l'Univers, son culte
la Vertu, ses Fêtes la joie d'un grand Peuple rassemblé pour resserer les doux noeuds de
la Fraternité, et lever la mort des Tyrans

Figure 9 Celebration of the *Etre Suprême*: homage to Nature before the Chariot of Agriculture.

Figure 8 Allegorical study from Aix en Provence, from which the woodcutters of the Revolution derived their inspiration.

Figure 10 The Fountain of Liberty in an Alpine landscape, at which the peasants quench their thirst.

Revolution and the urban economy: maritime cities and continental cities

The political conflict during the Revolution is often seen as having been detrimental to the economy and to economic growth. This is due to the impact of civil disturbances and particularly of military operations upon the bulk of the population, especially the town dwellers. However, situations varied and the historian needs to exercise caution. It is necessary to divide the towns of France into two distinct groups: the Atlantic ports and the continental cities. We cannot overestimate the influence of the wars which began in 1792. Their impact was decisive as economic development, at least in some sectors, collapsed with the onset of maritime war in 1793.[1]

Preliminary remarks

The urban economy suffered directly from the effects of the Revolution. First, the productive potential of some towns was undermined by military operations or civil disturbances, but such destruction was quite limited in space and time.[2] Secondly, the majority of the towns suffered from bouts of paper money inflation. This undoubtedly had serious consequences because it coincided with many merchants and manufacturers losing their working capital through the combination of a sharp rise in costs, price control under the Maximum and the payment of government orders in depreciated *assignats*. Finally, the consequences of the diversion of resources to military purposes and the heavy burden of taxation should not be underestimated.[3]

The impact of war on the urban economy was more important than the direct effects of the Revolution, however. The wars which affected Europe almost continuously from 1792 to 1815, and particularly the maritime conflict between Britain and France from 1793, had a serious impact on economic development through the dislocation of international trade. Trade dislocation occurred throughout the whole war period and not only during the Continental Blockade.

In addition to these interruptions to economic development, we have to allow that each French town had its own pattern of difficulties: on the French maritime front, the Atlantic seaboard was bound to suffer, of course, but the situation was rather different for the inland cities. On the maritime front, similar difficulties had been experienced during the wars of the eighteenth century, but during the Revolutionary and Napoleonic wars the situation was much worse because the British, thanks to their superior sea power, imposed major restrictions on seaborne trade which caused the decline and eventually the almost complete suspension of that trade. French colonial trade had been the most dynamic sector of the economy: it had increased tenfold between 1716 and 1787.[4] We need to bear in mind this expansion when measuring the scale of the losses incurred by the Atlantic ports.

Cities and merchants on the French Atlantic front

The rapid expansion of the West Indies

A study of commercial trends affecting the French Atlantic ports in the eighteenth century highlights the spectacular growth of the 'Jewel of the West Indies' – the French half of Santo Domingo – in the years before the slave revolt of August 1791 and the naval war of 1793, when the burning of plantations and the threat to safety on the seas destroyed the base on which it rested.[5]

The French Windward Islands – Martinique, Guadeloupe and Tobago, a recently acquired colony – were certainly far from inactive in trading networks as they, like Santo Domingo, provided sugar, coffee, cotton and indigo, which were then redistributed throughout France and beyond to Europe as a whole. The Greater Antilles were, however, the main driving force in colonial trade. Santo Domingo drew the largest number of French ships, varying between 550 and 600 per year in 1787 and 1788. These figures include both 'direct' shipping, plying regularly between the Caribbean and the homeland by the most direct and therefore most profitable route in terms of time, and merchant vessels which put in for long periods on the coast of Africa. Over 480 ships used the regular direct trade route to deliver food, flour, wine, salted meat and oils, which were indispensable for feeding the planters and their workforce, along with equipment such as sugar mill wheels, boilers and various iron fitments, which were needed to run the plantations. In addition to these goods, the same ship would also bring to the colonists – keen to keep up with the latest fashions – articles such as carriages, saddles, handkerchiefs, shoes, fine-quality shirts, mirrors, fine wines, fruit preserved in brandy and meat conserves. Over a hundred vessels exporting cotton, fabrics, sheets, armaments and brandy to the coast of Africa supplied Santo Domingo with about 28,000 slaves per year between 1786 and 1789.

A large number of coasters either extended this trade or competed with it, providing a link between the French Cape or Port au Prince and Jamaica, Spanish America and various North American ports. A great many cargoes of valuables, shipped from French ports as goods intended for private sale (*pacotille*), disappeared on the Spanish Main.

Before the French Revolution, sugar and coffee carried most weight in the balance of trade, both in terms of volume and value. France received about 95,000 tons of sugar, of which 71,000 tons came from Santo Domingo alone; and over 39,000 tons of coffee, about 34,000 tons of which were sent from the Greater Antilles. West Indian sugar attained a value of 90 million *livres*, and coffee came close to 88 million *livres*. The value of cotton goods unloaded came to less than 22 million *livres*, which was less than 10 per cent of the total value of West Indian produce.

It is important to note the degree to which both the density of traffic and the value of trade with the West Indies depended upon the development of the plantation economy; this becomes especially clear if one's analysis is confined to French imports alone and is further limited within this context to sugar, coffee and cotton. In fact, a large proportion of the commodities produced were directed towards foreign markets, either illicitly or under perfectly legal conditions following the partial lifting of the *Exclusif*, the Trade Monopoly, in 1784. French merchants were aware of these trade developments and in the 1780s they voiced their resentment at losing considerable profits through direct trade links being established between other European countries and the colonial markets. French Atlantic trade felt the threat of falling profits. The French failed to follow the commercial initiative of English and American shipowners who reduced the time ships spent anchored in West Indian ports and cut the size of crews, thus enabling gains in productivity to be made on a scale that their rivals never matched. As French ports faced up to the crisis of the Revolution, they were, without doubt, much less prosperous than they were generally thought to be.

The transformation of trade and dislocation in the maritime towns

The Santo Domingo slave revolt of August 1791 and the maritime conflict during the Revolution and Empire put an end to a golden age in West Indian – or Atlantic – trade, even if it had not seemed so golden to many merchants at the time. The violence of the Revolution considerably weakened trade; the plantations were ruined by the slave revolts and dangers abounded at sea.

The dislocation of international trade was serious and we have to appreciate the permanent injury inflicted on the various industries in the ports and their hinterlands which had been making consumer goods for overseas markets. François Crouzet has argued that there was a lasting de-industrialisation or pastoralisation of large areas, with a definite shift of capital from trade and industry towards agriculture.[6] In Bordeaux itself there is some evidence for this transition among great merchants such as Paul Nairac, a major protestant shipowner and member of the Constituent Assembly in Paris, who showed a readiness to give up business to become a landowner.

To the east of Bordeaux, the town of Tonneins had 700 ropemakers in 1783, 1,000 in 1789 and only 200 in 1800; in the same town, a tobacco factory that had 1,200 workers in 1789 had fewer than 200 in 1800. In Bordeaux and Bayonne shipyards registered a decrease in their production despite a demand for ships from privateers which was quite significant during the Directory. Bordeaux and Nantes also had sugar refineries, distilleries, glassworks, linen manufacturing for slaves and cornmills producing fine flour for export to the West Indies (in Montauban, near Toulouse, the cornmills employed 1,800 workers and a further 3,000 were engaged in the manufacture of woollens). All these industries were badly affected. Bordeaux, for instance, had forty refineries before the Revolution and only ten in 1809. In Nantes cotton printing was almost completely wiped out.

The great seaports were very seriously affected: few ships anchored in their harbours. In March 1808 – somewhat later, it is true – the American Consul in Bordeaux painted a bleak picture of what had become a hopeless situation:

> From the Baltic to the Archipelago nothing but despair and misery is to be seen. Grass is growing in the streets of this city [Bordeaux]. Its beautiful port is deserted except for two Marblehead fishing schooners and three or four empty vessels which swing on the tide.[7]

The reduction in commercial activity led to an actual decline in the population of towns such as Bordeaux and Marseille: Bordeaux had 110,000 inhabitants in 1790 (as compared with only 60,000 in 1747), but by 1806 the population of the city had dropped to 93,000.

The rise of the Americans

It is, however, worth qualifying the impression this picture gives. Santo Domingo was not so cut off from Europe as is generally claimed. Sometimes French merchants used British and American staging posts, so that some trade with the Greater Antilles remained possible, although it was carried out under very difficult conditions. Coffee production, in particular, remained quite high as it depended less on the huge working gangs of slaves which had been broken up by the revolt. The main point of interest, however, is not that some merchants in Bordeaux or Nantes made efforts to keep up trading links and that they occasionally met with success. It is far more important to observe how the North Americans and the English took a hold in the West Indies and to note the transformation of trade which accompanied this development.

The United States had profited from the opening of the Spanish American ports to foreign trade (this opening had coincided with Cuba's first boom in sugar production) and from the naval war between France and Britain.[8] From 1793 onwards the conflict had forced the French Indies to depend on foreign traders. The Anglo-Spanish war in 1796 provided the Americans with even greater opportunities to intervene in trade. They, along with the Danes, remained the only neutral nation which could offer to carry out transactions in relative safety. A report written by a Bordeaux merchant in November 1799, at a time when American trade was suffering an embargo in France, recognised the importance of American shipping, which 'was flourishing and has gone on to fare even better during the early years of the war because we have been able to trade indirectly with our colonies by sailing under the American flag'.[9]

It should be emphasised that some American companies who took advantage of the improved opportunities for shipping established themselves in Bordeaux, Nantes and Bayonne. In a recent study, John Chase showed that a significant number of vessels plying between New York and Europe were clearing from French ports. Bordeaux was the major port throughout the period, followed by Nantes and Le Havre. Well behind came Lorient, Cherbourg, La Rochelle, Dieppe, Rouen and Marseille, all occasional ports of call.[10] Naturally, American merchants forged links with firms in these ports and could also form their own firms.[11] Equally there were traders from France or of French origin who settled on the American side of the Atlantic between New York and Charleston; they were often partners in West Indian companies or had trading posts in Cuba, Santo Domingo or Guadeloupe. Although these links were in place before the Santo Domingo revolution, they were greatly strengthened as a result of it. Merchants and planters from the Greater Antilles withdrew to the coast of America. E. H. Schell has studied the network of Dutilh, for example. Etienne Dutilh, whose brother Jean was living in Jamaica, joined the Wachsmuth firm in Philadelphia.[12] Pierre Changeur, a merchant from Bordeaux, also set up his firm in Philadelphia at the time of the Directory.[13]

The Atlantic coast of the United States was essential as a staging post for the 'indirect' shipping which linked France to its possessions in the West Indies. In Europe, two different zones were exploited for the purpose of Franco-American commerce. The north European ports, mainly Hamburg, were used to store colonial commodities and were also supplied by British merchant shipping. Similarly, the northern coast of Spain from Corunna to San Sebastian was frequented by American ships because merchandise could be dispatched from there to Bordeaux and Paris via Bayonne with relative ease. Cotton from Lisbon, one of the main centres of neutral trade, was transported by cart from Bayonne to Paris.

As a result of the blockade, relations between companies on either side of the Atlantic tended to fluctuate. Accordingly, in the spring of 1797, the crisis in Franco-American relations caused Etienne Dutilh to concentrate more on trade with India and China, as well as on direct trade with Cuba and the American ports. Two years later,

Dutilh used Spanish staging ports to ship tobacco and sugar to France: he had agents in El Ferrol, Corunna and San Sebastian.

French firms retained their reputation by shipping valuables, vintage wines, Lyon silks and high-quality cloth. Some French shipowners even took advantage of the neutral status afforded by the American flag and in the midst of the war continued to ship standard cargoes, of which food and equipment made up the largest part of the tonnage. This trade was bound for Santo Domingo or Guadeloupe. Wartime business in Bordeaux was not able, of course, to undergo any spectacular growth. The city's inhabitants survived the war years with difficulty; the population fell by 7,000 and business failures multiplied in 1793–94, 1799 and 1805, when trading conditions deteriorated. But ingenious ways were devised to continue the trade indirectly. Privateering again became an important substitute for regular trade: from 1796 to 1801, 163 privateers left the port of Bordeaux and during the period 1793–1814, 209 privateers were operating. 'Corsairomania' became fashionable in Bordeaux under the Directory,[14] the most striking feature being the number of merchants who arrived in the city between 1795 and 1800. The composition of this mercantile community differed markedly from that of the *ancien régime*. Newly established merchants were able to make great fortunes from maritime commerce and privateering, yet their total income seldom came from that source alone. The successful merchant invested in urban real estate and in vineyards thanks to the opportunity he was given to buy *biens nationaux*. Yet many merchants of the *ancien régime* had been ruined in 1793–94, even if the big firms generally survived and sometimes extended their business. We can guess that the total number of merchants was roughly 650–700 (there were more than 560 firms), and this number was the same as in 1789.[15]

On a microeconomic level, company histories convey some idea of how businessmen in France under the Directory, and to an even greater extent under the Consulate and the early days of the Empire, were consistently deluded about the situation in the West Indies and America. The business world was seized by feverish hope whenever peace negotiations led it to anticipate a return to 'normal conditions', for instance in 1797 and 1801–02. Periods of peace or negotiations meant, in effect, that merchants could resume traditional maritime trade and enjoy a return to their former prosperity. During these periods new trading companies that had set up in Paris and the main ports flourished, bringing together bankers, merchants and former

Santo Domingo planters. The existence of an American circuit trading in cotton and cloth from India, and of a rival British circuit, helped to feed ambitions which were, however, founded less and less on concrete realities.

Louis Bergeron has analysed the relatively effective policies of men like Oberkampf and Ternaux who led the French markets in prints and cotton. Spanish America continued to provide outlets for these manufacturers with the assistance of American staging posts. Bayonne emerged as a place of primary importance in controlling access to this market on account of its ties with Cadiz, Oporto and Lisbon.[16] Even politicians were closely involved in these business speculations, men such as Fouché and Tallien being prime examples at the end of the Directory. All trade carried out under these conditions remained extremely shaky, however, as it depended heavily on foreigners. France's most positive gain during this period lay in industrial developments which centred on overland trading networks.

The presence of American merchants both on the Caribbean and European fronts prevented French colonial trade from being completely stifled, and thus seaports such as Bordeaux, Nantes and Bayonne managed to continue their activity. However, this did not bring about any basic modification in major commercial trends or in the long-term development of trade. Despite certain tensions, North America remained closely involved in British interests. In New York, on 6 July 1797, the French merchant Michel Olive voiced his disappointment at the signing of the Anglo-American trade treaty:

> The English have never been totally eradicated from this country and their power is still on the increase . . . they get carried away by England's power . . . they are constantly indebted to their homeland's former glories and yet they use it to acquire such huge advances on goods that they fear circumstances might force English merchants to engage rather less freely in the shipping of products which they hold on to for a long time and which are one of their principal sources of finance.[17]

French merchants adhered to a traditional concept of trade, the foundation upon which the prosperity of colonial trading under the *ancien régime* had been built, namely respect for the Monopoly and the use of foreign trading partners for illicit dealings if necessary. Although the French business world had connections with American companies which were often quite effective during the Revolution and the Empire, the French do not seem to have been genuinely aware of the economic 'revolution' which was taking place, or, more specifically, of the major roles which New York and London had come to play in this. In 1815, when the Lesser Antilles were surrendered to the France of Louis XVIII, the sole ambition of French traders was to resume their former relations with the colonies within the framework of a fully restored Monopoly, and they still hoped to regain a foothold in Santo Domingo.

The investment switch from commerce to the land

We cannot over-estimate the diversion of capital towards agriculture as merchants increasingly became landlords. The most important developments in this respect arose from the sale of *biens nationaux* between 1791 and 1800. Opportunities for commercial employment and for the accumulation of capital which could be shifted later to more productive industries had decreased sharply. Instead, more and more people were interested in the switch of capital towards viticulture which could give a high level of profits through the sale of high-quality wines (1798 saw the best vintage of the century and outlets were available thanks to the efficiency of merchant networks on the European market). To judge from merchants' letters, the sales of Rhine wines were decreasing in northern Germany at the time of the Directory, whereas Bordeaux wines improved their position in Hamburg, Lübeck and Stettin.

Rents from landed property were increasingly attractive, too; yet even before the Revolution, great merchants had been deeply involved in the seigneurial regime and land ownership. In August 1791 Boyer-Fonfrède, the future Girondin leader who was also a shipowner, had an interest in the financial compensation arising from the loss of seigneurial rents in the countryside around Bordeaux.[18] Most merchants had similar rights and regarded them as an investment in relation to their trade. However, it should be pointed out that the argument that there was a shift of great fortunes from trade to land in Bordeaux under the Directory is supported by little real evidence. Those merchants most involved in privateering and in trade, such as Lacombe or Balguerie, invested heavily in real estate, but they did not give up their business interests. Debt-ridden merchants and others who had suffered from the times did not play an active role in the land sales.

Indeed, it is worth emphasising the point. Even during the golden age of trade before the Revolution, Bordeaux merchants were not people who appreciated risk-taking. The rapid increase in trading activity looks impressive, but even before the Revolution merchants were attracted by landed and seigneurial property. During the Revolution their behaviour was not much different: they were skilled in mounting trade ventures; they were attracted by investment, and land purchase was just one such investment.

The economy of the continental cities

There was also a second type of urban economy, for which the consequences of trade dislocation were not as negative as they had been in the Atlantic sector. This was the inland sector involving cities like Clermont-Ferrand or Limoges. Clermont-Ferrand had about 31,000 inhabitants in 1806, and the development of regional trade was the reason for its growth between the American War of Independence and the Empire. The city also had an important urban network in the Auvergne, consisting of seventeen towns of 2,000–10,000 inhabitants. Along the Garonne, Toulouse had 52,000 inhabitants in 1806. It, too, possessed a quite extensive urban network, with Montauban, Albi, Castres and Carcassonne numbering 24,000, 10,000, 10,000 and 15,000 inhabitants, respectively. During the Revolution the decline of these cities was slower than that of Bordeaux, where the loss of overseas markets created a condition of hopelessness. Civil disturbances and military operations were the main factors affecting the cities of the South-west (we should bear in mind the important government orders given to merchants for military purposes, such as the provisioning of the Army of the Pyrenees). Some merchant-manufacturers, Jean Boyer-Fonfrède for one, did try to organise cotton mills on the British pattern, but they were hindered by inadequate infrastructures.

It is interesting to draw a parallel between the resilient economies of the inland cities of France and the expansion of the textile industry in the northern and eastern parts of the country. This parallel should not, however, be exaggerated. There is no doubt that during the 1790s French industrial output did collapse and, although it recovered from 1796 onwards, by 1800 it was at best 60 per cent of its pre-1789 level. The causes of this disaster were many, but the interruption of French foreign trade was one of the most important. However, the damage was not completely beyond repair and in many towns, such as Paris or the towns in the northern or eastern areas, the wool and silk industries revived sharply under the Directory and Napoleon. There was relatively rapid progress in the cotton industry, with the growing concentration of this branch of European industry in northern and eastern France, Belgium and north-west Germany, a characteristic persisting throughout the nineteenth and early twentieth centuries. A shift of industries from the seaboard to the heartlands of Western Europe also took place. Because the British had monopolised overseas markets, the French wars forced most French industries to become inward-looking, focusing instead on the national market. In France, the Revolution created a national market which was relatively large, and manufacturers for whom war and post-war conditions had made access to foreign markets difficult were encouraged to confine their ambitions within their own borders.[20]

The new industries which developed during the wars and which were able to modernise and take over large markets were established in northern and eastern France, particularly in Paris. In Rouen, the pre-1789 condition of the textile industry had been bad, as it had in all the industrial cities of Normandy following the free trade treaty of 1786 between Britain and France. But around Paris and in eastern France, there was a spectacular rise in the number of new industries before the Revolution, notably the Oberkampf textile printing works in Jouy-en-Josas. After the difficulties of the Terror, capital investment had all but ceased. But the Directory was a time of prosperity, and from 1796 onwards machine spinning increased substantially following the modernisation of the cotton mills. At the turn of the century, cotton mills using water-frames were introduced. The prohibition of British goods increased the demand for locally produced yarns, and cotton printers were induced to start spinning mills. During the Revolution these industries took advantage of the creation of a national market and of sustained protection against British competition, and as a result the output of cotton goods increased. The cotton industry was the only one which did not collapse during the Revolution and even managed to increase its output. Some textile centres developed fast during the Directory and the early 1800s, particularly Paris and Lille; around 1800 French consumption of raw cotton was slightly greater than it had been before 1789.

In Paris, the resilience of the merchants played a key role in the increase of trade at the end of the eighteenth century. Many merchants from provincial areas went to Paris; often they were 'renegades' from the Atlantic bourgeoisie and they gave the new trade the necessary stimulus. Louis Bergeron has depicted these merchants who opened new businesses in Paris, men like Jean-Pierre Deville, a Bordeaux merchant residing in the Gironde before 1793 who came to Paris by way of Switzerland in 1795. Another example is Marc Antoine Grégoire Michel, a merchant who was protected by Cambacérès and who worked on government clothing orders for the Army of the Pyrenees in 1793. In 1796 he was in Bordeaux in partnership with his brother before moving to Paris in 1798, while during the Consulate he was the partner of Ouvrard in the great speculation in Mexican funds. Ouvrard was protected by Barras and was heavily involved in navy provisioning in 1798.

Paris was the centre where successful merchants placed their investments – in order of importance – in government bonds, banks, and provisioning of the army and navy, and in urban real estate and land. The city was the focal point of both national and international trade. Some merchant-manufacturers from Normandy, like Henri Grandin from Elbeuf, came to Paris to play a leading role in the Spanish wool trade and to sell wool to the manufacturers of Louviers, Sedan and Elbeuf. Other big merchant-manufacturers divided their business between manufacturing and overseeing the large trading networks in French and foreign ports. As early as 1782 Ternaux *père* began to do business in Paris while running his manufacturing operation in the provinces. His firm continued to grow during the Revolution and by 1798 Ternaux *fils*, who also had extensive interests in Leghorn, had built up a considerable fortune in Paris. Examples of this kind of business are numerous. In 1796, for example, Lenoir was partnered in a manufacturing venture by a certain Richard who had begun his career smuggling British dry goods, textiles and linens.

The markets which were open to these trades and manufactures were, of course, the national market and the continental market which functioned behind a wall of tariff protection. The exploitation of this continental market attracted entrepreneurial energies which had ceased to be tied up in overseas trade. But the study of New York merchants by John Chase shows that the origins of manufactured imports passing through that American port were much more diverse during the Revolution than had been the case before 1793, or would be again after 1815. Most studies have stressed American dependence on British manufactured goods, yet the evidence suggests that New York merchants had a fairly broad range of alternatives during the war years. Dry goods were entering New York from Hamburg, Amsterdam, Le

Havre and Bordeaux, as well as from British ports. These included textiles that had been manufactured on the Continent, not in Britain. Luxury dry goods of French origin were on offer in New York, although these seldom reached America directly from France. French manufactured goods from Paris and Lyon were highly prized in New York.[21] Some agricultural products, particularly cognac, were regularly imported through New York, too, although London always dominated the mixing and merchandising of cognac. In 1800 a new direct trade route was tried by cognac firms such as Otard and Hennessy.[22] The brandy was different, in that it was not treated with Madeira wine as it was for the British market.

Some American-born merchants were involved in smuggling and in the colonial trade. These firms did a lot of business in French ports and particularly in Paris. Most of them invested in urban real estate and the construction of elegant town houses. They were also interested in speculating in *biens nationaux*.[23]

A broad range of activities was offered by Paris, from banking and speculative ventures to maritime trade. All in all, the manufacturing sector must have provided jobs for around 40,000 people. The domestic market and the foreign market were consuming the products of this industry and Parisian consumers, boosted by prosperity under the Directory, were demanding more and more luxury goods. Watch-making, ribbon-making, glass-making, jewellery and earthenware all contributed to the reputation of the so-called 'articles de Paris'.

So, in the 1790s and 1800s, the economy of Paris rested on a few big businesses, luxury dry goods, government bonds and army pro-visioning, all of which helped to secure Paris's reputation as a com-modity and exchange market. Clear progress had been made during the Revolutionary period. Thanks to the decline of the seaports and their hinterlands, Paris began to attract resources from these ports and to increase its business. Entrepreneurs based in Paris and possessing substantial capital resources took over the smuggling and privateering activities operating out of the ports. In this way, Paris became the first 'commissionnaire' of the French economy.

However, we should not overlook three basic facts. The first is that Paris was already exploiting its potential before the Revolution by taking over important sectors of the economy, be they banking, manu-facture or trade. Moreover, Lyon also enjoyed a revival after the Terror.

The second basic fact concerns the investment in rent. A sharp rise in rentiers' profits occurred before 1789 with the speculative boom launched by Calonne, and this resumed under the Directory. There also were the opportunities presented by the sale of *biens nationaux*. However, the argument advanced by Alfred Cobban concerning the fossilisation of French wealth should not be disregarded completely. Honoré de Balzac would soon be chronicling the world of rent in early nineteenth-century Paris.

Finally, we should not overlook the fact that the most important shift in the urban economy derived from the difficulties faced by the ports. But we have to allow that the crisis in the colonial economy may have pre-dated the Revolution. In the 1780s quite a few of the Bordeaux merchants were aware of the internal problems of commerce and in particular of increasingly-vigorous foreign competition. They blamed this competition for their falling profits and doubtless failed to realise that powerful innovative measures were called for in order to make their ventures pay. When innovation did receive the support of the law, as had been the case when the Monopoly was lifted in 1784, they simply called for protection through a return to the old structure of the privileged market. During the turmoil of the Revolution, when the sugar mills of the Greater Antilles ground to a halt and ships ceased to cross the Atlantic, their sole desire was to return to the familiar prosperity of times past.

Notes

1   J-Cl. Perrot, 'Voies nouvelles pour l'histoire économique de la Révolution', *Annales historiques de la Révolution Française* (1975), pp. 30–65, shows the difficulties inherent in the statistical approach.

2   F. Crouzet, 'Wars, blockade and economic change in Europe, 1792–1815', *Journal of Economic History*, XXIV (1964), pp. 567–88. Crouzet gives an illuminating analysis of the *conjoncture* that we have applied to the cities.

3   P. Mathias and P. O'Brien, 'Taxation in Britain and France (1715–1810)', *Journal of European Economic History*, V (1976), p. 601 and *passim*. French taxation was less heavy than that of the British. During the Revolution, due to the civil disturbances, direct taxation, *emprunts forcés*, etc. varied. It is difficult to discern a trend.

4   F. Crouzet, 'Angleterre et France au XVIIIe siècle, essai d'analyse comparée de deux croissances économiques', *Annales E.S.C.*, XXI (1966), pp. 254–91.

5   P. Butel, 'Traditions and changes in French Atlantic trade between 1780 and 1830', *Renaissance and Modern Studies*, XXX (1986), pp. 124–45.

6   Crouzet, 'Wars, blockade', p. 573.

7   *Ibid.*, p. 571 n. 4.

8   S. Stein, 'Caribbean counterpoint: Vera Cruz vs Havana, war and neutral trade,

1797–1799', in J. Chase, *Géographie du capital marchand aux Amériques*, Paris, 1987, pp. 21–45.

9 J. Chase, 'War on trade and trade on war: Stephen Jumel and New York maritime commerce (1793–1815)', in *Bulletin du Centre d'Histoire des Espaces Atlantiques*, 4 (1988), pp. 111–63. This American development is studied using the example of New York.

10 *Ibid.*, p. 140.

11 It is possible to identify two big American firms set up in Bordeaux under the Directory – Morton and Russell and Strobel and Martini, which were successful until 1805.

12 E. H. Schell, 'Stephen Dutilh and the challenge of neutrality: the French trade of a Philadelphia merchant, 1793–1807', Conference on Franco-American Relations, 1765–1815, Wilmington, 1977.

13 P. Butel, *Les négociants bordelais, l'Europe et les Iles au XVIIIᵉ siècle*, Paris, 1974, p. 46.

14 'La corsairomanie prend beaucoup vu les prises nombreuses que nous faisons. Tous, jusqu'aux femmes, s'intéressent dans les armements et ils ont ici relevé bien des fortunes', see Bibliothèque Municipale de Bordeaux, fonds Bernadau.

15 Archives Départementales de la Gironde, 4L 312, Directory of the Department of Gironde, An VIII.

16 L. Bergeron, *Banquiers, négociants et manufacturiers parisiens du Directoire à l'Empire*, Paris-Lille, 1975, pp. 664–5.

17 Archives Municipales Bordeaux, Papiers Monneron, correspondance New York.

18 Archives Départementales de la Gironde, Etude notariale Rauzan, acte responsif, 18 August 1792, between Boyer-Fonfrède and Barthelemy Rateau, lawyer in the *ci-devant* Parlement of Bordeaux.

19 J.-P. Poussou, *Bordeaux et le Sud-Ouest au XVIIIᵉ siècle, croissance économique et croissance urbaine*, Paris, 1983, p. 224.

20 Crouzet, 'Wars, blockade', pp. 585–7.

21 Chase, 'War on trade', p. 141.

22 Codman papers, Boston, letter from Otard and Dupuy, Cognac, to Codman. I am grateful to Professor Crouzet who sent me a copy of this letter.

23 F. Crouzet, 'Les Codman de Boston', *L'Atlantique et ses rivages, actes du colloque des Historiens modernistes français*, Bordeaux, 1983.

chapter four T. J. A. LE GOFF *and* D. M. G. SUTHERLAND

The Revolution and the rural economy[1]

There is a widespread belief that the Revolution did much good for French agriculture since it relieved country people from centuries of fiscal and seigneurial oppression. Researchers who have looked more closely at the rural world are usually more cautious. They point out, for example, that by entrenching the rights of millions of smallholders and making it difficult to alter the old communal rights, the Revolution may have slowed down the pace of rural economic transformation and put a brake on the movement of labour into the cities and the factories. They also know that although the Revolution proclaimed the fiscal equality of all citizens and regions, this goal was not approximated until well into the nineteenth century.

Yet even among specialists a note of optimism persists. One thinks of the concluding sentence of *Les Paysans du Nord*, where Lefebvre writes that his peasants 'always approved the Revolution for uprooting aristocratic rule from their villages.'[2] In the same mode, the latest historian of the peasantry in the Revolution offers a judicious balance sheet but concludes that 'benefits there had been, and they should not be overlooked. For a majority of country dwellers the ending of seigneurial obligations and the tithe marked the watershed; for the minority it was access to land.'[3]

Most of these positive judgements rely on the supposed economic effects of institutional changes. And the evidence of these changes is incontrovertible. Consider the social arrangements abolished in that truly glorious summer of 1789 and in subsequent legislation down to 1793–94: church tithes, most seigneurial dues, seigneurial justice and the old patchwork of local and provincial government, which had so often reinforced the economic domination of the privileged. They were all replaced by rational public institutions. Taxes were to be levied on a fair basis and accounted for to the nation. Administrators and clergymen were paid on a uniform salary scale. The new system of *juges de paix*, which supplanted seigneurial courts as the tribunals of first instance, replaced an often capricious, and sometimes extinct or corrupt, judicial system with one which was both accountable and accessible. All of this was admirable.

But there are at least two difficulties in assessing the economic impact of such changes. First of all, there were immense local variations. Seigneurial dues, for example, had ranged from the symbolic and innocuous, through the vexatious and absurd, to the offensively heavy; in many regions, particularly when seigneurs and landowners were the same people or the same social group, their abolition made little difference. The regional incidence of church tithes had also varied considerably. But even more than the variety of local conditions, the changed environment of the Revolutionary and Imperial years makes it hard to isolate the results of institutional transformations, for they took place amidst shifts in rental values, population, consumer demand, political constraints and many other factors. Many positive institutional gains could have been enhanced, or cancelled, by the general context of the rural economy.

Many contemporaries of the Revolution and Empire did try to assess the impact of institutional changes on the economy, and came out with an encouraging result. Thus, the prefect of the Aude wrote in the Year X (1801–02) of how people in his department had better living standards since they had been freed from 'the tithe and dues on the land [*redevances foncières*]' and liberated from their debts 'as a result of the long period in which paper money circulated and lost value'. His colleague in the Aube claimed that 'the peasant made great gains during the Revolution, but used them to pay off his old debts and buy land. Only now that he has done this can he use his savings to get more livestock, repair his buildings and plant new crops.'[4] These were only two among numerous such reports administrators made to their superiors in Paris.

In these comments, the prefects were expressing what was fast becoming a government line, voiced by such writers as Jacques

Peuchet, bureaucrat, politician and indefatigable collector of fact under every regime since that of Louis XVI.[5] Its most effective spokesman was J.-P. Bachasson, Comte de Montalivet, Minister of the Interior from 1809 to 1814, who, in February 1813, produced for Napoleon's parliament a well-known report on the economic state of the Empire, much used by historians. In it, Montalivet went out of his way to show how the ordinary *cultivateurs* now enjoyed unheard-of prosperity; they can pay top prices for their land, they are better clothed and fed, they can rebuild finer and solider houses for themselves. All this because of the 'liberal laws which regulate this great Empire, the suppression of feudalism, of tithes, of mortmain, of monastic orders' (which gave property to the poor), because of partible inheritance, simpler property and mortgage laws, and rapid justice. 'These same causes and the influence of vaccine' had increased the population, as had military service, for it encouraged the rural elite to marry earlier in order to avoid conscription. To back up these claims, Montalivet published a great deal of statistical information, notably a summary, by 'agricultural region, of the prefects' figures for the harvests of 1810–12. Before the Revolution, he claimed, the average harvest was worth about 470 livres per head; the 1810–12 harvest was worth 520 livres per head; 'therefore our cereal production has increased by one-tenth'. Montalivet made sure of his claim by applying to the prefects' reports the methods of Napoleon's plebiscites: he increased the harvest of each agricultural region by exactly 12·5 per cent.[6]

When the chemist J. A. C. Chaptal, one of Montalivet's predecessors as Minister of the Interior (1801–04), published his treatise *De l'Industrie françoise* six years after the appearance of Montalivet's report, he announced that he had consulted the prefects' reports, local studies and various experts. He too produced statistical tables, including one for cereal production by department. Its figures, like Montalivet's, have also been used by many historians, among them J.-C. Toutain[7] and Alexandre Chabert,[8] but none could tell how representative they were. Comparison with the original prefects' reports shows that Chaptal took most of his data from the harvest summary of 1812 and worked out estimates for departments whose results were, in his view, unsatisfactory.[9] However, perhaps aware of the way that Montalivet had cooked his results, Chaptal declared that he would abstain from quantitative assessments and concentrate on qualitative comparisons. This allowed him to conclude, though with some precautions, that if we compare agriculture with what it was in 1789, we will be astonished at the improvements that have been carried out: harvests of all sorts cover the ground, numerous robust cattle plough and fertilise the land. Healthy and abundant food, clean and commodious lodgings, simple but decent clothing: such is the countryman's lot. Poverty has been banished from his life; his well-being results from free access to all produce.[10]

Chaptal, though by far the most perceptive of these witnesses, fell victim like all the others to the belief that since the institutional changes had been for the better, the economic context in which they operated had to reflect that beneficence.

Thus, one might say, did the surgeons pronounce their operation a success and the patient cured. Much of the thinking of Chaptal, Montalivet and others can be traced back to the early days of the Constituent Assembly, and indeed to the circles around the enlightened ministers and officials of the *ancien régime*. For generations they had held to the 'physiocratic vision', the notion that a rational tax system and the abolition of market controls would ultimately stimulate production by creating incentives to re-invest in agriculture. Embedded in the voluminous apologetics they left behind for historians to follow was the fundamental assumption that the Revolution, by rearranging public and private extraction from rural income, had left peasant families and landlords with a greater disposable surplus for productive investment as well as for consumer spending. By the time of the Empire, officials were well-primed to find a new prosperity everywhere they looked. They were even prepared to find benefits in the chaos of the Revolution, for they also assumed that various conjunctural changes, particularly the monetary disasters of the period, had eliminated debts and, by implication, rendered taxation innocuous for long periods of time, which likewise allowed peasants and landlords to invest their money more productively.

It is far from easy to evaluate contemporaries' assertions that an increase in agricultural production had in fact taken place. No one has produced a really satisfactory general account of economic change in this period.[11] One reason for this is that the continuity of the sources on which economic historians rely was broken in 1789. Harvest reports, which the royal administration had collected regularly after mid-century, ceased, or became fitful and unreliable, during the Revolutionary years, and the abolition of the tithe removed a source which historians of the *ancien régime* have often used as a proxy for production. The institutional chaos and introduction of fast-depreciating paper money between 1790 and 1797 disrupted the collection of continuous data on prices and turned the government's tax accounting into science-fiction at the height of the inflation. Only with great difficulty have demographers reconstructed the movement of population during these years from samplings in local archives. Private leases and accounts, which could partially fill these gaps, do exist, but are all too rare, and pose the obvious question of their representativity. The impressions and sporadic statistics left by officials from the period of the Consulate and Empire have long provided virtually the only overview used (and very often misused) by historians, but their authors had their own ambitions for the future and ambiguities about the recent past. We shall proceed then as medieval historians often must, working with fragmentary evidence, trying to deduce from a cluster of symptoms their unknown causes. The results must necessarily be tentative, but such a re-examination is surely better than accepting largely unsubstantiated assertions about the place of the Revolution in the lives of ordinary countryfolk.

How well, then, did the rural economy produce? No one knows, of course, and none of the rudimentary harvest surveys of the period 1789–99, particularly those of the Year II and Year V, can be trusted, since everyone quite rightly feared they were a prelude to requisitions. However, many of the original reports from the period of the Consulate and Empire, which Montalivet misused and Chaptal muddled, are still in central and departmental archives. They were part of a mass of statistical data gathered at a time when the Ministry of the Interior picked up the traditions of political arithmetic and national accounting which had begun to emerge under the *ancien régime* monarchy.

Between 1800 and 1813 the prefects were asked to produce information on most forms of agricultural output. The story of how this material was collected has been ably told by J.-C. Perrot and Stuart Woolf.[12] The most frequent and thorough of these enquiries were annual questionnaires on the prospects, and results, of the grain harvests. At first, the prefects estimated the amount or the fraction by which cereals for human consumption differed from the output and human needs of a 'common year' in their departments, but from September 1802 onwards they were asked to provide a figure for total cereal production for human consumption, and often the detail of the various crops, the estimates being made at the level of the basic administrative units, the communes and cantons.[13] Complete national records survive for the years 1810–13.[14] In 1813 the government's definition of a 'harvest' was enlarged to take in all grown foodstuffs, most notably oats, chestnuts and potatoes (the latter two being converted to a cereal equivalent). Fortunately, the Ministry kept a copy of the complete results, which makes it possible to reconstruct what would have been the result for that year under the previous system of collecting data on cereals for human consumption (Table 1)[15] and also to link the full results of that year with the virtually identical published material in the *Statistique générale de la France* for the period after 1815 (see Table 3).[16]

The 1810–13 data are the first proper national figures for harvest output since 1789, indeed the first systematic overall figures ever produced. They indicate an average annual production of 107·1 million hectolitres of grains for human consumption over the four years from 1810 to 1813 for the territory of France within its post-1815 frontiers.[17]

Table 1 *Cereal production for human consumption 1810–13*

Year	Hectolitres	Quintals
1810	98,845,554	65,238,066
1811	86,085,983	56,816,729
1812	119,942,185	79,161,842
1813	125,549,337	82,862,562
Average	107,056,871	70,657,535

Source: AN F[10] 252.

How representative were these years of the general level of harvests in the period? On the basis of the responses to the government's annual enquiries, we have developed a very tentative index of wheat, rye and maislin production in seventeen departments. These can be set beside other indicators bearing on both France and the annexed territories which were to be included in the Empire: surpluses and deficits of food cereals, cereal imports and exports, and national wheat prices (Table 2).[18]

These figures conform to what is believed to have been the general pattern under the Consulate and Empire: poor or middling harvests in 1800–03, and then some good harvests punctuated by the poor or bad years of 1806, 1809, 1810 and 1811 (Table 2). The year 1812 was considered reasonably good; 1813 was a record. However, regions varied widely in their performance because of climatic variations and the different weightings of winter and spring grains in local production.

The data in our index suggest somewhat higher average cereal production in the years 1804–09 than in 1810–13, but they leave out, or represent inadequately, the poor years 1800–03; if the latter could be included, output figures for 1810–13 would probably be similar to the average for the previous decade.[19] Full national data suggest a comparable level for the period 1815–25. Indeed, the whole period from 1799 to about 1825 appears as a long period of stagnation prior to a take-off in the late 1820s (Tables 2 and 3). Although no macro-economic evidence on production is available from the period 1791–99, it is difficult to believe that the chaotic Revolutionary years from 1791 to 1799 often surpassed these levels. Crops from 1795 to 1799 were probably adequate, but 1794 had witnessed a remarkably poor harvest and the results of the earlier years of the Revolution were considered less than sufficient.[20] The period 1810–13 therefore probably represents a good average for the Revolutionary and Imperial period. Evidence from leases points in the same direction, as we shall see.

How does this average production of 70·7 million quintals compare to what was grown in the 1780s? J.-C. Toutain estimated France's annual production at about 85 million quintals of bread cereals for the

Table 2 *Indicators of cereal production, exports and prices 1800–13*

Year	(1) Wheat, rye and maislin production (seventeen French departments) (1813 = 100)	(2) Food cereal surpluses and deficits in the 'Empire' (million hectolitres)	(3) Balance of foreign cereal trade for the 'Empire' ('000 quintals)	(4) French wheat prices (1813 = 100)
1800	82 (1)*	–	381·8	90
1801	74 (2)	–	20·2	100
1802	103 (4)	−11·9	−956·6	112
1803	137 (1)	1·2	−137·4	104
1804	87 (7)	9·3	307·5	83
1805	107 (5)	6·3	922·3	87
1806	83 (15)	2·0	107·7	86
1807	104 (11)	7·8	257·9	84
1808	126 (7)	22·6	554·9	73
1809	83 (2)	18·8	503·0	66
1810	75 (6)	−2·9	887·4	87
1811	66 (6)	−13·9	−981·6	116
1812	88 (17)	7·6	−1364·0	153
1813	100 (17)	–	−572·0	100

*Number of departments with usable information in brackets.
Source: As in note 18.

Table 3 *Harvest indices 1813–31 (1813 = 100)*

Years	Wheat, rye, maslin	All cereals	Potatoes
1813	100	100	100
1814	–	–	–
1815	73	81	94
1816	79	84	112
1817	86	94	207
1818	94	85	127
1819	–	–	–
1820	85	97	177
1821	107	110	187
1822	94	96	180
1823	50	76	195
1824	110	112	203
1825	106	101	–
1826	108	106	–
1827	102	104	–
1828	107	109	–
1829	116	114	237
1830	96	111	239
1831	101	116	287

Source: Ministère de l'Agriculture. Direction de l'Agriculture. Bureau des Subsistances, *Récoltes des céréales et des pommes de terre de 1815 à 1876*, Paris, 1878; AN F[10] 252.

period 1781–90.[21] If this were true, it would make the harvests of the later Empire look poor indeed, and suggest an absolute decline in grain production during a time of growing population, despite the return of stability and the expansion which is supposed to have taken place under the Empire. Dupont de Nemours, Tolosan and Lavoisier proposed lower estimates of average annual requirements and production for human consumption at the end of the *ancien régime*, but they based their calculations on a population which they estimated, wrongly, at about 25 million instead of the 28 million now considered the correct figure for 1789. J.-C. Perrot has suggested a revised version of their results in the range of 73–77 million quintals for the 1780s, reminding us, however, that contemporaries of Lavoisier, whose figures come at the top of this range, considered that he generally tended to underestimate.[22]

In any event, all of these results point in the same direction: performance in the last four years of the Empire at best only came up to the level of the most optimistic estimates of the political arithmeticians for the 1780s. Or, if Toutain's generous estimates for the 1780s are accepted, output in the later Empire represented a significant decline from pre-Revolutionary performance. The earlier years of the Empire may have seen a slightly higher output than that of 1810–13, but even this would not change the general picture of long-term stagnation.

Stagnation of supply was not apparently compensated for by a contraction of grain exports. During the *ancien régime* and after 1815 France exported some cereals, principally from western ports to the Iberian peninsula and the West Indies. This flow was frequently interrupted in the period 1792–1815. But total cereal exports had been rather small both before 1789 and after 1815: probably less than 1 per cent of French production.[23] Meanwhile, population rose – not by much in the Revolutionary decade, but somewhat more under the Consulate and Empire.[24] Even though the appetites of hundreds of thousands of adult men were 'exported' in the Revolutionary armies, where they fed at the expense of the rest of Europe, grain prices rose substantially, indicating tension on supply (Table 4). There was only one old-fashioned subsistence crisis, in 1794–95, but there were close calls in other years, notably in 1801–03 and 1810–11. People appear to have got by, as in bad years during the *ancien régime*, by eating cereals which would normally have fed animals, or not been grown at all. Thus, in 1811, the prefect of the Oise explained that 'si la cherté du blé se soutient [les orges] entreront au moins pour 1/6ᵉ . . . dans les fabrications du pain de la classe indigente des campagnes et contribueront d'autant à remplir le déficit en blé',[25] It is sometimes alleged that the spread in the cultivation of the potato during these years made up for the stagnation of cereal cultivation; thus Postel-Vinay claims that around 1820 potato crops provided 'from 25 to 30 per cent of the calorific equivalent of the wheat [*blé*] harvest'.[26] This is true, but misleading; the calorific equivalent of potato output came to only about 7 per cent of the total cereal harvest at this late date, and only 1–2 per cent of the equivalent of total cereal crops in 1813.[27] As Morineau has suggested, such growth in potato production as occurred may in reality be the replacement by the tuber of other potential substitutes such as barley and oats.[28] One is left with the impression that producers might have done better.

Was the apparently poor performance of the grain economy compensated by a shift to cattle-raising? Price movements (Table 4) and government requisitions certainly do not seem to have favoured such a shift before the turn of the century. A government enquiry into the bovine population carried out between 1809 and 1813[29] gives the totals for the post-1815 frontiers shown in Table 5.

Table 4 *Price indices for wheat, meat and wine (base 1776–89 = 100)*

Years	Wheat	Beef	Veal	Mutton	Pork	Wine
1776–89	100	100	100	100	100	100
1801–05	148	117	113	125	148	162
1806–10	120	122	115	126	135	171
1811–15	163	125	123	137	152	218
1816–20	171	138	136	150	179	277
1821–25	157	130	130	147	170	238

Source: Wheat prices: national prices in Labrousse, Romano, and Dreyfus, *Le prix du froment*, pp. 9–10; meat and wine: Strasbourg prices in A. Hanauer, *Etudes économiques sur l'Alsace ancienne et moderne*, Paris and Strasbourg, 1878, II, pp. 192–3, 337–8 (some missing years for Strasbourg 1776–89 interpolated from Mulhouse data). Wine prices are for new Châtenois ordinaire.

Table 5 *Bovine population, 1813 (frontiers of 1816)*

	Million head
Oxen	1·72
Cows	4·05
All bovines	7.88

Source: AN F[10] 510.

How did this situation compare with that under the *ancien régime*? Expilly and Lavoisier estimated between 7·1 and 7·9 million bovines of all species for the pre-Revolutionary decades, as compared to our figure of 7·9 million in 1809–13: in short, no apparent change. Lavoisier also produced figures for oxen and cows: 3·09 million oxen before 1789, as against perhaps 1·7 million in 1813 and 4 million cows compared to 4·05 million in 1813.[30] Montalivet, again, claimed advances had been made, but only by comparing cattle exports in the entire Napoleonic Empire at its height with those from France before the Revolution.[31] We are left again with a gloomy picture, and it might be thought that Lavoisier and Expilly had simply estimated too high for the period before 1789. However, an enquiry from the Year III (1794–95) offered a total of 8·7 million 'horned cattle', or 0·9 million more animals than in 1809–13. In that enquiry, the owners of cattle had an interest in minimising their holdings in order to escape requisitions; so this bears out the general opinion that the Revolution and its requisitions did no good to cattle-raising.[32]

A somewhat similar picture emerges from such statistics as are available on the sheep population during these years. Looking first at the end of the period, an enquiry prepared for Montalivet on the basis of information dating from 1809–11 put the national total at 25·5 million.[33] From Montalivet's figure of 35·3 million for the entire Empire, Toutain derived a figure of 27·3 million for 'France'; comparison of Montalivet's and the inspectors' figures show the Minister's figures, printed on a regional basis, to be higher in all but one case, but of course he may have had the advantage of later information.[34] Chaptal reproduces what are probably real *wool production* figures from the same enquiry, giving a national clip of 35·2 million kg; Toutain, on the basis of what is apparently a subsequent slip by Chaptal, estimated the sheep *population* at this figure. In any event, Montalivet's *production* figures are also inflated: almost one-third higher than the comparable wool output in Chaptal.[35] Compounding the confusion, Toutain cites Herbin's figure of 30·3 million sheep in 1803 without realising that it referred to the sheep population of both France and its recently annexed territories.[36] All this muddle has carried over into general works.[37] Further on, the official statistics for 1830 and 1836 indicate only 29 million and 32 million head, respectively, after much progress had presumably occurred. These make the 1809–11 total of 25 million a reasonable estimate for the end of the Empire.[38]

If an estimate of 25·5 million sheep at the end of the Empire is right, and if Lavoisier's estimate of 20 million sheep in 1789 is accepted, there would have been a reasonable increase in the bovine population, but Toutain is probably right to think the 1789 figures too pessimistic (the *abbé* Expilly had even estimated 32 million in 1778). An enquiry of 1794, cited by Peuchet, carried out when peasants had every interest in hiding their stock, indicated a total of 24·3 million head already,[39] or about the same as in 1809–11. This figure of 24·3 million head may derive from a version of the enquiry of the Year III, which enumerated 22·5 million *moutons et brebis*.[40] As with bovines, then, there may well have been as many, if not more, sheep in 1794–95 (and very likely in 1789 as well) than in the late Empire.

A slightly brighter picture is provided in the realm of viticulture. The production of wine would appear to have risen somewhat in the course of the period 1786–1815. It has been suggested that the momentary abolition of the drink excise and the growing numbers of troops under the colours led to greater demand for cheap wines, for direct consumption or distillation, which outweighed, at least in volume, the loss of many export markets for finer wines, and that the reintroduction of the drink excise in 1804 did not slake consumers' thirsts. Figures for average production from 1786 to 1788, 1805–08, 1810, 1812 and 1823–41 show a fairly dramatic leap during the Revolutionary generation, from 27·2 million hectolitres per year on the eve of the Revolution to 36.8 million hectolitres per year in 1805–12, a level not much less than that reached in 1823–41. But several reservations need to be expressed about these figures. The years 1786–88 came at the end of a long crisis in French viticulture; and were for years considered 'barely average', so that the normal pre-Revolutionary production capacity was probably higher. Secondly, wine production was notoriously volatile. Perhaps a more stable measure of the state of this sector is the total surface under vines, which rose only a little (6 per cent) between 1788 and 1808, from 1·58 to 1·68 million hectares, further increasing to 1.74 million in 1824. This is probably because a great deal of investment in wine production had already been made during the pre-Revolutionary generations. Favourable weather plus demand enhanced by the abolition of the excise finally made it worthwhile.[41]

If the macroeconomic figures are to be believed, then, only the viticultural sector provided some signs of dynamism in an otherwise stagnant rural economy at the end of the Empire. An examination of more disparate microeconomic sources tends to confirm this pessimistic hypothesis. One such source is the accounts and leases of sharecropping landlords found from time to time in private papers. Obviously, this is a less comprehensive source than overall production figures, but it has the merit of great precision. The results are instructive. The estate of Hauterive in the Mayenne, for example, remained the same size from the 1730s until early in this century, and collected its rents in kind at the same rate throughout the Revolution and Empire. Its accounts thus furnish a direct record of production; and except for the owner's incarceration as a suspect during the Terror and the Chouannerie, between 1794 and 1797, the estate carried on more or less unperturbed. Berset d'Hauterive took all of the former tithe for himself (thereby confirming an argument we have made elsewhere),[42] and when this is taken into account, his share of the harvest in grains floated within fixed limits. Indeed, with the 2,600 *boisseaux* (Laval measure) harvested in 1792, the estate reached a high point which was never exceeded even in the more settled conditions of the Empire which saw harvests fluctuate between 1,500 *boisseaux* and 2,300 *boisseaux*. Only in the 1830s was the 2,300 *boisseaux* ceiling broken and harvests of 3,000 *boisseaux* attained.[43] The *métairie* of Villeroy, owned by the Hospice of Sens, had maintained the same dimensions from the early seventeenth century to the 1850s and beyond. From 1777 until 1796 it collected 23·4 hectolitres of wheat and 32·8 of rye plus 6 pairs of pigeons; the new lease of 1796 took about 3 hectolitres less of rye, dropped the pigeons and added 176 *livres* in specie (once again, it seems clear that the landowner kept the tithe). In 1820 the administrators rounded up the wheat and rye to 30 hectolitres and dropped the money component.[44] In short, nothing changed. On the *métairie* of Varennes in Poitou (arrondissement of Châtellerault), about 100 *boisseaux* of rye plus accessory charges (firewood, chickens, capons, eggs, etc.) went annually as a proportional share of the harvest to the *curé* for his tithe, and to the owner, M. de Marans, on the eve of the Revolution. In the next lease, signed in 1798, Marans not only took over the *curé's* tithe, but doubled the amount extracted from the sharecropper, who now had to pay 200 *boisseaux* of rye as a fixed rent in kind plus more accessory charges, in part to compensate for the fact that the former *curé's* share no longer had to be hauled to the presbytery, perhaps also just out of greed. However, 200 *boisseaux* proved too much rent to bear; when Marans took on a new tenant seven years later, in 1806, he had to reduce his share of the profits to the pre-1789 level, with a fixed levy of 100 *boisseaux*.[45] But Marans still kept it all for himself.

Leases can also be used to estimate production, albeit indirectly and with a greater margin of error. As J.-P. Chaline points out, when we look at the yearly movement of prices and leases, we find that leases respond quickly in this period to price rises, but more slowly to falls, since leases usually ran for six to nine years.[46] The Hospice of Langres (Haute-Marne) specified payments in grain for many of its rural properties. J.-J. Clère has reproduced figures from three of them, which start in 1790 and run through this period; they show a rise of 15–18 per cent by 1809; this rise was probably the equivalent of the abolished tithe and possibly the *champart* in a region much burdened by such dues before 1789.[47] An index (Table 6) can be produced for a larger set of forty-one leases in kind held by this hospice; it does not have a big enough base for the period before 1793 but it does show clearly the limits of expansion once the tithe and *champart* were integrated in the lease: during the period 1793–1820 rental values moved up and down by only a few percentage points and declined after 1803.

Cash leases were more common. Zolla studied several score hospital leases from the seventeenth to the nineteenth centuries and collected what he could from nineteenth-century monographs.[48] From his series

Table 6 *Leases in grain, Hospital of Langres (Haute-Marne) (base 1816 = 100)*

Year	Index	Year	Index	Year	Index
1790	79	1800	111	1810	106
1791	88	1801	112	1811	104
1792	92	1802	113	1812	104
1793	99	1803	114	1813	106
1794	99	1804	112	1814	105
1795	98	1805	111	1815	101
1796	102	1806	110	1816	100
1797	106	1807	108	1817	100
1798	110	1808	107	1818	98
1799	112	1809	106	1819	98

Source: Clère, *Les paysans de la Haute-Marne*, pp. 340–3; (all leases in kind (excluding *terrages*) and the farm of Beauchemin).

and similar studies,[49] the indices shown in Table 7 can be ascribed to rents in 1789 and 1815.[50]

Table 7 *Comparison of cash rents on hospital lands (1789/90–1815) (index 1789–90 = 100)*

	1789	1815	(Number of leases)
Hospice of Rouen (10 farms near Rouen)	100	136	(140)
Hospice of Le Mans			
– Arrondissement du Mans (19 farms)	100	126	(126)
– Arrt of La Flèche (4 farms)	100	130	(139)
– Arrt of St-Calais (3 farms)	100	117	(116)
– Arrt of Mamers (4 farms)	100	136	(131)
– Arrt of Mamers, Le Mans etc. (additional group – 28 farms)	100	124	(132)
– Department of Mayenne (5 farms)	100	92	(95)
Hospice of Sens (4 farms)	100	159	(165)
Hospice of Bourg (Ain) (26 farms)	100	100	

Source: As in notes 48 and 49.

What was the timing and explanation of these rises? Zolla, drawing on the records of the Hospices of Rouen and Le Mans, and from other material on Beauvais, Sens and from the Seine-et-Marne, concluded that most of the increase – 10–20 per cent – took place in the Revolutionary decade from 1789 to 1799, and more specifically between 1790 and 1792.[51] This was the result of incorporating permanently into the lease the temporary provisions of the law of 11 March/10 April 1791, which had stated that the landlord could collect the equivalent of the tithe for the duration of the existing lease. Indeed, Zolla was able to show a close correspondence in the Sarthe between rent rises and the proportion of rent (about 10 per cent) represented by the tithe.[52] As more and more leases were renewed, these payments, and, later, abolished seigneurial dues, were successively put into the leases. However, as most of the farmers he studied were made to pay their rents in kind or in the current cash equivalent of specified quantities of produce during the years of currency instability, it could be some time before the leases reflected the true level of rent. The initial rise was followed by a levelling off or even a decline in the Consulate and early Empire, and finally by a sharper rise in the last few years of the Empire. Table 8 gives some indication of the timing of rent changes.

Table 8 *Chronology of cash rents on hospital lands (index: 1789 = 100)*

Locality	Period				
	1789	*1795–99*	*1799–1804*	*1804–15*	
				First leases	*Second leases*
Near Rouen	100 (10)*	125 (1)*	112 (8)*	110 (5)*	140 (10)*
Arrt of Le Mans	100 (19)	112 (13)	124 (11)	–	126 (19)
Arrt of La Flèche	100 (4)	–	116 (3)		139 (4)
Arrt of St-Calais	100 (3)	120 (1)	114 (2)		116 (3)
Arrt of Mamers	100 (4)	99 (2)	110 (4)		131 (4)
All leases (Zolla data)	100 (4)	112 (17)	117 (28)	110 (5)	131 (40)
Hospice of Bourg (Ain)	100 (26)	150 (26)	100 (26)	100 (26)	100 (26)
Grain prices (France)**	100	107	125	101	137

* Numbers of leases in parentheses.
** Base 1787–91 = 100 for grain prices.
Source: As in notes 48 and 49.

This compilation suggests an initial rise of (in most cases) 12–25 per cent between 1789 and 1799, then a long period of near stability, or occasional falls, and a final spurt of rents in the last years of the Empire leading to an overall gain of the order of 26–40 per cent, which is close to the figures which Zolla derived using a different method. Zolla concluded that the overall gains in rent were the result of the abolition of the tithe and seigneurial dues, rising prices, and falling taxes – and not of increasing production.

But if Zolla was able to show the close link between the tithe as a percentage of rent and the jump in leases around 1790–92, the link with prices was, and is, less easy to establish. If we take as the basis of an index average national grain prices for the five years 1787–91 inclusive and compare them with average prices in the periods which Zolla used, we get the results shown in Table 8. These figures suggest that, despite the 'bonus' given proprietors by the abolition of the tithe and seigneurial dues, leases never made a permanent advance on prices in this period, only gaining temporary advantages in 1795–99 and under the early Empire. This is a more pessimistic conclusion than Zolla himself reached, for it suggests a fall in real rents, and, indirectly, production. More sophisticated tests on Chaline's annual data suggest that Zolla was right to believe that in very favoured regions leases may have risen a little in real terms.[53] Further analysis of rates of increase of leases and grain prices confirms the initial surge in leases in the period 1790–99, well over the rise in grain prices. It also illustrates the stagnation of rental income in mid-stream (1795–1804 or 1795–1809), and, finally, a speculative boom in the later years of the Empire and early Restoration, when increasing grain prices prompted even greater rent rises.[54]

True, hospital properties may have been conservatively administered (though their leases were required by law to be awarded at public auction), and private landlords might have been quicker to seize opportunities. Unfortunately, there is apt to be less continuity in private leases, and more likelihood that the farm changed its dimensions or resources, which makes it more difficult to constitute continuous data. We have collected a series of eleven leases which both illustrate this problem and give some indication of the general tendency (see Table 9). Thus, the farmer of the Duc de Charost, in the rich Pays de Caux, to the north of Rouen, agreed to a rent of 1,200 *livres* in 1780, paid nothing but produce and labour between 1795 and 1804 according to a lease signed in Year IV, handed over 1,580 *francs* a year until 1813, and then 2,500 *francs* until 1825, but the increase here was at least in part because of some additions made to the property. Without these improvements, the duke's lease would conform to the general movement which Zolla detected.[55] The duke's luck in leasing out some meadows was a little different. In 1784 he claimed a rent of 1,400 *livres*, in 1806, 1,060 *francs*, in 1817, 2,100 *francs* (once again in part because of improvements).[56] The remainder of the series in Table 9 comes from leases on six farms in the Pays de Caux, two large farms in Picardy and a small tract of land in the Cotentin. We find a couple of dramatic rent rises, almost certainly justified by improvements, enlargement of the premises or special

Table 9 *Indices of leases on private holdings (index 1790 = 100)*

	Pays de Caux								Avran-chin	Ile-de-France/ Picardy	
Year	(1)	(2)	(3)	(4)	(5)	(6)	(7)	(8)	(9)	(10)	(11)
1774										65	
1777			91								
1778											69
1779	100	100									
1780						100	100				
1784							100			100	
1785		100									
1786			100		100				100		
1789										100	
1790				100							
1791		180									112
1792			109								
1793											
1794											119
1795									150		
1796					156						
1797				83							
1798											
1799	81										
1800											
1801				83		120					
1802											96
1803											
1804							131		190		
1805											
1806								76			
1807			127		253						
1812	119								200		
1813							208				
1817								150		110	
1818										110	

Source: As in note 57.

arrangements about tax payments, but in general the rise between 1789 and the Empire is of the order observed by Zolla: a rise at the outset of the Revolution, followed by a fall after the Directory and subsequent recovery under the Empire.[57]

None the less, rents and other private exactions like the tithe and feudal dues during the *ancien régime* were only part of the total levy on rural production. Taxes were the final element of this overall *prélèvement*. It is important to stress that total exaction from production had an upper limit. Each of its elements was interdependent, so that if one part fell, the others would, after a period of adjustment, rise to take up the slack. This was the logic of the Constituent Assembly's decision to assign the newly abolished tithe to the landowner in 1791, the same logic which the nineteenth-century economist Léon Say expressed when he claimed that 'quand une terre est favorisée par l'impôt c'est comme si sa fertilité s'était accrue' and that therefore it would rent for more than higher taxed land.[58]

To explore this hypothesis, based on assumptions common to landlords, tenants and economists alike, we have worked out estimates (Table 10) of the total and per capita amounts of direct taxes actually collected during this period within what became the frontiers of France after 1815.[59] As land taxes always represented about three-quarters of total direct taxes,[60] changes in the volume of all direct taxes can therefore stand as a rough equivalent for changes in the volume of the land tax. We have provided two sets of indices of total taxes and taxes per capita, one set based on an estimate of 220 million *livres* of direct taxes collected in the last years of the *ancien régime*, and another on the total direct taxes the French were expected to pay in 1791 according to the new tax reforms.

Despite the hopes of the Constituent Assembly for a greater tax yield after the abolition of the tithe, direct taxes effectively collected in the Revolutionary years stayed well below *ancien régime* levels until about 1797, then rose to a level about one-third above. It took the crisis of the Empire after 1810 to bring direct taxes up to the level legislators had hoped for in 1791.[61] The level of the land tax in the late Empire and early Restoration put severe strains on the peasantry, particularly when agricultural prices began to fall after 1820, and it was accordingly reduced again.

Here, then, is the probable explanation for the rhythm of rent movements in this period. Peasants could bear rising taxes when prices rose but refused to sign higher leases when prices fell and taxes stayed high. Government failure to enforce the heavy direct taxes imposed in 1790 left landlords a breathing-space in which to incorporate the tithe

Table 10 *Estimates of direct taxes and surtaxes collected 1789–1829*
(post-1815 territory of France)

Years	Tax collected) (million lv/fr)	Indices 1789 = 100		Indices 1791 = 100**	
		Tax	Tax per capita	Tax	Tax per capita
	(1)	(2)	(3)	(4)	(5)
Pre-1789	220·0 (200·0)**	100	100		
1781 levy*	400*			100	100
1791–92	180·4 (225·0)	82	82	45	45
1792–93	106·1 (181·3)	48	48	27	27
1793–94	81·0 (192·3)	37	37	20	20
1794–95	35·0 (394·4)	16	16	9	9
1798–99	340·9	155	150	85	83
1799–1800	352·8	160	154	88	85
1800–01	298·0	135	130	74	72
1801–02	275·0	125	119	69	66
1802–03	303·3	138	132	76	73
1803–04	312·4	142	135	78	75
1804–05	312·4	142	135	78	74
1807	306·7	139	131	77	73
1808	300·6	137	128	75	71
1809	312·8	142	133	78	73
1810	306·2	139	130	77	72
1811	308·9	140	131	77	72
1812	315·4	143	133	79	74
1814	426·1	194	180	107	99
1815	313·0	142	131	78	73
1816	413·2	188	172	103	95
1817	440·4	200	183	110	101
1818	396·1	180	163	99	90
1819	373·7	170	153	93	84
1820	326·2	148	133	82	73
1821	359·2	163	145	90	80
1822	345·3	157	138	86	76
1823	344·1	156	137	86	76
1824	348·8	159	138	87	76
1825	346·7	158	136	87	75
1826	338·8	154	132	85	73
1827	324·4	147	126	81	69
1828	324·9	148	126	81	69
1829	325·2	148	124	81	69

* Base 1791 = total direct taxes and surtaxes *assessed* (but not collected) in 1791.
** Nominal receipts in parentheses.
Source: As in note 59.

and seigneurial dues into their rents. Allowing for a certain lag, the new effectiveness of tax collection after 1797 probably helps to explain the subsequent fall or stability of so many leases in the years after the turn of the century; similarly, the tax rise after 1809 or so helped to freeze rents after 1813, and especially when prices slumped in the 1820s.[62] Over the long run from 1790 to the 1820s, the delayed rise of direct taxes, and particularly of the land tax, explains the relatively slight overall increase in rents, despite the disappearance of tithes and seigneurial dues.

In the long upward movement of agricultural production in the century from 1750 to 1850, then, the period of the Revolution and Empire represents a pause. It is difficult to believe, however, that this setback was caused by population hitting a Malthusian ceiling on resources. The subsequent history of nineteenth-century growth, so much of it within the framework of the old agricultural economy, argues against that.[63] Some of the difficulties can be explained by poor harvests. But the effect of human decisions cannot be ignored either.

In effect, the physiocratic vision that production could be increased by strengthening property rights and by reforming taxes collided with the structural realities of the French countryside and the way the foreign war was financed. In the first place, only certain classes of producers benefited from fiscal reform and from the abolition of the tithe and of seigneurialism. Much depended on the status of the individual peasant family, and whether it owned or rented its land. Much also depended on the attitude towards investment held by owner-occupiers, tenants or landlords, and their short-term response to the very chaotic economic circumstances of the years 1789–1820. No one has ever seriously investigated these responses in this period. But it can hardly have been a propitious time for investment in improvements; especially when it was so much easier simply to buy more land when rural property values collapsed after 1793.[64] It might also be wondered (though it is a hard-hearted question to pose) whether the real progress accomplished towards greater tax equity within communes[65] did not decrease the investment capacity of the better-off peasants by taking more from them in order to relieve the burdens of the poor.

Further to that point, the assumption that inflation cancelled debts to rentiers and landlords[66] is also misleading. As one estate steward in upper Normandy pointed out, his tenants could not buy out their debts with inflated currency because controlled markets and requisitions reduced their remaining marketable production to practically nothing.[67] A study of notarial contracts in that same region concluded that rural creditors and debtors were both quite aware of the precautions that had to be taken in the face of inflation.[68] In addition, shrewd landlords demanded their rents in kind, even going well beyond the emergency measures of the law of 21 July 1795 which authorised them to collect half their rents in produce. Many managed to take the entire rent in cash or kind, as it suited their needs, no matter what the law said.[69] Finally, if inflation favoured some debtors in the brief period 1792–95, lenders' fear of it did them a disservice, for it drove up interest rates on hard currency loans for long afterwards. In April 1793 usury rates were abolished, ironically (as one disabused revolutionary later noted), just as the Convention was about to impose controlled prices; inflation did the rest. Records in the range of 30–34 per cent and even higher were attained in 1798–99, but even officially published rates stayed well above the pre-Revolutionary 5 per cent until the later 1820s and unofficial rates for rural borrowers, principally small peasant proprietors, were appallingly high, even after a return to regulated credit in 1807. Borrowing to invest in productivity was not a likely alternative in this generation. Some borrowed to buy land; more, to relieve hardship. Peasant indebtedness was widespread: over a third of owners were 'obérés et grevés de dettes onéreuses' over vast areas of central and southern France, the south-east of the Paris basin, in the Calvados, Moselle and the Bouches-du-Rhône, according to a questionnaire returned by cantonal mayors in 1814–18.[70] Swingeing interest payments made the path of small peasant capitalism – the much-vaunted 'voie paysanne' which is supposed, in neo-Marxist literature, to have triumphed at this time[71] – a hard slog, if not a treadmill; maybe a dead end.

The higher wages which agricultural labourers were able to claim from around 1794 onwards must also be seen in this context. As a result of manpower shortages caused by military conscription, nominal and real wages shot up very early in the Revolution and stayed fixed on a higher level (Table 11).[72] This was all to the good for the worker, and, in so far as the claims of Montalivet and his like are based on real-life impressions of rural prosperity, it may have been the lessened misery of agricultural labourers that they saw. But higher wages did not make the producer's life easier, if he used much wage labour.

What the agricultural labourer, the rentier and usurer did not take, the state, sooner or later, did. The revolutionaries set direct taxes at an astronomic level in 1791, and only inflation, conquest and procrastination mitigated the burden. But even at the height of currency

Table 11 *Provincial labourers' wages 1790–1819*

Years	Wheat	Salary
1790–94	100	100
1800–04	121	140
1805–09	98	158
1810–14	132	171
1815–19	139	167

Source: As in note 72.

inflation, a surprising amount of tax was collected.[73] Thus, in 1793, producers were obliged to use the receipts for supplies requisitioned at officially fixed prices (*bons de réquisition*) to pay back taxes and two-thirds of the current year's taxes; there was no inflationary benefit for producers here.[74] The artificially low prices imposed on rural producers by the maximum laws of 1793 and 1794, and rigged markets for specie in rural areas,[75] also made certain that producers would pay more tax than the official conversion rates for assignats, which we have used in Table 10 for the period 1791–95, would suggest. After 1797 taxes actually collected approached or surpassed *ancien régime* levels. It was only the later 1820s which brought partial relief. This, again, could hardly have encouraged investment.

But another main culprit appears to have been the controlled economy of 1793–97 and its sequel, the depression of 1797–98. It is a common error to believe that the Maximum of the Year II was the revolutionaries' sole attempt to manage the economy, or that they returned France to a free market economy by abolishing controls late in 1794. In fact, the grain market was strictly regulated until the end of 1797. The Convention gave local officials greater enforcement powers after Thermidor than they had in the Year II, including the ability to imprison offenders, to hold rural mayors hostage and to billet gendarmes and soldiers on recalcitrant communes. In any event, decreed prices and the obligation to accept rapidly depreciating paper currency worked as a covert tax on agricultural surpluses. Indeed, requisitions even diminished rural capital when cattle, horses and carts were seized. Thus, however much the Maximum and its successors helped military suppliers and urban consumers, the countryside paid the price; and the necessary funds to replace lost animals, labour and equipment took time to recover.[76] Then, from 1797 onwards, taxes plus all arrears had to be paid at their full value. To obtain the cash – which the Revolutionary administrators were now prepared to collect, when necessary, by billeting troops on obstinate peasants – producers flooded the market with produce. Prices, low in any case because of abundant harvests, plummeted. As Schnerb says: 'Les ruraux troquèrent le maximum et les réquisitions contre la mévente et un plus grand besoin d'argent.'[77] In both cases the very people who were supposed to be the agents of physiocratic development ended up financing not an agricultural boom but the expansion of France's frontiers.

These difficulties, together with the destruction caused by the civil war in western France, made it hard for livestock raisers to profit from the brief period in the early Empire when grain prices declined and higher wages seemed to promise a wider market for meat. A well-informed observer in 1805 blamed high meat prices on cattle shortages, and put the responsibility for the latter largely on the events of the previous decade: 'la Révolution et ses évènements les ont rendus beaucoup plus rares. ... La Vendée et le Cholet depuis les guerres civiles, produisent moitié moins d'élèves qu'avant la Révolution. ... Les marais de Rochefort ont ... conservé leur belle espèce [mais] ils fournissent beaucoup moins qu'avant la Révolution. L'espèce est prête à manquer partout.' Fodder shortages forced early slaughtering; early slaughtering produced less meat. 'La Révolution, la guerre, les besoins extraordinaires, les sécheresses de l'an 10 & 11 [1802–03] ont encore ajouté en faisant périr beaucoup de bestiaux de toute espèce.' The result was a general lack of cattle for food and labour. Although the Loire-Inférieure was a department specialising in breeding and raising cattle, the local prefect had had to forbid slaughtering; and public works in Nantes harbour, which had previously been done with oxen, had to be carried out with superannuated nags.[78]

On the demand side as well, there were many reasons why the physiocratic dream of free markets did not encourage expanded production and structural innovation. The de-urbanisation of France during the years of the Revolution and Consulate and the crisis in secondary rural industries must have hampered recovery. Paris lost 100,000 inhabitants between 1790 and 1806; Bordeaux, 20,000; Toulouse, 2,000, and so on.[79] Parisian demand for articles of common consumption had fallen drastically by the end of the Directory and the beginning of the Consulate; no doubt the same was true of other towns as well. It revived a little during the early years of the Empire, then sank again.[80]

But changes in the urban and industrial sectors must also have had an effect on investment. It is a well-established fact of the *ancien régime* economy that extra earnings from secondary activities such as cottage industry, part-time craftsmanship and seasonal agricultural labour contributed vitally to small producers' incomes, allowing them to invest in livestock, equipment and other necessities. Economic changes under the Revolution and Empire seriously undermined this source of capital. This context of uncertainty is worth remembering when we consider apparently rising rural salaries in the Revolutionary and Imperial periods. Not all rural labour was salaried: rural cottage industry was paid mainly by piecework, and thereby subjected to the many industrial crises of this period. It was not just the explosive growth in cottons under the Empire which provoked the decline of the woollen and silk industries. The map of wool production had been considerably rearranged and shrunk by 1810 beyond even its reduced size in the 1780s. The sheep population was down considerably because of requisitions, because the clearing of commons permitted by the law of 10 June 1793 reduced pasture and because alpine communities prevented seasonal transhumance from the lowland plains. In and around St-Quentin before the Revolution there had been 12,000–14,000 looms; in 1802, no more than 3,000; the female spinners, in much reduced numbers, were earning half the pre-Revolutionary wages, and exports to America and Eastern Europe were reduced to zero. In and around Troyes, hat and stocking-making were down by one-quarter, dyed cloth by one-third. There, even cotton suffered. In 1784 the city boasted 2,000 cotton looms; in 1802, only 800, nearly half of which were out of use. The collapse of rural silks was staggering. The women lace and ribbon-makers of the Haute-Loire saw their piece-rates drop by over 50 per cent in the 1790s, and lace-making became 'une ressource quasiment nulle'. Since the export of these textiles paid for the grain which the region had to import because it was not cereal country, everyone suffered and the surrounding region became notorious for its draft-dodging, banditry and general crime.[81] Few textile regions were hit as hard as this, but whenever the loss of animal stocks and the decline of textile production reduced the secondary sources of family income, the ability to recover was considerably impaired.

All of these developments ruined the hopes generated by the physiocratic vision, and most of the destruction took place in the Revolutionary decade, to 1799. Conscription created shortages of labour, animals and grain; the war eliminated export markets, and inflation undermined marketing structures. The more positive achievements of the Empire and Consulate should be seen as a recovery from these bad times. It follows that the redistributed surplus from the abolition of the tithe and seigneurial dues and from fairer, or momentarily diminished, taxation, must have gone largely to buffer the impact of the economic crisis. De-urbanisation, the dislocation of traditional market structures, and all the rest worked against using the new surplus to invest in cattle, new crops and new rotations.

But this does not mean that the Revolution was a mere interlude in the long interaction between population, social structure, landholding and production; on the contrary. Population rose by about 2 million during the Revolutionary and Imperial periods, and more in the countryside than in the towns, putting pressure on the shape of the landholding pyramid. In the region around Chartres, for example, the number of landowners went up by 30 per cent between 1790 and 1820, but the peasant majority ended up with most of the holdings of less than 5 hectares.[82] Similar phenomena occurred in the Seine-et-Oise.[83] Entrenching smallholders may have had social benefits, but it surely weakened demand and reduced the number of those with disposable capital. The experience of the Pas-de-Calais in the nineteenth century seems to suggest that owners of small properties could not make much of a contribution to agricultural growth through the cereal economy; their heirs had to await the coming of the railroad before they could transform themselves into market-gardeners.[84] In this case, the Revolution both delayed growth and then affected the sort of transformation which would subsequently take place.

Viewed from the perspective of probably most people who had to live through it, the Revolution was long and hard. We do not, of course, wish to darken the picture unnecessarily, but rather to make the point that unintended consequences for the rural world flowed from those political decisions which have so stirred generations of historians, who have seen the Revolution from a fundamentally urban point of view. The financing of the war and the Terror, and the impact of civil disturbances, we would argue, put a new burden on the neglected majority of the population, the countrymen and women so despised by the *sans-culottes*. Our figures suggest that rural production suffered particularly after 1793. The recovery was lengthy and difficult because the Revolutionary crisis was severe and prolonged. Thus, we should not shrug when we find production figures in 1810–13 so close to those of the last years of the *ancien régime*. There was no horizontal dotted line to fill the blank intervening period with a hypothetical and reassuring stability. Instead, there was, we suggest, a saucer-shaped curve, a lost generation for economic growth and development.

Notes

1 This revision of our original paper has benefited from the criticisms of those present at the Manchester conference, and also from the remarks of James Riley. We wish to acknowledge the material assistance of the Killam Foundation, York University and the University of Maryland.

2 G. Lefebvre, *Les paysans du Nord pendant la Révolution française*, Paris-Lille, 1924, p. 886.

3 P. M. Jones, *The Peasantry in the French Revolution*, Cambridge, 1988, p. 269.

4 C.-I. Brugière de Barante, *Observations sur les états de situation du département de l'Aude envoyés au Ministre de l'Intérieur...*, Paris, An X, p. 3; C.-L. Bruslé de Valsuzenay, *Tableau statistique de département de l'Aube*, Paris, An X, p. 56.

5 J. Peuchet, *Statistique élémentaire de la France*, Paris, 1805, pp. 278–80.

6 J.-P. Bachasson de Montalivet, *Exposé de la situation de l'Empire présenté au corps législatif, dans sa séance du 25 février 1813*, Paris, 1813. The harvest results were printed, grouped into regions considered to have comparable agricultures but also concealing the results of individual departments. The summary of the original prefects' reports can be found in A[rchives] N[ationales] F^{10} 252; many, but far from all, of the detailed reports are in AN F^{11} 454–67 and in series M of the departmental archives.

7 J.-C. Toutain, 'Le produit de l'agriculture française de 1700 à 1958: I. Estimation du produit au xviiie siècle', *Cahiers de l'Institut de Science Economique Appliquée*, Sér AF, No. 1, No. 115, 1961, pp. 77–88; Toutain has since published slightly revised estimates, in 'Le produit intérieur brut de la France de 1789 à 1982', *Economies et sociétés. Cahiers de l'I.S.M.E.A. Série Histoire quantitative de l'Economie française, No. 15*, 1987, but this concerns mainly the nineteenth century and beyond.

8 A. Chabert, *Essai sur les mouvements des revenus et de l'activité économique en France de 1798 à 1820*, Paris, 1949.

9 It is sometimes said that his figures covered fourteen years of Napoleonic rule, but this is incorrect.

10 J.-A. Chaptal, *De l'Industrie françoise*, Paris, 1819, xix, pp. 127ff.

11 A. Soboul, 'Le choc révolutionnaire 1789–1797' and 'La reprise économique et la stabilisation sociale 1797–1815', in F. Braudel and E. Labrousse (eds), *Histoire économique et sociale de la France*, III, 1, Paris, 1976, pp. 5–64, is weak on the economy before 1797 and closely paraphrases Chabert's *Essai* thereafter. M. Agulhon, G. Desert and R. Specklin, *Histoire de la France rurale III. Apogée et crise de la civilisation paysanne 1789–1914*, Paris, 1976, also says little about the economy; other brief treatments in R. Sédillot, *Le coût de la Révolution française*, Paris, 1987 (pessimistic), pp. 149–74; and F. Hincker, *La Révolution française et l'économie: décollage ou catastrophe?* Paris, 1988 (optimistic). See also the rather inconclusive round-table discussion in *La Révolution française et le monde rural*, Comité des Travaux Historiques et Scientifiques, Paris, 1989, pp. 199–231, including a contribution by M. Morineau, 'Les moissons de la Révolution'. The most recent synthesis is a brilliant essay by G. Postel-Vinay, 'A la recherche de la révolution économique dans les campagnes 1789–1815', *Revue économique*, XL (1989), pp. 1015–45, which appeared while the final version of this

article was being completed. We are in agreement with most of its conclusions, but are more pessimistic about the growth of cereal and animal production.

12 *State and Statistics in France 1789–1815*, Chur, 1984; see especially S. Woolf's essay 'Towards the history of the origins of statistics: France 1789–1815', pp. 81–194, which supersedes 0. Festy, 'Les enquêtes agricoles en France de 1800 à 1815', *Revue d'histoire économique et sociale*, XXXIV (1956), pp. 43–59; see also M.-N. Bourguet, *Déchiffrer le France. La statistique départementale à l'époque napoléonienne*, Montreux, 1988.

13 To judge from surviving records, not all departments were asked for full details, or at least did not provide them, until 1810. In 1812, and subsequently, the figures were tied to statistics on the total land under cultivation for each crop, a method that was to continue under the Restoration and July Monarchy. In that year as well, the prefects provided the old type of estimate for the Ministry of the Interior and the new ones for the Ministry of Commerce and Industry; the two sets were, however, concordant. In 1813 both sets of figures went to the Ministry of the Interior.

14 AN F^{10} 252; the preparatory material for the grid is in F^{10} 254.

15 Total production under the new criteria of 1813 came to 157,984,711 hectolitres for France within its post-1815 frontiers but this has to be both increased to take account of potential production of the 'missing' departments of the Ardennes, Ariège, Côte-d'Or, Haute-Marne, Meurthe-et-Moselle, Nord and Pyrénées-Atlantiques (unavailable, presumably, because of the imminence of an Allied invasion at the end of 1813), and reduced to remove grain used for animal consumption, brewing and distilleries; the latter calculation was made on the basis of consumption requirements in 1821–25 in *Archives statistiques du Ministère des Travaux Publics de l'Agriculture et du Commerce*, Paris, 1837, pp. 132–3; the following percentages of each product were estimated as necessary for seed or human consumption: wheat, 99·6; maslin, 99·2; rye, 98·3; barley, 68·0; buckwheat, 85·6; maize and millet, 83·7; oats, 10·9; *légumes secs*, 82·2; other vegetables, 28·4; we have estimated that half of the potato and other farinaceous crops was used for human consumption.

16 Cf. the incorrect assumption of Chabert, *Essai* . . ., pp. 50–4 that the Imperial statistics cannot be linked to those of the Restoration.

17 Chabert, *Essai*, p. 52, produced a harvest output figure for 1805, but for the whole Empire, computed from the prefects' estimate of how much production exceeded an unspecified 'common year'; Chabert calculated a common year from Montalivet's inflated statistics for 1810–12.

18 Production indices from A[rchives] D[épartementales] Eure, 7M 3, 7M 4, AD Eure-et-Loir 7M 5, 7M 6; AD Seine-Maritime 6M 1223-7; AD Yvelines (formerly Seine-et-Oise) 13M 1; AD Oise M (unclassified series, 1810–13); R. Durand, *Le Département des Côtes-du-Nord sous le Consulat et l'Empire (1800–1815). Essai d'histoire administrative*, Paris, 1926, pp. 38–41; AN F^{10} 252, F^{11} 454, 456-7, 462-3, 465-7 for the departments of the Aisne, Ardèche, Charente, Côtes-du-Nord, Eure, Eure-et-Loire, Mayenne, Nièvre, Oise, Seine-Inférieure, Seine-et-Marne, Seine-et-Oise, Deux-Sèvres, Vendée, Haute-Vienne and Yonne; barley for human consumption is included in the figures for the Eure, Eure-et-Loir and Seine-et-Marne. In some of the departments, figures from the earlier years are net harvest yields and had to be increased by seed estimates, which were taken from the actual amounts sown in 1812 according to the 1813 reports. Surpluses for all territory under French domination in AN AF^{IV} 1058: *Ministère de l'Intérieur. Résultat des tableaux de la situation des récoltes en grain de la France dans les huit années qui ont précédé 1810* [18 June 1810], which includes surplus grain from previous years; figures for 1810–13 from AN F^{10} 252 with 1813 total adjusted downwards as in Table 1. Close analysis of the documents suggest that the range of cereals

considered suitable for human consumption widened over this period, but this source does at least reflect changes from year to year. Exports taken from C.-A. Costaz, *Histoire de l'Administration en France*, II Paris, 1843, p. 60; cf. slight discrepancies with AN F^{IV} 1058 *Résumé des tableaux* . . .; wheat prices from E. Labrousse, R. Romano, F.-G. Dreyfus, *Le prix du froment en France au temps de la monnaie stable (1726–1913)*, Paris, 1970, pp. 9–10.

19 On annual variations, see also the various remarks of the prefects in the sources listed in note 18. Our index under-represents the weight of the great grain-producing departments like the Eure and the Eure-et-Loir, which are notably less brilliant than the average in the years before 1810, and uses very generous seeding estimates drawn from the 1813 harvest to estimate total harvests in certain departments which only provided net harvest figures before 1808; finally, there was probably an increasing tendency to cultivate lesser grains and potatoes at the expense of 'elite' cereals during this period, which leads to overestimating the size of earlier harvests in relation to those of 1810–13.

20 R. Schnerb, 'La dépression économique sous le Directoire après la disparition du papier-monnaie (An V–An XIII)', *Annales historiques de la Révolution française*, XI (1934), pp. 27–49; J. Merley, *La Haute-Loire de la fin de l'Ancien Régime aux débuts de la Troisième République (1776–1886)*, Le Puy, 1974, pp. 288, 294–5; J. Fourastié, 'Les comptes du domaine de Farcheville', *Bulletin de la Société d'Histoire Moderne et Contemporaine*, January (1956), pp. 1–10.

21 J.-C. Toutain 'Le produit de l'agriculture française de 1700 à 1958: I. Estimation du produit au xviiie siècle', pp. 77–88.

22 See the convenient summary in J.-C. Perrot's introduction to his edition of A. J. Lavoisier, *De la richesse territoriale du Royaume de France*, Paris, 1988, pp. 129, 182–5.

23 Export volumes in Costaz, *Histoire de l'Administration*, II, p. 60; directions of flow before 1789 in Bibliothèque municipale de Rouen, MS Montbret 155.

24 Total population estimates within present-day frontiers are 28·6 million in 1790, 29·1 million in 1800, 29·5 million in 1805 and 30·6 million in 1816 according to J. Dupâquier *et al.*, *Histoire de la population française*, III, Paris, 1988, pp. 67–70, 123.

25 A.D. Oise, M (fonds non classé), *Questions adressées à Mr le préfet* . . ., 2 October 1811.

26 Postel-Vinay, 'A la recherche', p. 1022.

27 In 1813 the potato harvest came to a little less than 23 million hectolitres while cereals came to over 163 million hectolitres; that is, potato output represented only 1–2 per cent of the calorific equivalent of total cereal crops; see AN F^{10} 252 and Ministère de l'Agriculture. Direction de l'Agriculture. Bureau des Subsistances, *Récoltes de céréales et des pommes de terre de 1815 à 1876*, Paris, 1878. Calorific equivalents are given in C. Chatfield, *Tables de composition des aliments pour l'usage international*, Washington, 1949, pp. 8–11.

28 'La pomme de terre au xviiie siècle', *Annales: Economies, Sociétés, Civilisations*, XXV (1970), pp. 1767–85.

29 AN F^{10} 510 *Ministère de l'Intérieur. Recensement des bêtes à cornes. Circulaire du 11 mars 1809*. Another, apparently earlier, version of this document appears in M. Baudot, 'L'enquête de 1813 sur les bovins', *Actes du quatre-vingt-douzième Congrès national des sociétés savantes. Strasbourg et Colmar 1967. Section d'histoire moderne et contemporaine*, I, Paris, 1970, pp. 51–68; the same data are given (straightforwardly, but with some variants), in Montalivet, *Exposé de la situation* . . ., pp. 41–2, Table 22; and (without calves) in Chaptal, *De l'industrie françoise*, p. 197.

30 Lavoisier, *De la richesse territoriale* (edited by Perrot), pp. 185–90.

31 Montalivet, *Exposé*, p. 12.

32 AN F[10] 500. It is also possible to compare the results of the 1813 enquiry with the statistics which twelve departments sent up to Paris for the same enquiry of the Year III. Seven of the twelve departments had more head of bovines in 1794–95 than in 1813. In all twelve departments, there was an overall loss of 14·4 per cent of the bovine population between the two dates; see Baudot, 'L'enquête de 1813'.

33 AN F[20] 534 *Travail demandé par Son Excellence concernant les tournées d'inspection pour les dépôts de mérinos et la statistique des bêtes à laine [1812]*.

34 Montalivet, *Exposé* . . ., pp. 32–5; unlike the harvest figures, the increment varies from region to region, so the information could well be genuine.

35 *Ibid.*, and Chaptal, *De l'industrie françoise*, I, pp. 179, 222.

36 P. E. Herbin, *Statistique générale et particulière de la France et de ses colonies*, I, Paris, An XII/1803, 289.

37 E.g. R. Haurez-Puech, 'Agriculture et paysannerie', in J. Tulard (éd.), *Dictionnaire Napoléon*, Paris, 1987, pp. 40–9: G. Lemarchand, 'L'apogée des campagnes (1794–1880)', in M. Clavel-Levêque, M.-T. Lorcin and G. Lemarchand, *Les campagnes françaises, précis d'histoire rurale*, Paris, 1983, p. 238; see also Postel-Vinay, 'A la recherche', p. 1,028, which is too sanguine.

38 Chaptal, *De l'industrie françoise*, I, p. 179; Toutain, 'Le produit de l'agriculture française', pp. 169–70.

39 *Essai d'une statistique générale* . . ., p. 42.

40 AN F[10] 500. The twelve complete returns from the departments, in O. Festy, *Les animaux ruraux en l'An III*, Paris, 1941–46, 2 vols, in response to the questionnaire of that year show virtual stability between 1794–95 and the results of 1809–11 (for *moutons* and *brebis*).

41 M. Lachiver, *Vins, vignes et vignerons. Histoire du vignoble français*, Paris, 1988, pp. 368–93; on the increased consumption of spirits, see *inter alia* M. Marion, *Histoire financière de la France depuis 1715*, II, Paris, 1919, pp. 95–8; on the post-1760 viticulture investment boom, E. Labrousse, *La crise de l'économie française à la fin de l'Ancien régime et au début de la Révolution*, Paris, 1943.

42 T. J. A. Le Goff and D. M. G. Sutherland, 'The social origins of counter-revolution in Western France', *Past and Present*, XCIX (1983), pp. 65–87, and 'Religion and rural revolt in the French Revolution: an overview', in J. M. Bak and G. Benecke (eds), *Religion and Rural Revolt*, Manchester, 1984, pp. 123–46.

43 AD Mayenne, 179 J 27, 62, 64–5, Chartrier d'Hauterive.

44 F. Lallier, *Du revenu de la propriété foncière aux environs de Sens depuis le xvie siècle*, Sens, 1858, especially pp. 42–3.

45 P. Massé, *Varennes et ses maîtres. Un domaine rural, de l'Ancien Régime à la Monarchie de Juillet (1779–1842)*, Paris, 1956, pp. 125–31. After 1812 the new tenants signed on for fixed proportions of the harvest, so it is difficult to see what was actually being demanded of them.

46 J.-P. Chaline, 'Les biens des hospices de Rouen. Recherches sur les fermages normands du xviiie au xxe siècle', *Revue d'Histoire Moderne et Contemporaine*, LXVI (1968), pp. 185–202; see also the methodological remarks in C. Gindin, 'La rente foncière en France de l'Ancien Régime à l'Empire', *Annales Historiques de la Révolution Française*, LIV (1982), pp. 1–34.

47 J-J Clère, *Les paysans de la Haute-Marne et la Révolution française*, Paris, 1988, pp. 340–3: leases at Hortes, Beauchemin and Langres. We have reduced these to a common index (base 1790 = 100), interpolating values for 1799–1814 by loglinear regression for Beauchemin:

Year	Index	Year	Index	Year	Index
1790	100	1800	114	1810	123
1791	100	1801	115	1811	123
1792	100	1802	115	1812	123
1793	100	1803	115	1813	124
1794	100	1804	115	1814	124
1795	100	1805	115	1815	124
1796	100	1806	116	1816	127
1797	100	1807	116	1817	117
1798	112	1808	123		
1799	114	1809	123		

48   D. Zolla, 'Les variations du revenu et du prix des terres en France au xviie et au xviiie siècle', *Annales de l'école libre des sciences politiques*, VIII (1893), pp. 299–326, 439–61, 686–705, IX (1894), pp. 194–216, 417–32, and, especially, 'Recherches sur les variations du revenu et du prix des terres en France. Deuxième partie (1789–1815)', *Annales agronomiques*, XIV (1888), pp. 49–78.

49   P.-C. Dubost, 'Recherches sur la production agricole. La rente et la valeur du sol', *Journal des Economistes*, 3rd Series, XVIII (1870), pp. 329–51, XIX (1870), pp. 17–37; Lallier, *Du revenu.* . . .

50   The indices given translate in the first instance Zolla's own percentages based on sums of revenues from groups of farms; a recalculated aggregate from the indices of each farm is given where possible in parentheses.

51   See especially Zolla, 'Recherches . . . Deuxième partie', pp. 50/1.

52   D. Zolla, 'Recherches sur les variations des revenus fonciers (Suite)', *Annales agronomiques*, XIII (1887), pp. 444–76.

53   Chaline, 'Les biens des hospices de Rouen'. These leases, unlike most, did not revert to payments in kind during the years of unstable currency. These data represent a 'best case' for rent rises. They come from the farms of the Rouen hospital, in one of the best agricultural areas of France, with the biggest rent rise among the leases Zolla used. They show lease rises coming out at the end of the period 1790–1815 between 3 and 22 per cent higher than grain prices. But if Zolla's more than plausible estimate of the tithe as the equivalent of 10 per cent of rent is subtracted from this gain, the real rent rise, even in this rich area, drops back to somewhere between − 7 and + 12 per cent. Using a loglinear regression to provide a closer fit to the curve described by Chaline's leases and by national grain prices, we obtain the trend values for prices and leases in 1790 and 1814 shown below; national wheat prices are taken from Labrousse, Romano, and Dreyfus, *Le prix du froment*, pp. 9–10 with estimates for the period 1793–96 from E. Labrousse, *Esquisse du mouvement des prix et des revenus en France au xviiie siècle*, Paris, 1933 (reprinted 1984), p. 105, converted to hectolitres. Regional price variations, which we have tested, make little difference in this sort of comparison during this period.

	Length of periods (years)					
	20	25	30	25	30	35
	1785–1814	1785–1819	1785–1824	1790–1814	1790 1819	1790–1824
Grain prices	128	132	114	118	126	106
Rouen leases:						
I	131	137	149	130	138	155
II	139	141	146	140	142	148
Difference (%):						
Grain-Rouen I	3	5	35	12	12	49
Grain-Rouen II	11	9	25	22	16	42

54 Annual rates of increase (per cent) in wheat prices and leases

Period	Wheat prices	France (Chabert)	Leases	
			Rouen (Chaline)	
			I	II
Ten-year periods				
1785–94	2·6	–	1·4	1·3
1790–99	−0·6	–	2·2	1·9
1795–04	1·1	–	−0·9	−0·9
1800–09	−3.3	2·2	0·7	1·2
1805–14	2·8	3·2	3·2	2·9
1810–19	0·0	1·0	1·9	1·0
Fifteen-year periods				
1785–99	1·4	–	1.8	1·6
1790–1804	1·2	–	0·6	0·9
1795–1809	−1·2	–	−0·1	0·7
1800–14	0·2	2·8	2·1	2·2
1805–19	2·5	2·2	2·8	2·2
1810–24	−3·0	–	3·2	1·8
Thirty-year periods				
1785–1814	1·1	–	1·1	1·4
1790–1819	1·0	–	1·4	1·4

55 AD Seine-Maritime, 7J 37, 77; this farm, in the commune of Clères, contained about 48 hectares. Subsequently, the rent was reduced to only 2,000 *francs* until 1845, although (a sign of the times) the tenant was expected to share the costs of insurance and marling.

56 He doubled the acreage under meadow and wood each to 5 hectares. Subsequently, he raised the rent in 1825 to 2,200 *francs* and finally, after 1834, to 1,800 *francs*.

57 G. Lemarchand, *La fin du féodalisme dans le pays de Caux*, Paris, 1989, p. 541, using A. Lechevalier, 'Historique de la propriété rurale dans le Pays de Caux, et particulièrement dans le canton de Criquetot-l'Esneval', *Recueil des publications de la Société havraise d'Etudes diverses*, 1911, pp. 117–63, 273–302; and AD Seine-Maritime 3P4/215; we have used leases for Angerville-l'Orcher (1–2), Ecultot (3), ferme Dupillon

at Bacqueville (4), Anneville (5) and Bertreville (6); the others given in this set are either hospital leases or garbled. We have also used P. Brunet, *Structures agraires et économie rurale des plateaux tertiaires entre la Seine et l'Oise*, Caen, 1960, pp. 509–10; and A. Descoqs, 'Cent cinquante ans de fermages dans l'Avranchin', *Revue de l'Avranchin*, XIX (1923), pp. 387–9. See also, on the continuing depression in the Calvados between the First and Second Empire (1810–55), G. Désert, *Les archives hospitalières. Source d'histoire économique et sociale*, Caen, 1977, pp. 30–40.

58   Cited in Zolla, 'Recherches sur les variations des revenus fonciers (Suite)'; see also Dubost, 'Recherches', pp. 18–21.

59   *Contribution foncière, contribution mobilière, patentes* and, from 1798–99, the tax on doors and windows. The sources used were AN C 393 (503); AD IX 505, 583, 585–586; AF[III] 120 (559), 130 (608) B[ibliothèque] N[ationale] Lf[158] 16 *Etat des recettes et dépenses faites au trésor public . . .*, Paris, 1790–91; BN Lf[158] 19–20, *Compte rendu à la Convention par les commissaires de la trésorerie nationale de leur administration depuis le 1er juillet 1791*, n.d., n.p.; and *Deuxième Compte rendu par les commissaires de la trésorerie nationale . . .*, n.d., n.p.; Lf[158] 32–5, *Administration des finances . . .*, Paris, An VIII–1808, *Compte de l'administration des finances*, Paris, 1809–14; *Compte rendu par le ministre secrétaire d'état des finances*, Paris, 1817–24 and *Compte général de l'administration des finances*, Paris, 1825–59; 4°Lf[156] 26, *Comptes rendus par les ministres*, Paris, 1814–43; Lf[190] 3, *Département des contributions publiques. compte rendu par le ministre au 1er février 1793*, Paris, 1793; A. Bruguière, *La première Restauration et son budget*, Geneva, 1969; *Archives parlementaires*, 2e sér, XV, pp. 564–8; D.-V. Ramel de Nogaret, *Des finances de la République française*, Paris, An IX; A.-J.-V. Hennet, *Théorie du crédit public*, Paris, 1816; F. Braesch, *Finances et monnaie révolutionnaires*, II, Paris, 1936. We have added in a conservative 20 per cent for estimated departmental surtaxes and collection costs in the period 1791–95 and 10 per cent for the pre-1789 estimate, and converted the original values (given in parentheses) using the table in P. Caron, *Tableaux de dépréciation du papier-monnaie*, LII–LV, Paris, 1909. Per capita figures were calculated from L. Henry and Y. Blayo, 'La population de la France de 1740 à 1860', *Population*, XXX, numéro spécial, November (1975), p. 95. Other estimates for taxes in the early years of the Revolution, on a monthly basis, are in S. E. Harris, *The Assignats*, Cambridge, Mass., 1930, pp. 47–53; and in F. Braesch, *Finances et monnaie révolutionnaires*, I, Nancy, 1934, both of which are concerned with total taxes, but produce estimates congruent with our own.

60   According to a fiscal technician of the day, taxes bearing on the land had accounted for about 80 per cent of direct tax in the *ancien régime*; see Hennet, *Théorie du crédit public*. The proportion fell to about three-quarters after 1790 and stayed roughly at that level until the end of the Restoration.

61   Daniel Zolla believed that direct taxation had been falling throughout the period, on the grounds that the basic levy (*principal*) for the land tax (*contribution foncière*) went down steadily from 1791 into the nineteenth century; see 'L'impôt foncier' in *Etudes d'économie rurale*, Paris, 1896, pp. 139–213. But he did not take account of surtaxes (*centimes additionnels*) which varied from year to year and could be heavy, or of the impact of monetary inflation and delays in collection, which were very great in the Revolutionary period, nor did he work out the actual sums collected, which is what we have done.

62   Thus, after a relatively good harvest and falling prices in 1810, the prefect of the Eure remarked to the Minister of the Interior that 'en Beauce les fermiers sont aux abois pour payer impôt & fermage vu la baisse soutenue des grains'. AD Eure 7M 4. *Série de questions adressées à MM. les Préfets . . .* [draft reply, 4 October 1810].

D

63   See, *inter alia*, H. Clout, *The Land of France 1815–1914*, London, 1983, especially pp. 60–3 and the stimulating examination of this movement in G. Grantham, 'Agricultural supply during the Industrial Revolution: French evidence and European implications', *Journal of Economic History*, XLIX, (1989), pp. 43–72, both with very full bibliographical notes.

64   D. Zolla, 'Les variations des prix et du revenu des terres', *L'Economiste français*, II (1888), pp. 629–32.

65   Schnerb, *Les contributions directes . . .*, pp. 212–13, 221–35.

66   For this conventional view, see M. Marion, *Histoire financière de la France depuis 1715*, III, Paris, 1921, p. 47; and Jones, *Peasants*, pp. 261–2.

67   AD Seine-Maritime 7J 77, *Réponse faite par le régisseur de la terre de Clères aux observations du conseil de Madame de Charost*, n.d.

68   A. Dubuc, 'Le mouvement des prix et les rapports économiques dans la région de Jumièges au cours de la Révolution', *Actes du quatre-vingt-unième Congrè national des sociétés savantes, Rouen-Caen, 1956*, Paris, 1957, pp. 429–35.

69   See the leases for the farms of Beaumesnil, Jouannière and Hermeraie owned by the Comtesse de Charost in AD Eure, E 2640, whereby the farmers paid the landlord's taxes in assignats and requisitions imposed on her in lieu of rent, negotiated payments of arrears in labour or kind and paid cash or kind as the landlord demanded – all this despite formal provisions in the leases.

70   *Archives parlementaires*, 2e sér, IX, speech of Goupil-Préfeln, 39e September 1807; L.-J. Loutchitch, *Allure des variations du taux de l'intérêt (en France de 1800 à nos jours)*, Paris, 1930, pp. 45–54; P. Leuillot, 'L'usure judaïque en Alsace sous l'Empire et la Restauration', *Annales Historiques de la Révolution Française*, VII (1930), pp. 231–51; Y. Denis, 'La dette hypothécaire en France au début de la Restauration d'après une enquête du gouvernement', *Actes du quatre-vingt-neuvième Congrès national des sociétés savantes, Lyon 1964; Section d'histoire moderne et contemporaine*, I, Paris, 1964, pp. 347–63; Marion, *Histoire financière*, IV, pp. 120–9, Clère, *Les paysans de la Haute-Marne*, pp. 348–54; as late as the July Monarchy, interest rates in rural Burgundy ran from 8 to 12 per cent and upwards, according to P. Levêque, *Une société provinciale: la Bourgogne sous la monarchie de Juillet*, Paris, 1983, p. 355.

71   See especially F. Gauthier, *La voie paysanne dans la révolution française. L'exemple picard*, Paris, 1977.

72   Based on the 'salaire horaire moyen du manoeuvre de province', in J. Fourastié and C. Fontaine, *Documents pour l'histoire et la théorie des prix*, Paris, n.d., pp. xxii–xxiii; see also F. Simiand, *Le salaire, l'évolution sociale et la monnaie*, III, Paris, 1932, Tableau I: France moins Paris. Salaires masculins; Chabert, *Essai*, pp. 86–9, 171–90, 239–64; Postel-Vinay, 'A la recherche', pp. 1,025, 1,031, reporting on the unpublished work of Y. Crébouw, 'Salaires et salariés agricoles en France des débuts de la Révolution aux approches du xxe siècle', Thèse d'histoire, Université de Paris I, 1986; Schnerb, 'La dépression économique', pp. 42–7; wheat prices as in note 53.

73   Ramel de Nogaret, *Des finances de la République . . .*, pp. 30–1, 35, estimated the yearly intake of regular tax revenues even then at the equivalent of 300 million in hard currency, but this included some indirect taxes and other income.

74   C. Bloch, *Les contributions directes. Instruction recueil de textes et notes*, Paris, 1915, pp. 447–9.

75   On the manipulation of the assignat by tax receivers themselves, see R. Schnerb, *Les contributions directes à l'époque de la Révolution dans le département du Puy-de-Dôme*, Paris, 1933, p. 260.

76   See Jones, *The Peasantry*, pp. 256–7.

77 Schnerb, 'La dépression économique', p. 48; Marion, *Histoire financière*, IV, pp. 88–93.

78 A-N F^{10} 510: *Vrai point de vue sur l'Etat des Bestiaux en France* [1805]. It is interesting that many of the reports of meat-eating peasants referred to in Chabert, *Essai*, pp. 91ff. come from English travellers visiting France just after the Peace of Amiens, when the forage crisis alluded to here would have compelled peasants to slaughter their cattle; in general, the assumptions found in Chabert, *Essai*, pp. 220ff. and Postel-Vinay, 'A la recherche', p. 1,028, of a livestock boom in the Revolution and Empire need to be treated with considerable caution; on demand in Paris, and the recourse to foreign cattle there, see L. Bergeron, 'Approvisionnement et consommation à Paris sous le Premier Empire', *Paris et Ile-de-France*, XIV, 1963, [1964], pp. 197–232; and AN F^{10} 510: memorandum to the Minister of the Interior, 8 September 1810.

79 Dupâquier *et al.*, *Histoire de la population française*, pp. 77–80.

80 Marion, *Histoire financière*, IV, p. 201, n. 3; A. Husson, *Les Consommations de Paris*, Paris, 1856, pp. 149, 153, 154, 195; L.-F. Benoiston de Châteauneuf, *Recherches sur les consommations de tout genre de la ville de Paris en 1817 comparées à ce qu'elles étaient en 1789*, Paris, 1920, pp. 106–9; Bergeron, 'Approvisionnement et consommation à Paris sous le Premier Empire'; M. Lachiver, 'L'approvisionnement de Paris en viande au xviiie siècle', in A. Croix *et al.* (eds), *La France d'Ancien Régime: Etudes réunies en l'honneur de Pierre Goubert*, Toulouse, 1984, pp. 344–54.

81 F. Bonnaire, *Mémoire au ministre de l'Intérieur sur la statistique du département des Hautes-Alpes*, Paris, An IX, p. 64; L. Dauchy, *Statistique du département de l'Aisne*, Paris, An IX, p. 60; Bruslé de Valsuzenay *Tableau statistique du département de l'Aube*, pp. 60–72; Merley, *La Haute-Loire*, p. 298; S. Chassagne, 'L'industrie lainière en France à l'époque révolutionnaire et impériale (1790–1810)', in *Voies nouvelles pour l'histoire de la Révolution française. Colloque Albert Mathiez–Georges Lefebvre (30 novembre–1er décembre 1974)*, Commission d'histoire économique et sociale de la Révolution française, Mémoires et documents, XXXV, Paris, 1978, pp. 143–67; C. Engrand, 'Concurrences et complémentarités des villes et des campagnes: les manufactures picardes de 1780 à 1815', *Revue du Nord*, LXI (1979), pp. 71–7.

82 M. Vovelle, *Ville et campagne au 18e siècle (Chartres et la Beauce)*, Paris, 1980, pp. 222–6.

83 O. Tulippe, *L'habitat rural en Seine-et-Oise. Essai de géographie du peuplement*, Liège, 1934, pp. 315–21.

84 R. Hubscher, *L'Agriculture et la société rurale dans le Pas-de-Calais du milieu du XIXe siècle à 1914*, I, Arras, 1980, pp. 741–6.

The urban bourgeoisie in the French Revolution: Marseille, 1789–92

Telle est la nature des opérations de cette classe précieuse des sujets de Sa Majesté, que le sort d'un particulier est presque toujours lié à de grands intérêts, et que ses revers ou ses succès influent nécessairement sur la chose publique.[1]

According to Marx, the bourgeoisie has played a most revolutionary role in history. The French Revolution, according to such Marxist historians as Lefebvre and Soboul, was a triumphal stage in the bourgeoisie's rise to power, a key moment in the transition from feudalism to capitalism. Of the power and confidence of the bourgeoisie, and its fierce commitment to the expansion of capitalism, the *Manifesto* leaves no doubt.

Less clear, however, is the position of the bourgeoisie in *ancien régime* society. Certainly, under 'feudalism', the bourgeoisie grew in strength and assurance, as the capitalist mode of production somehow formed itself underneath, or in the interstices of, the existing but ailing feudal mode. But though ultimate triumph was predestined – whether as part of a poetic promethean myth or the result of a more mundane technological determinism (or both) – the French bourgeoisie was, before 1789, an oppressed class. Unlike the recent Marxist interpretation of George Comninel, Marx maintained that the bourgeoisie was not part (or not merely part) of a ruling class, stretching from king to the most humble office-holder, living essentially from the exploitation of the peasantry.[2] The bourgeoisie certainly were exploiters – but they were also exploited. No doubt the concept of exploitation is hardly clear when applied to *ancien régime* conditions: perhaps the bourgeoisie was exploited mainly through a 'manque de gagner' imposed by the corporatist, fragmented structure of government and society – exploited because they could not fulfil their potential to exploit others. Marx satirised the petty nature of the commercial endeavours of the merchants, their 'haggling, mean and niggardly spirit', as they perforce had to jostle for advantages and privileges.[3]

It might be interesting to explore the theme of 'les grandeurs et misères' of bourgeois, especially merchant, existence in late eighteenth-century France. Asserting, rather than proving, that 1789 saw a bourgeois breakthrough, with the commercial classes playing a bigger role than is often conceded, some aspects of merchants' activities and attitudes will be invoked, with special reference to Marseille, but also with reference to the activities and attitudes of other social groups. I am interested in how notions of strength and weakness changed – how features seen as weaknesses, either admitted as such by merchants or imputed to them by critics or opponents, might – in situations of conflict – turn into (or *be* turned into) strengths. Conversely, strengths, partly through being perceived as such, could become weaknesses, if they encouraged wishful thinking; or if confidence became arrogance, breeding opposition; if great wealth became 'luxury'; or if the undoubted dependence of the poor on the rich was pushed too far, or emphasised so much that it provoked revolt.

While recognising the appositeness of Professor Hampson's phrase 'the ambiguities of class conflict',[4] it is easy to recreate a self-image of the merchants which exudes strength and confidence.[5] The impressive commercial expansion of eighteenth-century France, and the even more impressive dynamism of Marseille, provides some basis for this, though in the 1770s and 1780s this commercial expansion faced difficulties stemming from French structural weakness combined with problems of intensified foreign competition, and these difficulties may have contributed to a discernible feeling of insecurity on the part of many prominent Marseille merchants on the eve of the Revolution.[6] But, undoubtedly, merchants dominated the city, eclipsing the nobility. They 'gave' employment to tens of thousands, set the tone of social life, dictated the time of day and night (that is, fixed lunch-time by the opening hours of the Bourse, curfew by the time it took their carriages to get them home from the theatre).[7] Even the Academy, as Daniel Roche admits,[8] was dominated by merchants: Pierre-Augustin Guys, connoisseur of Greece; Dominique Bertrand, friend of Raynal (who lived near Marseille); Dominique Audibert, who had alerted Voltaire to the plight of Calas; Jacques Seimandy, author of influential pamphlets in 1789; André Liquier and Michel Roussier, both elected to the National Assembly.[9] At the Academy, merchant values predominated: nobles, financiers, scientists were measured according to specifically 'merchant' criteria.[10]

In 1789 Jacques Seimandy branded the arguments generally used to proclaim the superior usefulness of *roturiers* as 'ces choses générales qui à force d'avoir été écrites sont devenues des lieux communs.'[11] Using such 'lieux communs' of Seimandy himself, we could show that Marseille – for Montesquieu the epitome of the triple marriage of trade, enlightenment and liberty – produced much literature stressing the twin growth of trade and enlightenment (unaccompanied by liberty) since 1614, thus not repudiating history but showing confidence that historical trends were working in the merchants' favour. The most eminent merchants protested at those who tried to confine their knowledge and competence to purely professional matters, while also arguing that trade, broadly conceived and boldly practised, united practical knowledge (and experience) with a command of theory. The merchant elite, unlike both the nobility and their inferior colleagues,[12] was well versed in questions of jurisprudence, foreign policy, administration, finance, geography and 'les intérêts politiques du Royaume' and would soon put 'la science économique' on a sound footing, as trading and intellectual horizons expanded with France's regeneration. Claiming election to the National Assembly, since they did not seek favours or exemptions, but were independent and self-reliant, merchants professed to represent all 'industry', from themselves down to the humble 'ouvrier travaillant pour lui-même'. With trade a 'rampart against despotism', and encouraging equality, merchants were the best defenders of 'la cause du peuple'. Disinterested, they pushed their claims to be consulted, as their colleagues were in Britain, and called for a parliamentary regime, with the accountability of Ministers. They condemned government confusion and extravagance, attacked courtiers and wasteful financiers who pushed up interest rates. They denounced trading and manufacturing monopolies which violated their natural and proprietary rights to trade where and how they wished,[13] as well as the creation of offices whose cost fell on the public and which drained capital and talent from commerce. Four of their number monopolised the Third's deputation to the Estates General. In the period of elections and *cahier*-drafting, merchants were deferred to fulsomely by clergy and nobility, and by other groups which struggled to see themselves as equals – lawyers and *bourgeois* for example. They were obviously treated as superiors by those dependent upon them for a livelihood – shipbuilders, caulkers, clerks, sailors – while packers (*emballeurs*) showed a touching existential sympathy for them since, because of obstacles to commerce, the merchants were 'sans cesse travaillés de soucis sur le succès de leurs entreprises, toujours prêts à sacrifier leur fortune pour le bien général'.[14] However, even guilds which recognised merchant supremacy could be critical.

Moreover, the smooth self-image of the merchant sometimes cracked. Sometimes this appeared relatively obliquely, as when Seimandy, a leading merchant who had been through several bankruptcies as well as several religions, and who was nearly but not quite a noble in 1789, argued that merchants had continually to resist temptation, to wage a perpetual struggle silently within themselves, between 'délicatesse' and 'intérêt'. 'Le but du commerce est la fortune; il est vrai . . .', he confided, but challenged its detractors to acknowledge the effort of hard-work and self-control involved.[15] Dominique Bertrand maintained that if trade had risen in esteem, it was because of the talent, 'lumières', and, especially, 'la noblesse' with which merchants exercised their profession, perhaps an admission of inferiority within an assertion of their worth.[16] Merchants were proud of their attainments, yet aware of their precariousness, especially since their recklessness and irresponsibility in the specifically commercial and credit crisis of 1774 had so tarnished their reputation. And even if the foremost merchants felt a basic, but by no means unalloyed, confidence within their city, and were even proud of forming, internationally, a Republic within Europe's monarchical system,[17] they knew that their region (Provence) was dominated by a backward nobility, their nation by a wasteful one. Hence, a strange, unstable mixture of confidence and insecurity. With the calling of the Estates General, French merchants felt isolated, in a minority, in the peripheral part of the 'two Frances', their voice likely to be drowned by unschooled peasants electing lawyers, magistrates, *militaires*, landowners and nobles.[18] Yet they were *also* able to state that there were as many merchants, *marchands* and manufacturers as there were *propriétaires* and peasants.[19] But their campaign for 'separate and special representation' failed: it was based both on their feeling of strength (in their contribution to

French wealth), but also of inferiority (numerically and in terms of status).

Moreover, attacks on the merchants were sharp enough to puncture any outward complacency. In January 1789 Mathieu Blanc-Gilly, future deputy of the Legislative Assembly, published a pamphlet against the local tax system (*octrois*, which provided all royal taxation, pushing up the price of bread and meat). Though denouncing mainly the tax farmers, Blanc-Gilly painted a dismal picture of a city whose lower classes lived in dire poverty, in enforced crime and immorality, and where trade and industry were smitten by periodic crises. A moralist rather than an economist, though himself a merchant, Blanc-Gilly deplored in a series of pamphlets 'cette mauvaise foi qui règne presque généralement dans le commerce . . . ces haines implacables que l'on se voue, et ces pièges de toute espèce que l'on se tend pour les assouvir'.[20] Dishonesty flourished, because honesty went unrewarded. For the rich owed their fortunes to their ancestors, to swindles or to chance. Trade had become a lottery. Marseille was a whited sepulchre, with only the appearance of wealth, but with 60,000 citizens, 'semblables aux frêles vaisseaux qui voguent sur une mer orageuse', exposed to shipwreck.[21]

Thousands of these, as well as many merchants (some of whom later retracted) signed one of Blanc-Gilly's diatribes. This cited an essay of André Liquier which had denounced the corrupting power of commerce, the social dissolution produced by the cash nexus – an essay which had been crowned, not without controversy, by the Academy in 1777, perhaps as a self-conscious demonstration of broad-minded enlightenment.[22] Blanc-Gilly noted the long-running complaints against soap-manufacturers (some of the richest being *négociants*) who sold defective produce and he also recalled the crisis of 1774 when 'five-sixths' of the city's merchants went bankrupt. This 'libelle licencieux' was condemned by Municipality and Chamber of Commerce, partly because Blanc-Gilly had sent it round the maritime cities of France, thus further damaging the already fragile credit of Marseille, exposing it to the attacks of rival ports, all the more dangerous now that Marseille's privileged but precarious 'free port' status, seen as the basis of its prosperity, was likely to be threatened by the Revolution. But Blanc-Gilly was not deterred.[23] Denouncing the unstable concentration of wealth at Marseille, he pilloried those who, content to enjoy rather than create wealth, had in the virtual absence locally of a 'real' nobility, aspired to become nobles and had therefore suffered in silence the contempt of their social superiors. At Marseille, 'une aristocratie de ton, arrogante, stupide, ignorante et féroce,' blasphemed the Revolution when they realised that, as well as destroying the nobility, it was to put 'les classes de la médiocrité et de la pauvreté' at their level. Far from glorifying the self-made man, Blanc-Gilly criticised the arrogance of merchants still besmirched by their rise from the dregs of the people. Moreover, this new aristocracy could not even see its own interests since those merchants who composed it did not understand that 'le commerce n'existe, ne fleurit que par la liberté, qu'il dédaigne les frivoles distinctions, qu'il abhorre les privilèges et qu'il ne puise ses ressources que dans les produits de l'agriculture et de l'industrie'. As so often, the mercantile interest was blamed for oppressing the interests of agriculture and industry, again not a mark of a fundamental confidence.

Thus were shattered some of the clichés about trade: that Marseille had preserved from Greek times a 'republican' virtue and a vigorous cultural life sustaining good *moeurs*, despite the city's opulence; that trade favoured freedom, and indeed an equality and fraternity within a meaningful 'trading community'; that trade enabled even the most humble to rise by dint of honest work. Indeed, the richest merchants, the Samatans, Périers, Clarys, showed a vicious and vindictive streak by (allegedly) sacking their employees, even a sea-captain, generally a person to be trusted and even cherished, for signing patriotic petitions.[24] They thus tried to silence guildsmen desperate for work. Merchants took control of a previously democratic guard, dragooning their employees and dependants to serve, a motley array of clerks, exchange-brokers, insurance agents, packers, porters. Thus the much-vaunted 'unity of commerce' was revealed as an oppressive sham.[25]

However, the fact that merchants (with officials, property-owners and *capitalistes*) had pushed the tax burden on to basic foodstuffs testifies to the fragile – or bogus – nature of a 'union' sincerely hymned in many *cahiers*. Certainly the *cahiers* of artisans and *ouvriers* had bitterly condemned this tax, sometimes with drafting help from the patriotic bourgeoisie. And the abolition of the *octrois* by popular insurrection on 23 March had relieved some pressure. Moreover, merchants who had argued, in good faith and following the principles of political economy, that the food taxes had been paid by them through higher wages, were refuted by patriots who, beside lawyers and journalists, included young merchants who met in cafés after the *comptoir* to discuss the plight of the lower classes. These argued that wages took account only of 'l'homme isolé,' not his wife and children. Unemployment, due to wars, industrial and commercial crises,[26] or to ill health and accidents caused by unhealthy work situations, was never considered, nor was the fact that the worker's need for work, literally a matter of life and death, was of a different order from the merchant's need for labour.[27] Moreover, so-called 'high wages' meant that artisans, not just merchants, had to charge a lot for their products and so could not easily sell them, either at home or abroad.[28] Or they competed ruthlessly, further endangering life and limb, or had recourse to fraudulent practices, further discrediting trade.

Merchants, conscious of their numerical inferiority in the city, fearing that their qualifications would not be recognised, clumsily manipulated the elections to the Estates General. They were condemned for this by the patriots and by royal officials, nobles Demandolx and Forbin-Gardanne, who informed the government of how merchants had packed the meeting of 'bourgeois' men of 'no profession' – *rentiers, propriétaires* and the like – with their merchant colleagues (but also with *va-nus-pieds*). Given the assumed subservience of most guildsmen, only commerce would be represented at Marseille, to the detriment of the countrymen and of 'l'industrie que le commerce anime mais qu'il ne doit pas opprimer'. Merchants had indeed branded the guildsmen as 'illiterates', unqualified to judge the interests of the town.[29] This intellectual arrogance[30] was compounded when merchants got excluded from the town *cahier* demands which displeased them, their manoeuvres being exposed by a patriotic lawyer's forensic examination of the drafting process and its results.[31] Even more serious, however (since *all* guild *cahiers* were sent to Versailles), was the fact that prominent merchants, including Audibert and Seimandy, secretly called royal troops into Marseille on 19 August,[32] with a prevotal tribunal in their baggage, to put the patriotic leaders on trial. While some merchants 'of the second rank' appeared among the accused, and others fled, their more eminent colleagues testified against them.[33] Thus, 'L'aristocratie de la richesse' or, in Mirabeau's words, 'cette petite portion de négociants dont se compose l'aristocratie de l'opulence, qui ne seront désormais . . . que les égaux de leurs concitoyens', seemed set to sabotage the Revolution.[34]

Pro-merchant propaganda tried to counter the effect of all this. Merchants provided employment and imported food. Peace and order, and hard work from the lower classes, were needed to protect the interests of trade, shared by all citizens. Even the 'timidity' of the merchants became a means of defence. If molested, disturbed, even slightly troubled, they and their capital would depart for Avignon or Nice:[35] what then would become of peasant, manufacturer, *fabricant*, artisan or worker?[36] The restless *inquiétude* of the holders of mobile wealth was no longer a mainly psychological weakness for moralists and academic essay-writers to deplore.

Criticism continued. Some Provençal nobles accused the rich commoners of Marseille of wishing to overthrow them – the protectors of the poor – only in order to increase their own exploitation and to pocket for themselves the alleged benefits of the abolition of noble privileges.[37] However, more common were patriotic allegations that rich merchants aped the nobility.[38] Certainly, merchants' attitudes towards the nobility were ambivalent. Seimandy, while condemning what 'la noblesse ... a d'injuste, d'oppressif et d'humiliant' for the Third, stressed that merchants did not wish to destroy their due prerogatives and honours, for the prospect of nobility encouraged emulation among merchants.[39] But another, anonymous, merchant deplored that the haemorrhage of *négociants* into the nobility 'empêche ceux qui pourraient se distinguer par de grandes vues dans le commerce de les étendre sur cette profession'. They therefore could not impart their knowledge to others and, disdaining their former profession, reduced it to 'une industrie individuelle', of restricted scope and ambitions.[40] It seems, therefore, that in the prevailing conditions of the *ancien régime*, individualism was not always a sign of strength. And we know that commercial partnerships were often fragile, breaking up in mutual recrimination. They did not last.

Merchants had not been too distressed when the March insurrection had got rid of the noble mayor, humiliatingly imposed upon them in 1766, perhaps as part of some 'feudal reaction'. Individual anti-noble feeling was expressed privately by Dominique Audibert, who, writing to Madame de Staël on 25 July 1789, said that his blood boiled to hear men whose only virtue lay in their birth lord it over 'la pauvre espèce plébéienne'.[41] Justifying *émeutes* and violence to overcome oppression and injustice, Audibert evoked Marseille's spirit of independence, its merchants' lack of servility towards *les grands*, their lack of subservience to officialdom. He acclaimed the new constitutional order which would recognise the individual's worth and talent. It is interesting that Audibert now anticipated that existing wounds would be healed by a revival of trade which, this time, would last. The *ancien régime* had been the era of the short term.

The new Revolutionary Municipality, from February 1790, under the *négociant* Etienne Martin, was 'bourgeois', even if its merchants were 'modest' and there were rather a lot of *fabricants* scarcely above the rank of artisan. But could merchants, in the new regime, be patriotic? Certainly, in the old, the most prominent had a reputation for incivism. Lacking public spirit, devoted only to their purses, they purchased petty offices to escape the drudgery of municipal service. If they did serve, they were accused of neglecting public affairs while, in turn, *they* complained of being humiliated before the people by the high-handed actions of even petty officials.[42] Merchant stewardship of hospitals generally left these in confusion and distress. In the Revolution, merchants were reprimanded for not attending electoral and sectional assemblies, lacking not only political zeal but the confidence or even energy to put their case, to defend even their own interests.[43] Merchants were lax in guard-duty, but if the artisans became exhausted defending the property of the rich, these would complain that their security was not assured and would threaten to emigrate – always this blackmail from a position of weakness (though more often from the *apologists* of wealth than from the wealthy).[44] Patriots sometimes called their bluff, threatening to recall those exiled for religious reasons, to show that the people were not utterly dependent on the existing merchants.[45] Rich merchants were rebuked for being afraid of freedom, afraid of politics, afraid of the people and, especially, afraid of equality.[46] Though patriots stressed that the people would always need and respect the rich, they themselves were accused of breaking the knots which, everywhere, link those who need with those who give work.[47]

Merchant claims that they imported grain, lent money to an insolvent Municipality, seemed merely conscence-salving, or disguised and even desperate threats to plunge Marseille into famine or bankruptcy, especially since merchants did not pay their taxes. Traditional accusations that merchants were 'égoïstes', that trade atomised society,[48] producing indifference and undermining family life, were reiterated as political polemics. The social resentment of peaceable *bourgeois* had long been directed against a disruptive merchant community which drew to the city vagabonds and criminals – *classes dangereuses* which were rarely *laborieuses* but which contributed both to fill the city hospitals and clutter its streets with their diseased and disgusting bodies.[49] Such problems were now blamed not on merchants, who preached law and order and the expulsion of vagabonds, but on the patriots, energumens whom the most prominent merchants would gladly have sent packing. But the patriots then retaliated with a moralistic critique, deploring the merchants' secret intrigues – their dinner parties, gambling sessions, *cercles* and *cénacles*, where disaffected nobles were entertained with rich abbots, emissaries of the princes, go-betweens for the recruiting of a lumpenproletariat for the counter-revolution. Merchants' cultured sociability turned sour. Their *bastides*, once a refuge or retreat from the hurly-burly of the town, a haven for quiet family pursuits, where summers and weekends were spent among fig and vine, amid a contented peasantry – these were now turned into centres of conspiracy.[50]

Equally serious were allegations of economic sabotage – to cease giving jobs, investing, paying tax.[51] The restrictive economic practices of the foremost merchants had long been criticised by patriots. The domination of trade by a Chamber of Commerce controlled by a few unaccountable Levant merchants, 'de vrais nobles possédant-fiefs', imposing taxes on raw materials needed for the town's industries (by the hatters, for example) was heavily criticised.[52] The Chamber prevented foreigners participating in the Levant trade and used underhand methods to exclude them from other trades, too, thus pushing up costs and limiting outlets.[53] Merchants severely restricted their captains' trading activities: this was intensely resented and, in the Revolution, successfully challenged. A campaign forced the calling of general assemblies of trade, to which manufacturers, retailers and sea-captains, as well as all merchants, were called. The Chamber itself was being democratised before its abolition (*de jure* rather than *de facto*) by the Constituent Assembly in September 1791.[54]

The narrow, corporatist attitudes of the merchants were frequently condemned. At the start of 1789 a patriotic lawyer, Bremond, had rebuked them – somewhat unjustly – for being over-concerned with their economic interests, neglecting the Estates General's main purpose of providing a constitution.[55] The local, privileged Royal Africa Company was urged to open share-holding to the public and the inconsistency of defending it, while calling for the abolition of the East India Company, was underlined.[56] The 'free port' itself was a privilege, however eroded, and it, too, came under attack, from manufacturers such as the *cordiers*, who accused shipowners of importing cheap second-hand foreign ropes, endangering their crews in the pursuit of profit.[57] Certainly, merchants had complained in the *ancien régime* that trade was 'mesquin', with little chance of thinking big or planning ahead, given inherent structural restraints and arbitrary government intervention.[58] But the Revolution hardly provided an ideal climate of expansion, though trade prospered until 1793.

Merchants felt unappreciated – their spokesmen outnumbered in the National Assembly (and their *députés extraordinaires* not always listened to), themselves misunderstood by Club and Municipality at Marseille, though until mid-1792 ceremonies of reconciliation tried to bridge the gap. If enterprising merchants risked accusations of speculation (and in May 1789 Payan privately confided that *négociants* might do well in a period of upheaval),[59] they sometimes in 1790 argued for the moral and economic superiority of a trade which gave a repeated number of 'small profits', shared out between a large number of medium-ranking merchants, over one providing a small minority with a few enormous windfalls.[60] Moreover, traditionally worrying questions of commercial morality were raised in a new context. Fraudulent bankruptcies – a prime example of a weakness turned into a strength and said to be a growth industry in eighteenth-century Marseille – harmed the artisans.[61] Yet just as merchants used to complain that nobles never paid their debts, now artisans accused merchants of a cavalier attitude to their obligations – not paying for goods delivered or services rendered, giving work only if the goods produced were supplied on credit. They, however, were pitiless in pursuing lower class debtors.[62] The quarrel over (or in) the soap industry grew more acrimonious, with the leading merchants accused of swindling the consumer and speculating in raw materials in order to bankrupt less resilient competitors who were purely manufacturers.[63] Conversely, 'petits marchands', trying to survive, were accused of falsifying the goods they sold to the people, in a cascade of dishonesty.[64] All the old arguments against 'luxury' were given a new edge.

Thus, merchants were open to suspicion. Commercial correspondence reveals acute mistrust.[65] Merchants always expected their colleagues to cheat them as to price and quality of goods. Moreover, such correspondence does show them speculating in essential foodstuffs and raw materials, despite their earlier opposition to the mass issues of *assignats* which made this so lucrative, if risky. Criticism of foot-loose 'capitalists', so common from staid and sedentary property-holders in the *ancien régime*, was now directed by patriots at merchants whose prided cosmopolitanism was viewed in the more exclusively negative terms of selling France and the French people short. Yet if they were not good patriots, where, conversely, was their universalistic humanism now, when they defended slavery and the slave trade against opposition which was now political and even popular?[66] Perhaps merchants' anti-Arab and anti-Jewish attitudes were more in tune with popular feeling, but their employment of foreign workers and sailors was obviously self-interested and pushed the 'native' work-force to acts of violence.[67] Labour disputes, including those between sailors and shipowners, were often ugly.[68] Merchants also ruthlessly exploited divisions within the guilds, where the atmosphere was far from fraternal.[69]

The patriots were genuinely distressed, as well as exasperated, by such developments, which tarnished a Revolution that had promised to give the merchants the freedom, security (and political hegemony) to which they had aspired. The Municipality tried to reconcile merchants and artisans, as forming 'un même peuple' with 'une même âme'.[70] 'La classe du peuple sera toujours soumise à celle de l'opulence', proclaimed Mossy *père* in his district assembly.[71] Plays in a patronising middle-class parody of Provençal tried to calm the people: 'Le commerço il réprèno sa courso . . . la révolution n'est-il pas assureyo? Il l'est aussi fermément qué lé roucas de notro Damo de la garda.' The moral? 'Le riche sera toujours riche. Mais le pauvre ne sera pas toujours misérable.'[72]

Patriots, who themselves often stressed their own respectability and responsibility as traders and manufacturers,[73] emphasised the benefits which the Revolution had brought to trade and traders – the abolition of the East India Company, the end of 'privilege', the confirmation of the free port, religious toleration which rescued protestants from 'l'état précaire où ils étaient réduits', the removal of obstacles and restrictions.[74] The expansive genius of commerce now soared without hindrance over the immensity of the oceans. But, even so, the Municipality was almost petulantly aggrieved and perplexed that merchants did not show more gratitude for its efforts to keep the peace, and though pleased that, in July 1791, its brutal expulsion of 'vagabonds' had momentarily reconciled it with 'messieurs les négociants', mistrust persisted.[75] Patriots repeatedly assured merchants of the people's good sense and pacific intentions – they knew that the first 'moments' of a revolution would not bring opulence but remained confident of a prosperous future. They urged merchants to activate their manufactures and to make their money circulate.[76] However, some moderate writers pessimistically portrayed the desolation which would ensue if the rich were threatened, while some bold conservatives even justified the gap between the very rich and the rest, arguing that Marseille's wealth was more beneficially distributed than if 'partagée entre plusieurs petits capitalistes encore exposés aux hasards et resserrés dans les privations qu'exige son économie et son avarice'.[77] The absolute dependence of poor on rich was stressed, mostly brutally, sometimes even sentimentally, with the 'humblest labourer' congratulating himself on belonging to the 'trading community'.[78]

However, there was very little harmony at Marseille. Divisions deepened among the patriots, some outbidding others in pledging themselves to assure peace to the merchants; others, notably in the Club, being more demagogically inclined. At Marseille, insults between revolutionaries were often couched in moral-economic terms. Jean-François Lieutaud, vainglorious commander of the National Guard, now servile champion of the rich, did not merely idolise La Fayette; his father had been so disgusted by his son's debauchery that he had disinherited him of a considerable fortune (or, alternatively young Jean-François had fled to the West Indies to enjoy the booty). It could therefore be said that 'les délits que la patrie reproche au Sieur Lieutaud ne sont que la suite des écarts d'une jeunesse dépravée'.[79] Belief that the sons of merchants were far too eager to enjoy their fathers' hard-earned fortunes, and that regular family life was destroyed by the restless pursuit of profit in a commercial town[80] – and that this also blighted other spheres (like education, for example) – made for a hopeless instability of relationships within the Revolutionary bourgeoisie. It allowed an easy birth for enmities of *amour-propre*, and nurtured avarice for power and fame even more than for money.

Lieutaud gambled. The rich gambled. Artisans, not content with their 'mediocre happiness', gambled. And if, as Blanc-Gilly had alleged, trade had been a lottery in the *ancien régime*, was it not a gamble in the circumstances of inflation and paper-money, in which 'hardiesse et imprudence'[81] could bring a merchant instant fortune or disaster? Most merchants approved of the constitution, many rushed to buy *biens nationaux* – whether for speculation or security, redoubled activity or withdrawal from business – but the torrent of Revolution and then war plunged Marseille into civil strife. But though merchants played a role in the federalist revolt, and suffered for it, continuities of fortune and personnel remained strong. However, the substantive history of the 'Revolutionary bourgeoisie' – at Marseille or in France – has yet to be written. It may provide as many surprises as it must surely bring rewards. We are still remarkably uninformed regarding their pursuit of profit in the period after 1792, a pursuit which was tortuous and almost clandestine, but not necessarily futile.

It is a *lieu commun* to say that the Revolution made the bourgeoisie as much as the bourgeoisie made the Revolution. It is also a commonplace to refer to 'the bourgeoisies' in the plural. However, if I have to some extent deconstructed the bourgeoisie – and I concede that many historians would fruitfully multiply distinctions between different professions, and between the inhabitants of different *quartiers*, as well as between different cities and regions – we must recognise in more than a merely rhetorical fashion, that the Revolutionary bourgeoisie (to reassemble the pieces once more) was involved in an international development of immense scope, whose potentialities and contradictions have far from exhausted themselves even today. The French bourgeoisie has had a very distinctive role to play, especially perhaps in the political and ideological spheres, but the full significance of its making (or unmaking) in the French Revolution cannot be understood in a merely national context.

I would finally suggest that even consideration of the 'economic' dimensions of the activities of the Revolutionary bourgeoisie must take into account questions of perception, *mentalité*, *moeurs*, of social and individual psychology. The perceived strengths and weaknesses of the bourgeoisie need to be kept in mind. After all, problems relating to, or deriving from, the insecurity of the French bourgeoisie (an insecurity *vis-à-vis* the bourgeoisie of other countries or stemming from threats from other classes within France, and perhaps intensified by repeated revolutionary experiences) – not only lie heavily across the history of the French bourgeoisie but have affected the history of France and indeed of Europe as a whole.

Notes

Abbreviations

ABR   Archives départementales des Bouches-du-Rhône, Marseille.
AC   Archives communales, Marseille.
ACC   Archives de la Chambre de commerce, Marseille.
AD   Archives départementales, (various localities).
AN   Archives nationales, Paris.
FP   Fonds de Provence, in Bibliothèque municipale, Marseille.

1   AN, Fonds of Calonne's East India Company, 8 AQ 326, letter of *procureurs du pays* of Provence, regarding the Marseille merchant Jacques Rabaud.

2   G. Comimnel, *Rethinking the French Revolution: Marxism and the Revisionist Challenge*, London, 1987, p. 196 etc.

3   Particularly interesting, in comparing the bourgeoisie of the eighteenth century and the proletariat of the nineteenth, as 'revolutionary classes', is F. Claudin, *Marx, Engels et la Révolution de 1848*, Paris, 1980. E. Sherover-Marcuse, *Emancipation and Consciousness*, Oxford, 1986, discusses parallels between Marx's concept of the proletariat and Robespierre's notion of 'the poor', rather than analogies between bourgeoisie and proletariat (with the latter, being 'nothing', struggling to be 'everything'). The quotation regarding merchants is from Marx and Engels, *The German Ideology*, Moscow, 1976, p. 80.

4   N. Hampson, *Prelude to Terror. The Constituent Assembly and the Failure of Consensus*, Oxford, 1988, pp. 83–98. Not, of course, that class conflict is *ever* unambiguous.

5   J. P. Ferran, *La haute bourgeoisie protestante marseillaise à la veille de la Révolution*, DES Mémoire, Faculté des Lettres, University of Aix, n.d.

6   Remembering that Marseille had to recover from the plague of 1720, which killed half its population. For the economic history of Marseille, see Charles Carrière, *Les négociants marseillais au XVIII* siècle*, 2 vols, Marseille, 1973.

7   AC, Série Affiches, that of 11 February 1789.

8   D. Roche, *Le siècle des lumières en province. Académies et académiciens provinciaux, 1680–1789*, 2 vols, I, Paris, 1978, p. 252.

9   For the role of these merchants, see the *Recueil des ouvrages présentés à l'Académie des Belles Lettres, Sciences et Arts de Marseille*, Bibliothèque municipale, Fonds de Provence (henceforth FP), 7911. Dominique Bertrand, at Academy, 25 August 1785. *Recueil*, vol. of 1783–86. FP, 7911.

10   See in the *Recueil*, Dominique Audibert's *éloge* of the bailli de Revel, 21 April 1784; his praise of Jean-Charles Campion, *directeur des fermes*, as a 'financier citoyen', attentive to the needs of merchants (*exceptionally* so), etc.

11   J. Seimandy [attrib], *Observations impartiales et libres*, Marseille, 1789, FP, 4717, *Délibérations municipales*, I. Much of the following characterisation of merchant attitudes is taken from this and from Seimandy's *Mémoire d'un négociant de Marseille à l'occasion de l'assemblée des Etats Généraux*, Marseille, 1789, FP, 4717(845). This latter was given general significance by being adopted – with some modifications, so as not to offend its recipients – as the Chamber of Commerce's address to the government, asking for a 'special representation' for merchants in the Estates General, ACC, A25, 23 January 1789.

12   Naturally, the merchants of the Academy – and the Chamber of Commerce – considered themselves superior to the broad mass of *négociants*. These tended to have 'narrow' views, to have insecure fortunes which made them adopt 'dishonourable' methods, including fraudulent bankruptcies, collaboration with Jews or Turks, smuggling, etc. However, there are numerous indications, not least from commercial correspondence, that some of the leading merchants were not too fussy about their methods or their contacts. The records of the Amirauté Court (see Fonds Lejourdan, XIF1–14, in ABR) do not show the best face of the merchants. On 3 December 1786 Castries expressed the great displeasure of the king at Samatan's business practices in trading with Tripoli, and he and his partner were summoned to Aix to receive a reprimand from the Intendant. ABR, C2647.

13   Such terminology was not new in 1789, of course. Archives of the Chamber of Commerce, B65, Chamber's letter to de Castries, against East India Company, 19 June 1786; B18, discussion of government proposal to establish an insurance company, with the Chamber 'invited' to be the leading shareholder, 9 April 1783.

14 J. Fournier, *Cahiers de doléances de la sénéchaussée de Marseille*, Marseille, 1908, *Cahier* of *emballeurs*, pp. 118–19.

15 Seimandy, *Mémoire d'un négociant.*

16 D. Bertrand, welcoming André Liquier into the Academy, 25 August 1785; *Recueil des ouvrages.*

17 Audibert's *éloge* of Borély, Academy, 25 August 1785; *Recueil des ouvrages.*

18 Seimandy [attrib], *Observations impartiales*, and *Mémoire d'un négociant.*

19 ACC, A25, *Réflexions d'un négociant sur la convocation prochaine des Etats généraux*, Marseille, 1788.

20 M. Blanc-Gilly, *Plan de révolution concernant les finances*, (January ? 1789), FP,4717, Impositions, I, and *loc.cit.*, *Mémoire sur la découverte de l'impôt unique*, Marseille, 1789. For more polemical works: *Très respectueuses représentations* and *Défense, apologie*, 27 June and 15 July 1789, respectively, both *loc. cit.*, 4717(845).

21 M. Blanc-Gilly, address to president of National Assembly, 27 October 1789, AN, DXXIX54, and *Appel à la nation*, 25 January 1790. British Library, F967(3).

22 A. Liquier, *Discours qui a remporté le prix: Quelle a été dans tous les temps l'influence du commerce sur l'esprit et sur les moeurs des peuples*, in *Recueil des ouvrages*, vol. for 1777.

23 M. Blanc-Gilly (and his lawyer Lavabre), *Mémoire à consulter pour le Sieur Blanc Gilli, négociant*, 15 September 1790. British Library, 1029(4). Also, against the aristocracy of parvenus, Blanc-Gilly, *Victoire glorieuse*, 31 October 1790, FP,4717, VIII.

24 Merchants named in *Détail historique des principaux événements*, Marseille, 1790, FP 4528F; also, for coercion, *Avis impartial sur la garde nationale*, 1790, FP, 5102; Blanc-Gilly, *Défense, apologie*, Marseille, 15 July 1789, FP, 4528S.

25 M. Blanc-Gilly, *Patrouilles bourgeoises*, August 1789, FP, 4717, Garde nationale, I.

26 Liquier, *Discours qui a remporté le prix*; and P. A. Guys, *Marseille ancienne et moderne*, Paris, 1786, debated the causes and impact of commercial and industrial crises on the labouring classes.

27 The debate on wages, taxation, etc. was far more complex (and interesting) than can be shown here. See A. Patot, *négociant* [attrib.], *Réflections d'un citoyen de Marseille*, I, Marseille, 1789, FP, 4717; and, in particular, Eymar *aîné*, *négociant* [attrib.], *Réflexions sur l'impôt*, Marseille, 1789, FP, 4717, Tax, *(impositions)*, II.

28 The *caissiers* (box or crate-makers) argue this in their *cahier*, J. Fournier, *Les cahiers de doléances de la sénéchaussée de Marseille*, Marseille, 1908, p. 34.

29 Consult AN, Ba50, letters on elections to the Estates General.

30 One wonders about the intellectual security of a group like the *négociants* whose *cahier*, while calling for a free press, also prescribes for schools 'des livres élémentaires . . . approuvés par le gouvernement et dont les instituteurs ne puissent s'écarter, avec surveillance des officiers municipaux'. Fournier, *Cahiers de doléances*, p. 178.

31 Chéry, *avocat*, *Observations pour servir de supplément au cahier général des doléances*, n.p., 1789, FP, 5013.

32 AC, AA7, *Comparant*, 19 August 1789.

33 AN, DXXIX 54 and 55; BB 30 15 (etc.), for documents including interrogations before Bournissac.

34 Mirabeau, *Discours sur la procédure prévôtale*, 26 January 1790, FP, 4717, Justice prévôtale, I.

35 Often commented on during the *ancien régime*; AC, BB288, Municipality to Breteuil, 21 March 1788; in 1789, Blanc-Gilly referred to the fragility of merchants' fortunes: 'Après tout, le négociant ne possède un véritable avoir que quand il se retire du commerce': *Plan de révolution concernant les finances*, FP, 4717, tax, I. Another

contributor to the debate on tax, an anonymous *abbé*, urged that Marseille merchants be encouraged to buy land, so as to 'attach' them to the city, *Réflexions d'un patriote sur les taxes municipales, loc. cit.*, II.

36   P. le Pelley, *Discours prononcé à Messieurs les citoyens*, at the rich Section Saint-Ferréol, 25 March 1790, FP, 4717, IV.

37   AN, H1240, letter to government from Veinfer, *citoyen*, Marseille, 4 June 1789. See also the manuscript extracts from the *Observations impreimées* of the Provençal nobility, British Library, 936 c 27(38). At FP, 4717, II, *Dialogue entre la ville d'Aix et celle de Marseille*, 1789, with 'Aix' defending the nobility and accusing the merchants of selfish designs.

38   See, of particular virulence, *Brûlot des uniformes illégaux*, 1789 or 1790, FP, 4717, Garde nationale, I; and, in 1791, *Avis pressant aux tribunaux de justice de Marseille*, from Toulon, *loc. cit.*, III.

39   Seimandy, *Mémoire d'un négociant*.

40   ACC, A 25, *Réflexions d'un négociant*.

41   The letters, from which the following citations and references are drawn, are at the Bibliothèque municipale, Besançon, Ms. 1413.

42   For the often rather peculiar offices, see AC, BB250. Many patriots, including Blanc-Gilly, lamented the humiliation of Marseille, a former (Greek) republic, at the hands of 'subaltern' officials. *Mémoire à consulter*, British Library, 1029(4).

43   *Réflexions impartiales d'un ami du bien public*, 1 September 1790, FP, 4717, VII.

44   *Discours prononcé par M. Martin, maire, à l'Assemblée patriotique*, 11 April 1791, FP, 4717, X.

45   *Réflexions adressees le 25 mai 1790 . . . à Mirabeau*, British Library, F 290(7).

46   All these were favourite themes of *L'observateur marseillais*, Bibliothèque nationale, L¹¹c 635(95); No. 1, 16 May 1790; No. 4, 22 May 1790, (etc.), and of the *Annales patriotiques*, (BN, L¹¹c 635(93)), No. 9, March 1790.

47   *Réflexions impartiales d'un ami du bien public*, 1 September 1790, FP, 4717, VII.

48   A common accusation: see, for example, *Pensez-y bien*, July 1789, FP, 4528Q.

49   AC, BB289, letters of Municipality to Breteuil, 7 June 1788; to Intendant, 9 and 27 June 1788; also reflected in many memoranda on different topics, BB374 and 375.

50   The 'Lieutaud affair' – concerning the future counter-revolutionary agent Jean-François Lieutaud, commander of the National Guard until his brutal replacement in September 1790 – produced a mass of documents. See the dossier of his abortive trial before the District Tribunal of Marseille, ABR, L3293. Also, *Adresse de Monsieur Blanc-Gilly*, 11 September 1790, FP, 4528AG.

51   In the *Vie de Phocion*, 20 August 1790, merchants were accused by Blanc-Gilly of not paying their debts, refusing to give employment and even imposing deprivations upon themselves, in order to plunge the lower classes into distress, FP, 4717, VII.

52   Chéry, *avocat, Observations pour servir de supplément au cahier général des doléances*, n.p., 1789, FP, 5013.

53   ACC, E148. Castries, Minister for the Navy, was shocked by the subterfuges suggested and rejected them, letter of 12 March 1786.

54   For a comprehensive project for the Chamber's reform, *Adresse du Conseil général de la Commune de Marseille à l'Assemblée nationale*, early 1791, FP, 4717, IX.

55   Bremond [attrib. – possibly Antoine Bremond Julien, a young *avocat*], *Lettre aux Marseillais sur l'objet de leur députation*, early 1789, FP, 4717(845).

56   By Chéry, *Observations*.

57 AC, HH403. The *Mémoire du corps des cordiers à chanvre*, 16 December 1790, blamed 'l'avarice de certains armateurs et capitaines' for making them use inferior foreign or 'renovated' ropes.

58 This was a 'lieu commun'. See, among a wealth of materials, *Mémoire et consultation pour le corps de marchands*, Marseille, 1786, FP, 2236. Of course, merchants tended to defend what privileges they had – the free port, and the colonial '*Exclusif*' etc. For the latter, see ABR, C2562, memorandum of 10 January 1785.

59 AN, fonds Greffulhe, 61 AQ 154, letter of Jean Payan, 17 May 1789. I am grateful to the Duc de Gramont for permission to consult this valuable series.

60 This was accepted by a committee of the Chamber of Commerce, led by Seimandy, reporting on the free port, 16 November 1790. Musée Arbaud, Aix, *liasse* 153; see also, *loc. cit.*, *liasses* 206 and 207 and ACC, E107, for documents from the sea-captains putting forward similar views.

61 By 'Philopatrie', in his letter to Necker of 12 April 1789, AN, Ba50. For lawsuits, often involving bankruptcy, see Fonds Lejourdan, of Amirauté Court, ABR, XIF1–14, and Série XIIIB, Tribunal de commerce, *loc. cit.* However, Joseph Dubuisson *aîné* seems genuine when complaining of being ruined in the pre-Revolutionary crisis. Because nobles of Aix did not flock to the foire Saint-Lazare at Marseille, September 1788, he laments: 'je ne sais comment dans cette affaire me retourner dans cet état désespéré, chagrin de me voir détruit dans un seul moment, après avoir travaillé toute ma vie comme un forçat … et plutôt de supporter l'ignominie, je me brûle la cervelle …' Letter of 5 October 1788, to Intendant, ABR,C4664.

62 Chéry, *Observations*, criticised the merchants for their ruthlessness to debtors, in particular their barbaric desire to preserve 'la contrainte par corps' (admittedly their *cahier* mentioned only the colonies, Fournier, *Cahiers de doléances*, p. 184). Many guild *cahiers* were concerned with the problem of debts – including the payment for goods and work supplied to merchants who then went bankrupt. Fournier, *Cahiers de doléances*, p. 38 for *caissiers*, p. 113 for *emballeurs*, etc. One of the first acts of the patriots in 1789 was to organise a *quête* for the release of persons unfortunate enough to be in prison for debt.

63 For the disputes over soap, ACC, H143, H146; AC, HH428 and 429, among numerous dossiers.

64 AN, H1315, letter of Antoine-Joseph Armelin, to king, 20 March 1789.

65 For commercial correspondence, AN, Fonds Greffulhe, especially 61 AQ 151 and 152; AD Aube, Troyes, Fonds Fromageot, 3F159-173; AD Aveyron, Rodez, Fonds Solier de Camarès; AD Rhône, Lyon, 2F417, 2F418 etc.

66 ACC, B20, Chamber of Commerce's address to king, 16 November 1791, condemned in *Opinion de Pierre Micoulin*, FP, 5285.

67 Few memoranda from the Chamber on the Levant trade omitted derogatory remarks on the Jews, Greeks, Armenians, Levantines. ACC, J1561, J1562, etc. Liquier, *Discours qui a remporté le prix*, pp. 76, 78, 79, was frankly 'anti-Arab'. Clearly, such questions are far too delicate and complex to be more than mentioned here. On the problem of 'foreign' workers – and many well-established workers at Marseille were foreign, especially if this meant 'from outside the city' – see municipal proclamation of 19 December 1790, FP, 4717, IX, etc. See also AC, HH 434, for *Mémoire*, n.d., of *ouvriers tailleurs de habits*, complaining that masters prefer foreign workers.

68 In July 1790 there were violent demonstrations by sailors and their wives to get the reimbursement of money deducted from their wages. AC, BB292, letters of Municipality, 14 July, 24 July 1790, etc.

69 A comment based on a survey of the Série HH of the Archives communales.

70   AC, 1I702, Municipal proclamation of 15 May 1790.

71   Mossy *père*, speech of 11 February 1790, at District du Concert, FP, 4717, III.

72   B.S. Bonnet, ci-devant Bonneville, *Les Fêtes de la liberté*, 14 July 1790, FP, 4430.

73   F.-O. Granet, *Brèves observations*, February–March 1790, FP, 4717, IV.

74   *Réflexions impartiales d'un ami du bien public*, FP, 4717, VII.

75   AC, 4D1, letter of Municipality to deputies of Marseille at Constituent, 10 July 1791.

76   *La paix! La paix!*, Marseille, 1790, FP, 4717, VIII; *La contre-révolution éventée*, FP, 4528AF; *Lettre de M. Jean-François Lieutaud*, FP, 5188; *L'Echo du peuple marseillais*, September, Marseille, 1790, FP, 4717, VII; *Lettre d'un vieillard*, FP, 5198.

77   *Abbé* Ouvrière, *Adieux d'un cosmopolite*, Marseille, 1790, FP, 5088.

78   *Les révolutionnaires convertis*, 1790, FP, 4717, VIII.

79   For allegations against Lieutaud, see Bertrand, *homme de loi, Les grandes prophéties*, 1790, FP, 4717, Garde nationale, III; la veuve Marrot, *Mémoire en réclamation*, 1790, *loc. cit.*, IV; and accusation by Etienne Seytres at Lieutaud's trial, *Plaidoyer*, loc. cit., IV.

80   The accusation that the sons of merchants were indecently impatient to get their hands on their fathers' fortunes is made by the Marquis des Pennes, at the Academy, 25 August 1786, *Recueil*, FP, 7911; and features in P. A. Guys, *Marseille ancienne et moderne*, Paris, 1786. Liquier's academic essay, *Discours qui a remporté le prix*, has much on the degradation of family life, while L. Bérenger considered that 'la jeunesse de ce pays-ci est non seulement débauchée, mais plus dépravée encore, qu'on ne la remarque dans toutes les grandes villes commerçantes'. *Soirées provençales*, 3 vols, I Paris, 1786, pp. 128ff, for this, and other myth-puncturing remarks of Bérenger. For an idyllic picture of merchant family life, Dominique Audibert on Borély, 25 August 1785, Academy, *Recueil des ouvrages*.

81   A phrase used by the *négociant* Jacques Bouillon, on 21 February 1792, letter to Banque Greffulhe, AN, 61 AQ 152.

Artisans, *sans-culottes* and the French Revolution

Pour combattre Jean-Jacques . . . il suffit de l'opposer à lui-même: car, s'il a dit
que le gouvernement fédératif était le seul qui convient à un grand peuple qui
voulait être libre, il a dit aussi que le seul moyen de rendre libre un grand
empire serait de brûler une capitale aussi immense que Paris. Or, je vous le
demande, Messieurs, voulez-vous brûler Paris?[1]

Few scraps of paper have acquired the fame of the definition of a
sans-culotte written in an uncertain hand by a thirty-year-old Parisian
soldier and nailmaker named Jean-Armand Vingternier in 1793. The
beginning is, by now, very familiar: 'Un sans-culotte, Messieurs les
Coquins? C'est un être qui va toujours à pied, qui n'a pas de millions,
comme vous voudriez tous en avoir.' The concluding sentences are
rather less well known, but are no less striking, not only because of their
vigour but also because they are in English:

> Brethren and friends, will you to assure the revolution? Knock down the
> Snake Brissot, the Vipere Guadet, the reptil Vergniaud, the rascal
> Barbaroux, the Sweet Petion, the Dog and hypocritical Rolland and all
> others Scelerates of the clique Gensonne, Boyer-fonfrede, Rabaud,
> Buzot, etca, etca, etca, etca and that'il do.[2]

The aim of this chapter is to show that the mixture of French and
English in Vingternier's celebrated definition of a *sans-culotte* was not
entirely idiosyncratic. It was, instead, an effect of a developing argument over what kind of revolution the French Revolution was. That

argument ranged widely over the many modalities of political analysis available in late eighteenth-century France. In doing so, however, it was obliged to engage with one particularly prominent feature of the Revolution: the fact that it had been a successful urban and, more specifically, a Parisian insurrection that had destroyed many of the recognised prerequisites of monarchical government. There was little, however, in the vocabulary of late eighteenth-century French political analysis that could capture that combination of insurgent action and its distinctively Parisian context which, together, served to identify the fall of the Bastille as both the moment of Revolution and the point of departure of a new political and constitutional beginning. Conventional political analysis in eighteenth-century France (apart, perhaps, from that produced by Mably) did not, on the whole, have much that was positive to say about insurrections, the people who participated in them or the political implications of insurgent action.

It was this conceptual gap that was filled by the term *sans-culotte*. As Camille Desmoulins put it towards the end of 1789, 'les sobriquets populaires sont en général des indices sûrs de l'état d'une nation. En France, on appelle le peuple, la *canaille*; en Angleterre on l'appelle: *John Bull*, le taureau'.[3] Two years later, however, he had found a word with rather more positive connotations than the pejorative *canaille*. He did so by inserting a term of abuse (which was what the expression *sans-culotte* originally was) into a style of political rhetoric that had developed in fifteenth- and sixteenth-century Florence, had flourished in seventeenth- and eighteenth-century England and, in recent years, has come to be known as 'civic humanist', 'old Whig', 'commonwealth' or 'neo-machiavellian'.[4] By 1792 the Parisian equivalent of John Bull had become the *sans-culotte* (however different the political dispositions evoked by the two terms may have been). The French term came to represent an image of the Revolution that was popular and urban in character, in which Paris and its people were the authors and architects of Revolutionary politics, and in which the identity of the Revolution itself was grounded upon the needs and actions of the Parisian people.

The juxtaposition of French and English in Vingternier's definition of a *sans-culotte*, was, therefore, more than a linguistic eccentricity. It was redolent of a wider dialogue between the rhetoric of neo-machiavellian republicanism and the conditions of political life in post-Revolutionary France – a dialogue that began soon after the fall of the Bastille. By the time of the insurrection of 10 August 1792, the word *sans-culotte* had come to stand for popular participation in Parisian politics and, above all, to justify the hegemony of political clubs, and the Parisian Jacobin club in particular, over representative institutions. Since many of the supporters and members of such clubs were Parisian artisans, many artisans came to recognise themselves as *sans-culottes*.

It has been usual, however, to describe the relationship between artisans and *sans-culottes* in stronger terms. Ever since the publication of Albert Soboul's *Les Sans-Culottes parisiens en l'an II*, the equation between artisans and *sans-culottes* has been grounded upon certain putatively distinctive features of the late eighteenth-century urban economy. That equation has been coupled with a claim that the Year II represented a major, if short-lived, break with the politics of the earlier years of the Revolution. In this respect, the work of Soboul, as well as that of Richard Cobb and George Rudé, was as much heir to a long political tradition as it was an attempt to isolate those social determinants that meant that the politics of the Year II were irreducibly different from those of the early years of the Revolution. Nineteenth-century historians, hostile to the politics of the Year II, emphasised a series of political ruptures, running from 10 August 1792 to 31 May 1793 to 5 September 1793, caused by Jacobin demagoguery and its appeal to the rootless, hate-filled and violent population of late eighteenth-century Paris. Soboul, however, explained the same series of ruptures in terms of a fragile alliance between a Jacobin political elite and a heterogeneous population of artisans and retailers whose vital resources – corn and bread – had been jeopardised by the combined effects of war, inflation and rural profiteering upon the city's economy. The chronology of political transformation remained the same, even if the explanation was very different. According to Soboul, the sequence of *journées* was the product of growing pressure from below, forcing the Jacobins to accept price controls, agree to the creation of an *armée révolutionnaire* and surrender much of the power of the Revolutionary Convention to the *comités révolutionnaires* and *comités civils* of the capital's forty-eight sections.[5]

The matrix constituted by artisanal workshops, the market for corn and the institutions of the Parisian sections of 1793 was central to this analysis because each of its component parts could be set within the wider history of capitalist development and the labour movement to which Soboul subscribed. Examination of each of the features of the matrix – the characteristics of artisanal workshops, the vagaries of the market for subsistence goods, and the social composition of the Parisian sections and popular societies in 1793 − 94 – made it possible to combine historical explanation (by interpreting the politics of the Parisian sections in the light of the economic and social circumstances of artisans) with political realism (by emphasising the radical difference between pre-capitalist and capitalist societies). As Soboul presented them, the politics of the Year II were at once the outcome of an autonomous social movement but, given the inchoate character of pre-industrial society, were incapable of becoming the class-specific movement associated with large-scale industrial production and an organised working class. In this sense, 1793 was both an imperfect counterpart to, and confirmation of, the integrity of 1917.

Thirty years on, it has become apparent that this characterisation of the relationship between artisans and the politics of the Year II has lost a great deal of its explanatory power. It has become increasingly difficult to explain the emergence of the *sans-culottes* in terms of the interaction between artisanal workshops, the market for corn and the membership of Parisian sectional assemblies and popular societies. Although there were many artisans in Revolutionary Paris, and a significant number of them adopted or identified themselves with the political positions of the *sans-culottes*, it does not follow that they did so because they were artisans. Richard Andrews has shown, on the basis of the claims for small coin made by employers in 1790 and 1791, that many of the more prominent sectional leaders of the summer and autumn of 1793 were by no means the small-scale manual workers poised between independence and dependence that Soboul (or the rhetoric of the Year II itself) had suggested.[6] Since many *sans-culottes* were drawn from a much wider social spectrum than the matrix implied, it has become very much less easy to demonstrate that there was any necessary link between the politics of the Parisian sections and the circumstances of small-scale artisanal consumers.

It is also clear that artisanal workshops themselves were part of a more complex urban economy and a more sophisticated legal and political culture than Soboul had imagined.[7] There was a gulf between the small-scale, self-contained world of manual labour posited by the rhetoric of the Year II, and the elaborate divisions of labour, unstable hierarchies of contractors and sub-contractors, fleeting arrangements between masters and journeymen, and protracted legal argument over precedents, rights and obligations that characterised the world of the trades during the eighteenth century. Neither the economy of eighteenth-century Paris nor the multiplicity of products, product markets, networks of credit and formal and informal forms of association among master artisans and the journeymen they employed bore much relationship to the circumstances or processes that shaped Revolutionary politics. In short, the social determinants of the politics of the Year II simply did not exist (at least in the form in which it was assumed that they existed). The idealised artisanal workshops from which the concerns of the *sans-culottes* supposedly emerged had little in common with the artisanal workshops that actually existed in late eighteenth-century Paris. Whatever the social determinants (and the term allows for many interpretations) of the popular movement may have been, they could not have been those supplied by the matrix of artisanal workshops, the market for corn and the popular societies.

The unreality of the putative economic and social conditions associated with the *sans-culottes* has been matched by an increasing recognition that much of what seemed distinctive of the political projects and rhetoric of the Year II was already present in 1790 and 1791.[8] Conflicts between the sixty districts and the Municipality of Paris in the winter of 1789–90, and between the sections and the departmental or municipal administrations of the capital in 1791, were couched in terms that were very similar to those of 1793 and 1794. In 1791, as in 1793, local institutions emphasised the accountability of their elected representatives in terms of the undiluted sovereignty of the nation or the people, and attached particular importance to their right to associate freely, petition collectively and initiate legislative measures that exceeded the formal scope of their institutional entitlements. The difference, of course, was that these claims were made not by artisans, or in the name of *sans-culottes*, but by men (and women) who had little direct connection with the trades. There was little, in other words, in the modalities of political participation and accountability adumbrated in the direct democracy of the Year II that was specific to the social identities or ordinary concerns of the political actors who dominated Paris after the expulsion of the Girondins. The members of district or sectional assemblies who challenged municipal or departmental authorities in 1790 and 1791 did so not because of their occupational or social circumstances but because of their membership of district or sectional assemblies and their beliefs about the political rights that such membership conferred.

Finally, the large number of local histories of the social origins of royalism (particularly in south-eastern France) and federalism (in Lyon, Marseille and Bordeaux) undertaken since the publication of Soboul's thesis have revealed many occupational similarities between opponents of the Revolution or the Jacobin Republic and the *sans-culottes* themselves.[9] It is clear, in the light of the widespread popular support for royalism in Nîmes or federalism in Lyon, that there was no necessary relationship between being an artisan and following any particular course of political action. The relationship between being an artisan and becoming a *sans-culotte* was, in this sense, a contingent one. Any explanation of that relationship, like the relationship between artisans and royalism in Nîmes, or artisans and federalism in Lyon or Bordeaux, can only be historical, in which such social determinants as there were, were overlain by the issues and outcomes of more specific political choices and conflicts.

It is unlikely that there can be any viable analysis of the politics of the *sans-culottes* if the implicitly Leninist terms of Soboul's explanation remain the same and it is assumed that the Revolution was an incremental process of politicisation.[10] For the concept is an ambiguous one. If it is taken to mean that artisans learned to use new political repertoires during the course of the Revolution, it is an unexceptionable enough descriptive term, although one that applies as much to any social group – from the clergy to the professions – as it does to artisans. If, however, it implies that artisans came to participate in politics in a distinctively artisanal way, it either assumes that they were bound to do so as *sans-culottes* or implies that artisans had no conception of politics until, by dint of their involvement in the political life of the districts, sections and popular societies, they appropriated an already established political vocabulary. Neither assumption is particularly satisfactory, partly because large numbers of artisans were participants in Revolutionary politics from the outset. Simply because they were the largest component of the 75,000 or so Parisians entitled to participate in politics from 1789 onwards, their presence in the political life of the Revolution was a constant one. They were, for these reasons, particularly well represented among the National Guard, as the social composition of those of its members whose occupations were recorded by the *commissaires* of the Châtelet between mid-July and the end of December 1789 indicates.[11] Artisans did not enter the revolutionary process in 1792 or 1793: for they were always present. What changed was the manner of their presence.

It is also apparent that the concerns of artisans were not bounded by the narrow horizons of markets, prices and the daily or weekly struggle to achieve an adequate income before the Revolution. The papers of the civil courts of the eighteenth century, as well as the surviving traces of journeymen's own utterances and correspondence, disclose a culture in which questions of legal entitlement and an awareness of prevailing modes of formulating rights and obligations were very widely disseminated. The frequency of disputes in the eighteenth-century French trades, both among master artisans and between masters and journeymen, ensured that artisans did not need a revolution to acquire a measure of familiarity with the power of institutions and the organisational procedures that could be used to put that power to purposeful effect. What needs to be explained, therefore, is not how artisans acquired a political consciousness of their own (because that kind of awareness existed well before 1789), but how artisans came to acquire the kind of political consciousness encapsulated by the term *sans-culotte*, so that, by 1792, the term had become one of the rhetorical resources of republican politics.

It is not apparent, however, that the connotations of the term meant, as Richard Andrews has argued, that the *sans-culottes* are best understood as paternalistic regulators of the plebeian population of republican Paris. This interpretation merely transposes the cleavage between artisanal workshops and the Jacobin administration that gave Soboul's work its architectural coherence to another plane.[12] Just as there is nothing to support the view that artisanal workshops housed a social stratum whose concerns and preoccupations necessarily found their expression in the politics of the *sans-culottes*, so there is nothing to support the view that the plebeian population of late eighteenth-century Paris (a term that begs many questions) was inherently hostile towards the values of civic commitment, republican duty and hard work that, it is assumed, the political rhetoric of the Year II was designed to inculcate. The rhetoric of the Year II cannot be ascribed (albeit as a counterpoint) to the spontaneous predispositions of Parisian plebeians any more than it can be ascribed to those of Parisian locksmiths or tailors. There was more to politics in Revolutionary Paris than this emphasis upon the inherent qualities of the plebeian population can address.

Politics have figured more prominently in François Furet's broader characterisation of the Revolution.[13] In his reformulation of Augustin Cochin's interpretation of the relationship between Jacobinism and 'pure' democracy, the logic of Revolutionary politics was determined by the dynamic of direct democracy. The trajectory leading from 1789 to 1793 derived from the incapacity of political actors to divest themselves of the belief that popular sovereignty was inconsequential without direct democracy. Since direct democracy was an unworkable abstraction, it was always possible for particular groups of people to claim to represent or incarnate the sovereign popular will with more justice, or greater effectiveness, than others. From this perspective, the emergence of the *sans-culottes* was entirely in keeping with the Revolution's flight towards abstraction. In a political process in which any actual group of people was obliged to present itself as a surrogate or embodiment of the popular will, a term that implied possession of the qualities that could be ascribed to the people (such as need, industriousness, fraternal solidarity or an earthy disrespect for holders of high office) was a very powerful claim to the exercise of power.

It is not altogether clear, however, how far this characterisation of the dynamics of Revolutionary politics is an explanation or a re-description. The premise of a democratic political culture upon which the argument rests is something of an artefact, a composite made up of statements by Tocqueville and Cochin that have been transposed to 1789 and used to explain the course of political conflict during the Revolution in a functional, rather than a causal, manner. Even if it is accepted that the mechanisms engendered by continued appeal to the popular will led to the Terror (rather than, as might also be argued, by the more causally direct mechanism of a purposeful attempt to establish a classical republican dictatorship – which was, after all, how Marat and, later, the Committee of Public Safety justified Terror), the analysis does not address the question of why some revolutionaries not only claimed to embody but successfully claimed to embody the popular will, while others did not. Nor does it explain why some revolutionaries came to equate the people with the *sans-culottes*, while others did not. In the last analysis, it fails to address the related questions of why revolutionaries came to have the beliefs that they did, and why they acted upon those beliefs in certain distinctive ways.

Matters are complicated further by the very considerable changes that occurred to the connotations of the word *sans-culotte* itself during the Revolution. Before 1789 the figurative sense of the word *culotte* evoked scenes of sexual disorder or misconduct. One of the staples of the popular print industry of the rue Saint-Jacques in Paris and its offshoots in Orléans and Chartres was an engraving variously entitled *la culotte disputée, la lutte pour la culotte, le partage de la culotte*, depicting the age-old struggle between husband and wife over who should wear the trousers.[14] In a more literal sense, a man who was *sans-culottes* was someone found, usually by an outraged husband, father or guardian, in compromising circumstances with a young woman. According to the writer Louis-Sébastien Mercier, a play entitled *Le Sans-culotte* (which may have owed something to Rousseau's account of the young Saint-Preux's encounters with Julie de l'Espinasse) was performed as a satire upon a poet named Gilbert's unsuccessful candidacy for admission to the *Académie française* some years before the Revolution.[15] A man found *sans-culottes* was an object of derision because he had been caught with his trousers down.

This was the initial sense of the term during the early years of the Revolution. Between 1790 and 1792 royalist writers like the journalist François Marchant used it to refer, in a satirical or scatalogical way, to their political enemies. Marchant was the editor of a newspaper named *Les Sabbats Jacobites* and author of a pamphlet entitled *La Nation sans-culotte* published in November 1790. In 1792 he produced a series of scatological portraits of the principal members of the political clubs entitled *Liste des sans-culotte de Paris, avec leurs noms, surnoms et demeures*. Initially, therefore, the word *sans-culotte* denoted a condition rather than a person, and had a pejorative rather than a positive sense. By the time of the insurrection of 10 August 1792, however, it had acquired a wholly different, and more familiar, set of connotations. It referred to men who wore ordinary working clothes, rather than *culottes* and stockings, and who, by virtue of their simplicity, decency, hard work and civic commitment, embodied all that was most admirable in a republic.

The process of transformation can be followed with some precision. It occurred during the months that preceded and followed the elections to the short-lived Legislative Assembly in September 1791.[16] It was not the product of any challenge to the new political order by artisans as such, although a number of disputes in the Parisian trades served to raise the issue of the political status of informally constituted associations at a time when the relationship between political clubs and representative institutions was being particularly hotly debated.[17] This debate was an aspect of the intense campaign against the projected constitution of 1791 involving a cluster of overlapping individuals and groups drawn from the Jacobin and Cordelier clubs, the various *sociétés fraternelles des deux sexes*, the *Cercle social* and the *Point central des arts et métiers*. The political divisions associated with these conflicts, which culminated in the establishment of two rival political clubs to contest the Parisian elections to the Legislative Assembly in September 1791, formed the context in which the word *sans-culotte* began to acquire its positive connotations.

By September 1791 the term had lost its exclusively 'aristocratic' sense. In an address to the citizens of Paris read to the members of the club meeting in the *evêché*, the republican military strategist and future member of the Convention Dubois-Crancé denounced the 'calomnies' perpetrated by members of the rival *club de la Sainte-Chapelle* and their allies in the National Assembly who, he said, had used the word *sans-culotte* to besmirch the political reputations of men like Robespierre and Pétion. Instead of merely rejecting the label, Dubois-Crancé, to loud applause, declaimed: 'dussions-nous essuyer de nouvelles calomnies, dut-on ajouter encore quelques expressions injurieuses aux designations de *factieux*, de *sans-culotte*, dont les intrigants honorent les patriotes?'[18]

From that time on, the term became increasingly associated with the Paris Jacobin club, and particularly with those of its members who, like Dubois-Crancé, had refused to join the Feuillants between July and September 1791 and had been identified with the *club de l'évêché* during the elections to the Legislative Assembly. It was used in speeches to the club in the autumn of 1791 by Camille Desmoulins and the lawyer Pierre François Réal, both of whom had also remained Jacobins throughout the summer. Réal made the connection between the word and the electoral divisions in Paris particularly explicit. In a speech to the Jacobin club on 16 November 1791, he commended the people of Paris for electing Pétion to the office of mayor. The election, he said, was comparable to the insurrection of 14 July 1789 itself in revealing the character of popular opinion: 'C'est de ce grand mal dont ont tant à se plaindre ces ministériels et qui a donné tant d'énergie aux patriotes et aux sans-culottes de l'évêché.'[19]

The word, in other words, was a synonym for *patriote* and referred, particularly, to the members of the electoral club meeting at the *évêché* which had organised the Jacobin slate in the elections to the legislative Assembly and enabled the Jacobin rump to recapture its position in Paris after the secession of the Feuillant majority. It retained its association with political clubs when, in a speech to the Jacobin club on 27 May 1792, François Chabot recommended that affiliation to societies in large cities should be suspended: 'En général dans les villes, elles sont feuillantines, parce qu'elles sont composées de bourgeois, de marchands, qui détestent tout ce qu'on appelle *sans-culotte*.'[20] Only in June 1792 was the word used by an artisan when a 'citizen' from the *faubourg* Saint-Antoine presented an address to the Jacobin club complaining about the destructive effects of the conflict between Brissot and Robespierre: 'Si nous sommes sans-culottes, nous ne sommes pas sans sentiments, et s'il y avait seulement quarante citoyens de ma trempe, je ne doute pas qu'il n'y eût plus de vigueur parmi les patriotes.'[21]

The most prominent member of the Jacobin rump had, of course, been Robespierre, and it was Robespierre, in particular, who made the most striking use of the term in the spring and summer of 1793. 'Celui qui a des culottes dorées est l'ennemi né de tous les sans culottes', he stated in a speech to the Jacobins on 8 May 1793, calling for the creation of a popular militia, 'une armée populaire, non pas celle de Dumouriez, mais une armée populaire . . . composée de sans-culottes payés.' He returned to the charge on 12 May, again in a speech to the Jacobins:

> Cette armée ne peut être composée que de sans-culottes, ils ne peuvent en même temps manier la truelle et les armes . . . Il faut dans Paris une armée révolutionnaire, composée de sans-culottes qui s'exerceront au métier des armes et qui formeront une armée de réserve. Ces sans-culottes seront salariés aux dépens du trésor public.[22]

By August, the identification was complete: 'Nous autres, sans-culottes, n'avons point de femmes qui nous arracheront de la mort, lorsque les conspirateurs de Lyon nous poussent par centaines sous le couteau de l'assassin.'[23] The identification was maintained by Fabre d'Eglantine in his proposal to name the five additional days in the republican calendar *sans-culottides*. It was coupled with a somewhat optimistic (but conventionally neo-machiavellian) claim that, despite its initial 'aristocratic' usage, the term had a pedigree linking it to the liberties of ancient Gaul.[24]

The word *sans-culotte* was therefore used by members of the Jacobin club to appeal to a wider social constituency at three key moments: during the electoral campaign of the late summer of 1791, when electoral defeat would have meant the political collapse of the club; in the highly charged days leading up to the expulsion of the Girondins from the Convention in May 1793; and at the height of the political crisis produced by the federalist revolts of the summer of that year.[25] The term's continued identification with the Jacobin club throughout 1792 and 1793 makes it difficult to accept that it had any intrinsic association with artisans. It was, and remained, a term used by Jacobins to appeal to a popular, and artisanal, constituency.

The term's association with the Jacobin rump and then, successively, with Robespierre and his circle, Jacques Roux and Hébert is striking.

Brissot appears to have used the word very sparingly. In a speech to the Legislative Assembly on 9 July 1792 calling for the creation of 'une nouvelle commission de sûreté peu nombreuse et bien dêterminée à sauver la patrie', he made no use of the word in his concluding peroration: 'Soyez peuple, éternellement peuple; ne distinguez pas les propriétaires des non-propriétaires; ne méprisez pas les piques pour honorer seulement les uniformes.'[26] The Girondin Guadet implied, too, that the term had very specific associations in his speech denouncing Robespierre to the Convention on 12 April 1793: 'les vertus publiques se composent de vertus privées, et je sens combien il faut se défier de ceux qui parlent de sans-culotterie au peuple en même temps qu'ils affectent un faste insolent'.[27] Clearly, Guadet assumed that neither he nor his political allies – Brissot, Roland, Clavière or Servan – spoke of the *sans-culotterie* (and certainly did not affect 'un faste insolent'). The term cannot be divorced from the Jacobin context in which it was first, and most strikingly, used.

The political figure who played the most significant part in introducing the term to its Jacobin context was Camille Desmoulins. Desmoulins was steeped in the neo-machiavellian tradition of political opposition that had flourished in early eighteenth-century England and taken on a new lease of life during the Wilkes affair and the American War. Its key figures, as they appeared in the pages of *Les Révolutions de France et de Brabant* in 1789 and 1790, were Hampden, Milton, Harrington, Sidney, Toland, Trenchard, Gordon – and Machiavelli himself. In his speech to the Jacobin club on 21 October 1791 on the state of France after the Revolution, Desmoulins offered his audience an analysis couched entirely in neo-machiavellian terms. The Revolution had had no ineluctable causes. 'Les racines de notre liberté sont aristocratiques; le peuple de Paris n'a été qu'un instrument de la Révolution: l'histoire nous dira quels en furent les ingénieurs.'[28] Yet, if the origins of the Revolution lay in a series of ministerial miscalculations, its effect had been the creation of a republic, however much the polity remained nominally a monarchy.

Long-term changes in the nature of French society had no place in this explanatory framework. Instead, the analysis focused upon the relationship between monarchical government and its institutional foundations. The destruction of the privileges of the nobility, the clergy and the *parlements* that had taken place between July and October 1789 meant the demise of a monarchical constitution. France had become a republic even if the majority of the French people had not as yet recognised the fact. Yet few of the members of the National Assembly had been prepared to accept the implications of this state of affairs. This, Desmoulins argued, was why they had first attempted to model the new political order upon the English system. A hereditary House of Lords was, however, a political impossibility after the fall of the Bastille and, a *fortiori*, after 4 August 1789. This, he claimed, was why the constitution of 1791 had been laid out as it had. It was a surrogate for an English system that could be introduced only in piecemeal fashion. The first and most important move in this direction had been the failure to abolish the distinction between troops of the line and the National Guard, and, in the second place, the requirement that members of the National Guard should wear uniforms:

> et voilà les citoyens distingués en citoyens armés et non armés: par là, je fais tomber les fatales piques, et je désarme les redoubtables sans-culottes, qui ne peuvent se procurer un uniforme complet à 32 livres l'aune.[29]

The image of the armed citizens was, therefore, the meta-concept into which the term *sans-culotte* was inserted. As in its English equivalent, this ideal of political independence was set against an examination of the servility and dependence induced by government founded upon credit. In a later speech, to the Commune on 24 July 1792, Desmoulins was careful to emphasise the specifically Parisian implications of this characterisation of the Revolution. Both the size and occupational structure of the capital were the effects of the court-based system of credit and aristocratic consumption. The political divisions that had affected the nation as a whole had their social origins and actual source among the 'propriétaires, boutiquiers' and 'rentiers' of the capital. If, in 1789, they had made a revolution, they were now prepared to make a counter-revolution, 'pour échapper à un pillage imaginaire des *sans-culottes*'.[30] Yet four years of Revolution had left this social stratum with no choice but to throw in its lot with the committed revolutionaries of the capital's political clubs. The intransigence of both the invading armies and the Parisian *sans-culottes* meant that there was no room for compromise. Like their counterparts in London in 1643, the municipal officials of the capital should renounce their allegiance to the king and call for his destitution.

Desmoulins was, perhaps, a somewhat marginal figure in Revolutionary politics. Yet, although many other figures made use of the rhetoric of the commonwealth tradition between 1789 and 1793, no-one used it as consistently and as systematically as he did, from the first issue of *Les Révolutions de France et de Brabant* in the summer of 1789 to the last issue of *Le Vieux Cordelier* in the winter of 1793–94. Desmoulins was the first to use the term *sans-culotte* in a positive manner and did so in ways that were quite consciously designed to complement the contemporary English term John Bull.[31] In this sense, Marx's *boutade* about the politics of the Revolution being enacted in Roman garb may have been somewhat misplaced. For it was not Rome but England (or Rome mediated by England) that supplied revolutionaries in France with a vocabulary of political opposition and a justification of insurrection.

The place of that vocabulary within the political life of Revolutionary France has not been identified with much precision. For neither was it a style of political analysis that originated during the Revolution nor, it would seem, was it one that deviated in any particularly significant way from its earlier 'civic' or 'neo-machiavellian' incarnations. Its best-known French exponent before 1789 was Mably. Yet the circuits – both intellectual and interpersonal – which led from Mably and his noble interlocutors on the one hand, to Camille Desmoulins and his Parisian interlocutors on the other (and, perhaps in different ways, to the most celebrated of the French incarnations of the classical republican tradition, Gracchus Babeuf) may yet merit fuller investigation. Both the history of the word *sans-culotte* and the changing contexts in which the term came to be used are an indication of how much more remains to be discovered about the relationship between political vocabularies, political actors and political action before and during the French Revolution.

Notes

I am most grateful to William Doyle and Colin Jones for their comments upon an earlier version of this chapter. Its remaining defects are my own responsibility. The remarks that follow are provisional in the extreme and will be taken up in fuller fashion in a forthcoming essay on republicanism and the politics of the *sans-culottes*.

1   Camille Desmoulins, speech to the Jacobin club of Paris, 10 September 1792, in Aulard, *La Société des Jacobins. Recueil de documents pour l'histoire du club des Jacobins de Paris*, IV, Paris, 1892, pp. 278–9.

2   W. Markov and A. Soboul, *Die Sansculotten von Paris*, Berlin, 1957, p. 2.

3   C. Desmoulins, *Révolutions de France et de Brabant*, III, reprinted in his *Œuvres*, 10 vols, II, Munich, 1980, p. 120.

4   See C. Robbins, *The Eighteenth-Century Commonwealthmen*, New York, 1959; J. G. A. Pocock, *The Machiavellian Moment: Florentine Political Thought and the Atlantic*

Republican Tradition, Princeton, 1975, and his *Virtue, Commerce and History*, Cambridge, 1984; for fuller references see, most recently, T. Ball, *Transforming Political Discourse*, Oxford, 1988; T. Ball, J. Farr and R. L. Hanson (eds), *Political Innovation and Conceptual Change*, Cambridge, 1989. No trace of Desmoulins's relationship to this tradition can be found in the most recent biography: J. P. Bertaud, *Camille et Lucile Desmoulins. Un Couple dans la tourmente*, Paris, 1986.

5   A. Soboul, *Les Sans-Culottes parisiens en l'an II*, Paris, 1958.

6   R. M. Andrews, 'The Justices of the Peace of Revolutionary Paris, September 1792–November 1794 (Frimaire Year III)', *Past and Present*, 52 (1971), pp. 56–105.

7   M. Sonenscher, *Work and Wages: Natural Law, Politics and the Eighteenth-Century French Trades*, Cambridge, 1989.

8   G. Kates, *The Cercle Social, the Girondins and the French Revolution*, Princeton, 1986; M. Genty, *L'Apprentissage de la Citoyenneté. Paris 1789–1795*, Paris, 1987; R. B. Rose, *The Making of the Sans-Culottes*, Manchester, 1983.

9   A. Forrest, *Society and Politics in Revolutionary Bordeaux*, Oxford, 1975; G. Lewis, *The Second Vendée*, Oxford, 1978; W. Edmonds, ' "Federalism" and urban revolt in France in 1793', *Journal of Modern History*, 55 (1983), pp. 22–53, and 'A study in popular anti-Jacobinism: the career of Denis Monnet', *French Historical Studies*, 13 (1983), pp. 215–51.

10   Rose, *The Making of the Sans-Culottes*.

11   Of 339 non-commissioned officers of the National Guard who appear in the *minutes* of the *commissaires* of the Châtelet between 14 July and 31 December 1789, 105 (31.2 per cent) were artisans or members of the victualling trades, 84 (25 per cent) were merchants or wholesale merchants, 50 (15 per cent) were *bourgeois de Paris*, 22 (7 per cent) were drawn from the legal professions and the remainder from an assortment of office-holders, former soldiers, domestic servants or clerks. I owe these figures to Dr Dale Clifford and her 'The Real National Guard: Local Culture in Paris, 1789–90', paper presented to the Washington Conference on the French Revolution, May 1989. The proportions suggest an even higher participation by artisans among the ordinary membership of the National Guard (as is also apparent from the social composition of the company formed in the *district de Saint-Merri*; see Sonenscher, *Work and Wages*, p. 342).

12   R. M. Andrews, 'Social structures, political elites and ideology in Revolutionary Paris, 1792–94: a critical evaluation of Albert Soboul's *Les Sans-Culottes Parisiens en l'An II*', *Journal of Social History*, 19 (1985), pp. 71–112. Criticisms of the unwarranted assumptions underlying this approach are now well known: see, for some of the most cogent, A. Reid, 'Politics and economics in the formation of the British working class: a response to H. F. Moorhouse', *Social History*, 3 (1978), pp. 347–61; C. F. Sabel, 'The internal politics of trade unions', in S. D. Berger (ed.), *Organizing Interests in Western Europe*, Cambridge, 1981, pp. 209–44; J. Zeitlin, 'Shop floor bargaining and the state: a contradictory relationship', in S. Tolliday and J. Zeitlin (eds), *Shop Floor Bargaining and the State. Historical and Comparative Perspectives*, Cambridge, 1985, pp. 1–45.

13   F. Furet, *Penser la Révolution française*, Paris, 1978.

14   P. L. Duchartre and R. Saulnier, *L'Imagerie populaire*, Paris, 1925, pp. 34, 68.

15   A. Geffroy, 'Sans-Culotte(s)', in Institut National de la Langue Française, *Dictionnaire des usages socio-politiques (1770–1815)*, I, Paris, 1985. The association of the term with tutors is apparent in the Baronne d'Oberkirch's dismissive characterisation of Mme de Genlis as *gouverneur* of the Duc de Chartres's sons: 'C'est une femme à système, une femme qui quitte son grand habit pour les culottes d'un pédagogue'. See

Baronne d'Oberkirch, *Mémoires* (edited by S. Burkard), Paris, 1970, p. 317.

16 This paragraph is a very schematic summary of a complex series of conflicts in which what was manifestly at stake was often a surrogate for deeper objectives. The core of the conflict was the relationship between sovereign representative institutions (and the National Assembly in particular) and political clubs. The surrogate issues were the right to petition collectively, the rights of passive citizens and the conflicts in the Parisian trades. The celebrated Le Chapelier law is best understood in this context of conflict over political sovereignty rather than as an aspect of triumphant 'economic individualism'. The argument is developed at greater length in Sonenscher, *Work and Wages*, Ch. 10.

17 As J. Boutier and P. Boutry point out (without, regrettably, offering any evidence), 'les lois Le Chapelier (mai–juin 1791) proscrivant les "coalitions" sont parfois utilisées contre les sociétés'. See J. Boutier and P. Boutry, 'Les Sociétés politiques en France de 1789 à l'an III: une machine?' *Revue d'histoire moderne et contemporaine* XXXVI (1989), pp. 29–67 (p. 54).

18 Sonenscher, *Work and Wages*, p. 355.

19 Aulard, *Jacobins*, III, p. 249.

20 *Ibid.*, p. 614.

21 *Ibid.*, p. 657.

22 M. Bouloiseau, J. Dautry, G. Lefebvre, A. Soboul, *Œuvres de Robespierre*, IX, Paris, 1958, pp. 490, 514–15.

23 *Ibid.*, X, Paris, 1967, p. 63.

24 'Il nous a paru possible, et surtout juste, de consacrer par un mot nouveau l'expression de *sans-culotte* qui en serait l'étymologie. D'ailleurs une recherche aussi intéressante que curieuse nous apprend que les aristocrates, en prétendant nous avilir par l'expression de *sans-culotte*, n'ont pas eu même le mérite de l'invention.

Dès la plus haute antiquité, les Gaulois; nos aieux, s'étaient fait honneur de cette dénomination. L'histoire nous apprend qu'une partie de la Gaule, dite ensuite *Lyonnaise* . . . était appelée la Gaule culottée, *Gallia braccata*: par conséquent le reste des Gaules jusqu'aux bords du Rhin était la Gaule non culottée; nos pères dès lors étaient donc des sans-culottes'. M. J. Guillaume, *Procès-verbaux du Comité d'Instruction Publique de la Convention Nationale*, II, 2 Paris, 1894, p. 704.

25 It is particularly striking that Robespierre used the term only on a very small, but significant, number of occasions between April and September 1793: on 24 April, 8 May, 12 May, 26 May and 31 May 1793 (see his *Œuvres*). After then the word disappeared from his speeches until August 1793 in the context of a speech on the trial of Custine and the divisions within the Republic. Once Robespierre entered the Committee of Public Safety, Parisian matters and, *a fortiori*, Parisian insurrections were a secondary consideration.

26 *Choix de Rapports, Opinions et Discours prononcés à la Tribune Nationale*, IX, Paris, 1820, p. 223.

27 A. Vermorel (ed.), *Œuvres de Vergniaud, Gensonné, Guadet*, Paris, 1867, p. 301.

28 A. Aulard, *La Société des Jacobins*, III, p. 202.

29 *Ibid.*, p. 210.

30 Desmoulins, *Discours au Conseil général de la Commune . . . sur la situation de la capitale*, in his *Œuvres*, I, p. 412.

31 On John Bull in England, see J. Brewer, *The Common People and Politics, 1750s–1790s*, Cambridge, 1986; 'English radicalism in the age of George III', in J. G. A. Pocock (ed.), *Three British Revolutions, 1641, 1688, 1776*, Princeton, N. J., 1980); 'The

commercialisation of politics', in N. McKendrick, J. Brewer and J. H. Plumb, *The Birth of Consumer Society. The Commercialization of Eighteenth-Century England*, London, 1982. I am grateful to Dr Miles Taylor of Girton College, Cambridge for much information on John Bull.

Talking about urban popular violence in 1789

On 8 August 1789 the Comte de Quélen wrote to the Président de Saint-Luc to report on the resolutions of the night of 4 August. The distinctions based on privilege had been abolished, he said,

> pour ne faire à l'avenir qu'un même peuple sous la dénomination majestueuse de François, brûlant des châteaux, pendant, décollant, hâchant en pièces, sans formalité de justice, tous ceux qui déplaisent à cause de la grande liberté individuelle et enfin pour la plus grande gloire de Dieu. Quelle perspective heureuse pour l'avenir![1]

This association of popular violence and the Revolution was quickly to become the most potent theme of the counter-revolutionary argument. The more intelligent propagandists hastened to point out what such violence did to the revolutionaries' claim to legitimacy. The National Assembly was not, they argued, an expression of the general will of the sovereign people; its power was simply the product of violence. What France had got in reality was the rule of intriguers enforced by riot under the mantle of the sovereignty of the nation and of the Rights of Man, soiled by blood-letting. 'Qu'est-ce que ce principe de la souveraineté du peuple', wrote one of them late in the life of the Constituent Assembly,

> si ce n'est un moyen pour armer le peuple en faveur du pouvoir qu'elle [l'Assemblée nationale] exerçoit, en lui persuadant qu'il s'armoit pour sa liberté, si ce n'est le pretexte qui lui a fourni la force nécessaire pour changer la nature du gouvernement, et le rendre, non pas plus libre, non

pas plus populaire, non pas plus doux, sans doute, mais républicain de monarchique qu'il étoit auparavant?[2]

The less sophisticated propagandists simply equated the Revolution with lawlessness, the rule of the mob, murder and mayhem. The air of France was poisoned, they said, 'par l'inceste, l'assassinat, le brigand-age, et toutes les horreurs de la guerre civile'; the country had fallen into the hands of scoundrels who delivered the persons and properties of any opponents 'aux fureurs, au carnage, à l'incendie', while 'la plus vile populace fait et exécute des lois d'après ses passions et sa misère'.[3] At the end of 1789 the author of the significantly titled pamphlet *Rendez-nous la Bastille* agreed that the taking of the Bastille might well have been a founding act; but what it had founded was 'une anarchie sacrilège', a long bloody tumult of which the murder of de Flesselles and de Launay on 14 July, the murder of Foulon and Bertier on 23 July and the October Days were but the most striking examples.[4]

This was strong stuff. What made it potent was the fear of popular violence that inhabited the vast majority of men of property. They were very conscious of living in a society where, as the *abbé* Morellet expressed it in 1789, 'le gros du peuple est ignorant jusqu'à la grossièreté, pauvre jusqu'à la profonde misère, sans idée véritable d'ordre public, de propriété, de morale'.[5] This minor *philosophe* was simply echoing the views of his more celebrated counterparts who, in common with their educated audience, saw the *peuple* as essentially blind and irrational, brutal, violent and driven by passions – situated between man and beast, according to Voltaire.[6]

Indeed, in 1789 such perceptions surfaced frequently in commentaries otherwise favorable to the Revolution. Whatever the attempts to explain and accommodate popular violence within the Revolutionary process, descriptions of the turbulence at moments of crisis often initially used the emotive terms of 'canaille', 'populace' and 'brigandage'. Thus, for example, on the evening of 12 July, Paris 'est livrée aussitôt à la populace . . . il règne un brigandage affreux'; the sack of the Saint-Lazare monastery was the work of 'une horde de ces derniers et vils malheureux qui ne voient l'espoir d'une meilleure destinée que dans le sang et le pillage'.[7] The behaviour of crowds appeared to be unpredictable, the product of what Mirabeau called 'une inspiration soudaine'.[8] There was always a danger that crowds could not be controlled beyond a certain point: in pro-Revolutionary descrip-tions of mass events, phrases such as 'le peuple indigné et transporté de fureur n'écoute plus rien' or 'ce peuple est sans oreilles' commonly mark the moment of transition to violence.[9] By the same token, such commentators tended to explain the failure of crowds to turn violent at some critical junctures by the success of 'citoyens' or 'bourgeois' in influencing the people.[10] Even where they conceded a patriotic intent to crowds, some commentators would emphasise the potential for disastrous violence. Popular rejoicing was threatening because of its ability to degenerate into 'licence'.[11] The festive quality of popular violence (which commentators tended to equate with a rapid transition from a fury of rage to a fury of joy) puzzled and worried revolutionaries. 'Que cette joie me faisait mal!', wrote Babeuf on 25 July 1789.[12] Even someone as favourable to popular violence as Marat saw no more in the rituals of crowd violence than the barbarism of ignorance: in one of the more unguarded moments of his periodic bouts of despair about the people, he described the crowd of 12–13 July 1789 as 'la plèbe effrénée' and mocked the elaborate rituals of derision during the sack of Saint-Lazare as mere 'pantalonades'.[13]

For the great majority of Revolutionary commentators in 1789, then, the intervention of the crowd was threatening. The trouble with violence was that it was always likely to breed violence. 'Les scènes dramatiques ont un si dangereux pouvoir (sur le peuple)', noted Mirabeau.[14] Quite a number of analyses of the early turbulent crises of the Revolution were underpinned by the idea that two quite distinct forces were at work. Thus, Elisée Loustalot's classic account of the July Days began by juxtaposing 'le peuple' and 'les citoyens', the former running around aimlessly and destructively, while the latter proceeded from tearful silence to disciplined and armed organisation.[15] It is difficult to escape a sense in these early commentaries that the people were an alien intrusion into the Revolutionary business of the property-owners ('c'est la propriété qui fait le citoyen', wrote D'Holbach in the *Encyclopédie* under 'Citoyen'). This idea was made explicit in the discussions of the first violence of 1789 to have generated substantial pamphlet commentary, that is to say the clashes of 26–27 January at Rennes. The local nobility had incited their servants to attack the patriotic youth under the cover of demands over the price of bread, designed to provoke popular agitation. Third Estate pamphlets vehemently denounced this introduction of lower social groups into the conflict between 'citoyens' and 'aristocrates', and illustrated its folly by revealing that, although the people did not in fact riot, the workshops did close and workers broke into the arms depot.[16]

It is hardly surprising, therefore, that the news of the disturbances in Paris made 'l'impression la plus triste' on the National Assembly at Versailles on 14 July, and that deputies did not dissent from the description of them as 'malheurs'.[17] Certainly, by and large, the Assembly could not but welcome, officially at least, the outcome of 14 July. Yet anxiety over popular violence continued to run through the Assembly's debates over the next few days. It was exacerbated by serious grain riots at Saint-Germain-en-Laye and Poissy on 20 July. The National Assembly had tried to stop them by sending some deputies, including the Bishop of Chartres, to intervene. Their report had been sombre: they had arrived too late to prevent the murder of one alleged hoarder and, although they claimed to have saved another from being strung up by the crowd, the reality was that the man had been slipped into their coach by his friends as the deputies left in order to avoid witnessing the murder by a crowd they had failed to appease. In other words, the combined authority of old religion and new nation, of superstition and reason, had been unable to control the murderous fury of the mob.[18] This was the context for the recurrence of mass violence in Paris on 23 July with the murder of Foulon and Berthier accomplished on the Place-de-Grève with all the rituals of popular retribution, including the parading of their heads as well as Berthier's heart and the dragging of their corpses through the streets.[19] The barbarity of the event and the fact that the violence occurred when, for many, the peril of the Revolution seemed dissipated by 14 July made an enormous impression on the supporters of the legal Revolution of the National Assembly. In the Assembly, Gouy d'Arcy spoke for many when he referred to 'cette catastrophe', asked how such rituals and the accompanying rejoicing were possible 'dans un siècle aussi éclairé, dans un siècle de lumières' and predicted dire consequences since 'le peuple peut s'accoutumer à ces spectacles sanglants, se faire un jeu de répandre le sang'. In sum, it was both the antithesis of the regeneration of mankind by enlightenment and a premonition of the dissolution of society: 'la barbarie peut devenir une habitude'.[20] Observing 'ce carnage infâme' from outside the Assembly, Gilbert Romme, the future radical Montagnard and Prairial Martyr, agreed: 'le patriotisme seul ne peut pas être aussi sanguinaire'.[21]

Yet the action of the Paris crowd during the July crisis inescapably carried another meaning. 'C'est pourtant cette populace, méprisée des oisifs et des nuls, qui nous a sauvés de l'escalavage', wrote Loustalot on 16 July.[22] The Assembly knew – and a number of speakers underlined the point – that the Parisians had armed themselves for liberty. One could not dispute that crowd action had broken the yoke of despotism. Therefore, 14 July necessarily presented the revolutionaries with the problem of the place of popular violence in the process of revolution. How was such violence to be accommodated? In what terms could it be seen as legitimate? These questions were first explored in pamphlets and speeches which described and reflected upon urban disturbance during the summer months, principally in Paris but also in the provinces. The willingness to sanction some violence, even if only in the most limited and retrospective sense, probably marked the basic divide between supporters and opponents of the Revolution at this point. However, beyond that, there was considerable diversity of views. In part, this was an indication of the divisions beginning to emerge between revolutionaries. More particularly, it was evidence of the difficulty which the issue presented. Some commentators never got beyond the stock images of popular behaviour illustrated above, whereas others managed to move a long way. More generally, however, stock images and new perceptions tended to interweave, even when mutually exclusive in logic. Commentators were liable to produce in the same document several arguments which would later be indicative of quite distinct stances, more or less conservative or more or less radical. Analysis of the main themes does, therefore, confer a rather artificial coherence upon a debate which was more in the nature of an attempt to work out attitudes, at least until the October Days focused the issues more sharply.

The simplest initial reaction to disturbance in July was to argue that it was merely a natural part of the Revolutionary crisis, what Gouy d'Arcy described as 'l'effervescence qu'inspirent nécessairement l'anéant-issement du despotisme et la naissance de la liberté'. There was necessarily a price to be paid for the passage from slavery to liberty. However, the central point was that this was a temporary phenomenon. Loustalot was making a widely voiced comment when he wrote that, when the storm of revolution blew, the most sweet-tempered of peoples changed into the most ferocious and barbarian; 'mais dès que le calme renaît, il redevient lui-même' (the characteristic of counter-revolutionary comment was that it saw this change as permanent).[23] Indeed, said Loustalot, continuing the image, what one was witnessing was akin to a tree which, bent down by force (under the *ancien régime*), swings violently to and fro on release until it reaches a natural resting point in a free condition.[24] Of course, reassurance was the essential function of such an idea. However tormenting the disturbance, its brevity and its character as a mode of transition rendered it much less threatening. This kind of discourse tended, therefore, to play down the degree of violence and to insist on the speed of the Revolutionary victory.[25] There was a strong emphasis on a happy ending. The speeches of Lally-Tollendal (at the Hôtel-de-Ville) and Mounier (to the National Assembly) on 16 July were models of the genre. The references to the popular uprising were brief; the focus was primarily on the result which was presented as the golden days of union of king, deputies and nation; both deputies emphasised that peace was now breaking out.[26] The king's visit to Paris on 17 July was not merely a reconciliation between king and city. It was much more a deliberate affirmation of unity, or the end of conflict which threatened social order, a necessary fusion in wild applause for the monarch and the deputies: the message was explicit both in the speeches and in observers' reports.

This sense of turbulence as simply the rocky passage through to the sunlit plains of the future was not just the preserve of sophisticated moderates like Mounier. Exactly the same idea appears, for instance, in a naive chronology published in August by a provincial author, who concluded that 'les voilà donc arrivés ces jours de calme et de sérénité que nous espérions depuis long-tems'.[27] These images were, of course, rooted in the notion that the Revolution was indeed a brief passage. One of the clearest demarcations between revolutionaries quickly became how long that passage was seen to be and, thus, how much popular violence was admissible. The outrage felt by men like Lally-Tollendal, Mounier and Gouy d'Arcy at the murder of Foulon and Berthier proceeded from their sense that nothing remained to be accomplished after 14 July's defence of the legal Revolution. More radical figures went much further, but they shared the basic premise.

Of course, behind all this there was a strong desire to ward off further disturbance, to will unity and harmony into existence by speaking of them as present realities. It is striking how persistent the unanimist theme was in the descriptions of popular disturbance during these months. One pamphlet from Lyon carried this to the extreme.[28] In this city, the month of July was marked by recurrent rioting, the burning of customs posts, crowd-killing and street battles with the military. However, this account devoted itself to describing the conquest of Pierre-Scize, the Lyon equivalent of the Bastille. The crowd finds the entrance threateningly deserted and silent, but in the inner courtyard it discovers the governor, who has always silently regretted his duties, standing with the prisoners whom he has delivered and drawn up as a welcoming party. The governor declares this to be the sweetest moment of his life and the prisoners declare that they do not want to leave him. In the general rejoicing, the governor suddenly falls to self-reviling, revealing that there is a secret prisoner, who passes for dead. This man is then brought out, womenfolk are summoned from the neighbourhood and a festival begins. This stylised, quasi-mythical narrative is clearly both an allegory of the passage from *ancien régime* servitude to Revolutionary liberty and also a masking of the popular violence at Lyon. The crowd here is certainly the instrument of change, since it invades the fortress-*ancien régime*; but the supposed enemy is really on its side, the victims bear no grievance and harmony needs only be recognised.

None the less, although such an approach relieved one of the necessity to think in detail about crowd action and violence, it was inescapably based on the premise that mass action had a function. It followed, therefore, that, even if one did not envisage a function for such action in the future, it had been in some sense legitimate. Its legitimacy derived from the nature of the *ancien régime* which it had helped to destroy and from the nature of the future that it had helped to create. Even the most cautious definitions accepted that: Mounier associated expressions of pleasure at the end of the Bastille with his regrets at the violence of 14 July, and Lally-Tollendal called the Parisian grievances just. The mass action on 14 July was at least excusable because it was provoked by the conduct of the king's Ministers and advisers. Once again, Loustalot struck the note sounded by many commentators on 14 July:

> nos lâches oppresseurs nous y forcent: ils ont trahi leurs sermens, leurs devoirs; à la justice ils opposent la force; ils trompent la bonté du roi: c'est à nous de montrer que nos demandes sont équitables, et que la victoire est due à l'intègre justice.[29]

The introduction of resistance to oppression as one of the four rights in the Declaration of the Rights of Man was an extension of this perception. However, the critical point here was to decide just what behaviour was legitimated by the *ancien régime* and by the pursuit of liberty, and just what was not.

It is clear that all shades of opinion (outside the counter-revolutionary) saw a distinction between good and bad violence. There was quite simply a difference between riot and revolution and that difference was the one between licence and liberty. As one deputy put it succinctly in the National Assembly in July, one should not confuse 'le séditieux armé par la licence' with 'le citoyen armé pour la liberté'.[30] Undoubtedly, the social content of the term 'citoyen' suggests that the distinction meant here was between the resistance of the property-owners, even to the point of disorder, and the mob action of the poor. Yet such a distinction was unsustainable in face of the central role of the crowd on 14 July. One had to accept that, in certain circumstances at least, the poor were capable of behaving like citizens. This double and contradictory character of popular action was, of course, the starting point for uncomfortable ambiguities over the nation and citizenship. The most obvious solution was to criminalise or, rather, to continue the pre-Revolutionary perception of crowd action as criminal when it threatened life and property. This behaviour was still 'brigandage'. The distinction between 'brigandage' and acceptable crowd behaviour was given concrete form by attaching each to different groups: the latter to the people and the former to 'brigands et gens sans aveu'. Moments of great crisis produced, therefore, two sorts of people: 'tandis que les vrais Citoyens s'armoient pour la défense de leur liberté, d'autres s'armoient pour voler dans les maisons'.[31] The 'brigands et gens sans aveu' were taking advantage of the confusion; pillage and other acts of gross disorder were the sign of their presence.[32] In this way, the revolutionary contribution of the crowd could remain uncontaminated by frightening violence; the creative act was not perverted by the destructive. Intolerable violence was the work of men basically outside society – indeed, in some accounts (Mirabeau's defence of Marseille's record in 1789, for example), this was rendered explicit by attributing it to 'étrangers'.[33]

None the less, in 1789 commentators using these arguments mostly found it difficult to resolve the relationship between the people and the bandits. Some of them were unable to sustain the distinction and reverted in the course of their narrative to seeing the people as brigands; at this point, it was the poor who stood outside society and it became legitimate for the bourgeois to use arms to repress them.[34] As we have said, there was always a strong tendency to view the poor as unpredictable 'canaille'. Other, potentially more radical, commentators used the classic perception of the poor in a different way. For them, the ignorance and gullibility of the poor meant that they were easily misled. Thus, this approach could sustain the notion of a people capable of good acts without needing to deny popular participation in intolerable acts, into which they were, in this scenario, inveigled.[35] None the less, the acknowledged presence of threatening violence, the known character of the crowd, the propensity to move from liberty to licence, all jeopardised these attempts to accommodate popular action within the Revolutionary process. It is doubtless for this reason that so much emphasis was laid by some commentators on the good order of crowds and on the speedy end of disturbances. Loustalot, yet again, provides a clear example in his account of 14 July: 'que l'on examine', he invited his readers, 'avec quelle célérité l'ordre le plus exact, la discipline la plus sévère, se sont établis au milieu même du désordre'.[36] Another account even stated that the people gave the electors' delegates at the Hôtel-de-Ville a formal assurance that they would now return to work and keep quiet, 'à moins que des gens mal intentionnés, du parti de l'opposition à Versailles, ne voulût encore mettre des obstacles au bien public'.[37] These were obvious misrepresentations (to the point of mythification in the latter case). They were an extension of the technique of separating the people from the brigands; their function was, as the last quotation reveals, to demonstrate the crowd to be essentially orderly and devoted to the legal revolution of the National Assembly. In this way, popular action was further separated from its classic image.

At the very heart of the question of popular violence stood the problem of crowd-killing. It was over this issue that revolutionaries divided most clearly in 1789 and that a definably radical position can be discerned. By and large, those who accepted that 14 July had contributed to saving and consolidating the Revolution also accepted the deaths involved. Even the most moderate agreed that it was inevitable that, in the act of breaking despotism, the people would take revenge on those who had most sought to resist. The governor of the Bastille and the *prévôt des marchands* had brought it on themselves. It was regrettable but understandable; moreover, the constitution would soon be in place to soothe the wounds; indeed, the issue was relatively unimportant since there would be no recurrence as depotism was broken. Matters were rapidly put into quite a different light by the general growth of disorder and above all by the murders of Foulon and Berthier, as well as a number of equally barbaric crowd murders in provincial centres. The question was, to paraphrase Gilbert Romme, could blood and patriotism mix? In the answer to that question, there began to emerge, beyond the specific justification of specific murders, the outline of a more general argument about the virtue of popular violence in revolution.

It was the mark of the moderates, of those whose sympathy for the Revolution would soon evaporate, that they could see nothing but murder in crowd-killing; it was a direct challenge to the rule of law without which society would necessarily dissolve.[38] For others, the first step was to set aside a preoccupation with the barbarity of such killings. Some found that easier than others: Babeuf, for instance, was able to dismiss it as a cruelty learned from the public cruelty of despotism.[39] At that point, commentators were able to see these events as acts of popular vengeance. For the most part, accounts were careful to tie the murders to specific behaviour on the part of the victims. Thus, the justification of the murder of an alleged hoarder at Poissy on 20 July laid out his twenty-year record of personal harshness, speculation on grain and cornering the land market; similarly, one account of the death of the governor of the Bastille made doubly sure that the message was understood by having him tell the crowd: 'Ah! . . . j'ai trahi ma patrie!', whereas another preferred to get the same message across by having him shout 'chienne de populace'; Loustalot, who could only just stomach the manner of the death of Foulon and Berthier, felt obliged to invent the notion that Berthier was killed by a man whose father he had murdered; more generally, however, Foulon and Berthier were presented as responsible for many deaths by promoting famine.[40]

Clearly, the deaths of men such as de Launay, de Flesselles, Foulon and Berthier were easily portrayed as acts of justice as much as justified acts, since these men were deemed to be directly or indirectly murderers. However, at this early stage of the Revolution, it is not easy to find the notion, which was to become prevalent among radicals later, that popular action was an act of sovereignty and, hence, that crowd-killing was justice. Rather, the radical position over Foulon and Berthier, for example, was that they were out-and-out traitors and their deaths were just retribution.[41] This, in turn, quickly led to the argument that the function of such deaths went beyond retribution to be a dire warning to other traitors who might be contemplating a move against the Revolution.[42] At this point, crowd-killing had become incorporated into a wider perception of popular violence as an instrument for the defence of the Revolution.

The degree to which one was prepared to commit oneself to that perception and the degree of popular violence which one was prepared to tolerate depended ultimately on how serious one saw the threat to the Revolution to be. Radicals saw the menace of a great conspiracy. Robespierre made the point soon after 14 July in response to attempts to organise a national militia to repress the troubles in the country: there was, he said, nothing more legitimate than to rise against 'une conjuration horrible formée pour perdre la nation'.[43] Indeed, echoed Buzot, what guarantee was there that despotism had been destroyed by the Fall of the Bastille, and what defence would there be if the citizens could not or would not arm themselves? Several pamphlets appeared presenting in great detail what purported to be the orders for a military occupation of Paris, justifying thereby the insurrection of 14 July.[44] The sense of vulnerability was sustained through the summer by the belief in a famine plot. In the end, the point was that, to use the words of that cautious patriot Loustalot, however dangerous ignorance made the people 'lui seul est capable de certaines actions'.[45] All the same, there was little evidence of willingness during these summer months to provoke mass action as an offensive weapon against the enemies of the Revolution. Certainly, radical pamphlets did start to present the situation as a war against a vicious aristocratic enemy and as a combat against the hydra of despotism.[46] Yet the function of popular violence was at the most reactive and punitive. Suggestions beyond that amounted to no more than ambiguous hints. Thus, when the radical activist Bordier was executed at Rouen in July for incitement to riot, his friends only went as far as saying that 'nos ennemis, nos Bourreaux nous traîtent sans pitié: aujourd'hui Bordier, demain moi, après-demain vous. Quel parti prendre? *Les imiter*.'[47] In September Marat got closer to a general statement, but only implied the consequences: 'Jamais la machine politique ne se remonte que par des secousses violentes, comme les airs ne se purifient que par des orages. Rassemblons-nous donc sur les places publiques.'[48]

The October Days brought into focus the issues being debated during the summer. They polarised opinion because they presented a choice between approval and repudiation which it was hard to evade or to fudge. For those whose tolerance of popular disorder had been at the best retrospective and based upon the premise that it would not recur, the mass invasion of the Assembly by those outside the political nation, the killing outside and inside the palace, and finally the enforced removal of king and assembly to Paris were appalling acts. This was the 'canaille' at work and, in the evidence they gave to the judicial enquiry, those with this opinion invariably referred to the crowd as bandits and brigands.[49] Their premise always was that the killing was started by the crowd and they took care to recount every revolting detail and ritual of these deaths. The stock image of the natural ferocity, ignorance and gullibility of the people was developed into an argument, which the Châtelet adopted as its conclusion, that the violence had been orchestrated by ambitious men (principally, Mirabeau and the Duc d'Orléans).[50] It was, therefore, violence for political ends. The widespread credence given in this milieu to tales of men dressed as women was the symptom both of a need to escape the contradiction between the stock image of women and this perception of brigandage, and also of a need to sustain the plot thesis.

For patriots, however, there could be no doubting that the plot in October was the aristocratic one to destroy the Revolution. The insurrection had, therefore, been patriotic and salutary. 'Heureuse catastrophe', wrote a provincial clerk in his diary, thus capturing nicely the contradictory emotions of the moment.[51] The women were, according to one who claimed to be their spokeswoman, 'les libératrices de la Capitale, dont cet évènement doit pour toujours faire avorter les desseins des Aristocrates présens et futurs'.[52] The violence had liberated the Revolution from its enemies. Yet, although the end justified the event, even most radicals still did not deduce a prescription for the future. Their accounts played down the degree of violence; the deaths were provoked by the initial violence of the royal bodyguard against the crowd. This time, they thought, popular violence really had completed the transition from the *ancien régime*. Camille Desmoulins began the first number of the *Révolutions de France et de Brabant* in November with the words '*Consummatum Est*' and, reflecting upon the October Days, he told the National Assembly 'à présent vous n'avez plus d'ennemis . . . il ne vous reste qu'à gouverner la France, à la rendre heureuse'.[53] None the less, at the extreme, a new discourse was appearing. Discussing the march of the women in its second number in October, a violent little newspaper entitled *Le Furet Parisien* told its readers that they might as well kill themselves and their families if they had not the courage to kill those who sought to murder them by hunger and indigence. In November Marat produced the first unambiguous statement of a theory of revolutionary violence.[54] The people only rose when pushed beyond the limit of endurance, he wrote: the fact of insurrection was thus the evidence of its own necessity. Indeed, 'sa vengeance est toujours juste dans son principe'. As for the victims, what were a few drops of blood shed by the people for the recovery of their liberty when compared with the torrents shed in the course of history, from Tiberius and Caligula to Charles IX and Louis XIV? 'C'est donc aux émeutes populaires que nous devons tout'; only insurrection could ensure that the Revolution would come to term.

Confronted by the dilemmas posed by popular intervention in 1789, the response of the revolutionaries had been often contradictory, trying to reconcile profoundly held prejudices about the people, defined as the poor, with the repeated exigences of a revolution under stress. Yet, in the process, they had begun to formulate some of the principal arguments that renewed crises would refine over the next few years. The reactions to 14 July, the deaths of Foulon and Berthier, and the October Days foreshadowed the conflicting theses over 10 August and the September Massacres. The legitimation of Revolutionary violence by the violence of the enemy, the purifying quality of popular violence, collective violence as an act of sovereignty, insurrection as the sacred duty of the people were all ideas which began to germinate in the way popular violence was talked about in 1789.

Notes

1   P. de Vaissière, *Lettres d'"Aristocrates*', Paris, 1907, p. 17.

2   *Projet de protestation et de compte-rendu par M. de Bouville, député de la Noblesse du Bailliage de Caux*, Paris, 1791, p. 47.

3   [F. M. de Bressac], *A l'Assemblée Prétendue Nationale*, slnd; see, for example, *Tableau de la conduite de l'assemblée prétendue nationale, adressé à elle-même*, Paris, 1790, and *Appel au devoir de la noblesse française par M. le marquis de L.P.C.B.D.G.S.D.P.D.M.A.O.D.C.*, Paris, 1790.

4   *Rendez-nous la Bastille*, slnd.

5   *Lettres de l'abbé Morellet à Lord Shelburne* (edited by Lord Edmund Fitzmaurice), Paris, 1898, p. 279, letter of 24 September 1789.

6   H. C. Payne, *The Philosophes and the People*, New Haven, 1976, especially pp. 7–31.

7   *Paris Sauvé*, Paris, 1789, p. 8; A. Lamourette, *Désastre de la Maison de Saint-Lazare. A M. le Comte de T . . .* Paris, 1789, p. 13.

8   *Discours sur la Procédure Prévôtale de Marseille. Prononcé à l'Assemblée Nationale, par M. le Comte de Mirabeau, dans la Séance du 26 Janvier 1790*, slnd, p. 15.

9   *Révolutions d'Alsace*, slnd, p. 12; *Relations sur les scènes tragiques qui se sont passés à Saint-Germain et à Poissy*, slnd, p. 10.

10   E.g. *Ques-à-Co? ou Histoire des Troubles et Révolutions Modernes de Marseille*, 1789, p. 4; *Révolutions de Paris*, I, p. 7.

11   E.g. *Récit sanglant de ce qui s'est passé à Lyon, le 3 Juillet, au sujet des Réjouissances occasionnées par la réunion des trois Ordres*, 1789 and *Relation de ce qui s'est passé à Lille en Flandres*, Paris, n.d.

12   M. Dommanget, *Pages choisies de Babeuf*, Paris, 1935, p. 74.

13   *L'Ami du Peuple*, 672, 14 July 1792.

14   See note 8.

15   *Révolutions de Paris*, I; see *Révolutions d'Alsace*, slnd, pp. 13–14.

16   *Lettre sur les Evènemens arrivés à Rennes le 26 et 27 janvier 1789*, sl, 1789; *Discours et Mémoire des Avocats de Rennes: Délibération des facultés de droit de Rennes, concernant la malheureuse affaire, arrivée en cette ville les 26 et 27 janvier 1789*, sl, 1789; *Précis historique des Troubles de Bretagne*, slnd; *Lettre de Rennes, du Lundi 26 Janvier 1789*, slnd; *Relation de ce qui s'est passé à Rennes les 26, 27, et jours suivants du mois de janvier*, slnd; *Dernière relation de ce qui vient de se passer à Rennes*, slnd.

17   *Archives Parlementaires*, VIII, pp. 233–4, 14 July 1789.

18   *Ibid.*, pp. 249–50, 255; *Relations sur les scènes tragiques qui se sont passées à Saint-Germain et à Poissy*, slnd.

19   The best description is in *Mémoires de Bailly*, 3 vols, II, Paris, 1821–2, pp. 99–124.

20   *Archives Parlementaires*, VIII, p. 265.

21   A. Galante Garrone, *Gilbert Romme: histoire d'un révolutionnaire*, Paris, 1971, pp. 173–4.

22   *Révolutions de Paris*, I, p. 28.

23   *Ibid.*, II, p. 13.

24   *Ibid.*, VI, pp. 1–2.

25   A typical example is *L'Ouvrage des Six Jours ou Lettre d'un Membre du District des Feuillans, à son Ami, sur la révolution de Paris*, Paris, 20 July 1789.

26   For Lally-Tollendal's speech, see *Archives Parlementaires*, VIII, p. 246; for Mounier, *Récit lu dans la Séance du 16 Juillet 1789 par M. Mounier*, slnd.

27   *Récit des Evènemens remarquables qui ont opéré la Liberté des Français, par P. B. Ridet, de Saint-Chéron-les-Chartres*, slnd [Chartres, 1 August 1789], p. 8.

28   *Résurrection de M. le Marquis de Brunoy, retrouvé à Pierre-Encize*, slnd.

29   *Révolutions de Paris*, I, p. 5.

30   *Archives Parlementaires*, VIII, p. 254 (speech by Blesau).

31   *Le Grenadier Patriote, ou le Despotisme détruit en France*, Paris, 1789, p. 12.

32   E.g. Lamourette, *Désastre de la Maison du Saint-Lazare; Déclaration de la Jeunesse-Citoyenne de Marseille composant la Garde bourgeoise*, 1789; *La Grande Découverte ou les Menées Ministérielles dévoilées*, Paris, 1789; *Révolutions de Rouen. Extrait d'une lettre écrite de cette ville. Du Vendredi 17 Juillet 1789*, slnd.

33   *Discours sur la Procédure Prévôtale de Marseille*, pp. 6–7; the defence of Saint-Germain-en-Laye in *Archives Parlementaires*, VIII, p. 255.

34   E.g. *Révolutions d'Alsace*, especially pp. 13–14.

35   A good example in *Mémoires de Bailly*, II, pp. 113–14.

36   *Révolutions de Paris*, I, p. 27.

37   *La Mort Tragique de l'Intendant de Paris*, slnd, p. 4.

38   This position was eloquently developed by Lally-Tollendal in the National Assembly between 20 and 23 July (*Archives Parlementaires*, VIII, pp. 252–65).

39   *Pages choisies de Babeuf*, p. 74.

40   *Relations sur les scènes tragiques . . .*; *Révolutions de Paris*, I, p. 18 and II, p. 24; *Le Grenadier Patriote*, p. 27. Loustalot uses the same device over the killing of the Marquis de Belsunce at Caen, whom he accuses of having murdered his servant in Paris on groundless suspicion of dishonesty (VI, p. 46).

41   E.g. *Les Quatres Traîtres aux Enfers. Dialogue*, slnd.

42   See, as classic examples, *Les Quatres Têtes, ou la trabison punie*, slnd and *Le Deo Gratias*, slnd.

43   *Archives Parlementaires*, VIII, p. 253.

44   E.g. *Les Crimes Dévoilés. Ordre de l'Attaque de la Ville de Paris, projettée pour la nuit du 14 au 15 Juillet 1789*, 1789.

45 *Révolutions de Paris*, II, p. 6.

46 E.g. *Le Monstre Déchiré, vision prophétique d'un Persan qui ne dort pas toujours,* Ispahan (Paris), 1789.

47 *Les Iniquités découvertes, ou l'innocence reconnue des Sieurs Bordier et Jourdain*, Paris, 1789, p. 27. See (J–A. Bourlain, dit) Dumaniant, *Mort de Bordier, Acteur des Variétés*, slnd and *La Mort Subite du Sieur Bordier, Acteur des Variétés*, Paris, 1789.

48 *L'Ami du Peuple*, 8, 18 September 1789.

49 *Procédure criminelle instruite au Châtelet de Paris sur la dénonciation des faits arrivés à Versailles dans la journée du 6 Octobre 1789*, 3 vols, Paris, 1790.

50 *Discours pour l'Assemblée nationale sur l'affaire du 5 au 6 Octobre*, slnd. See *Compte-rendu d'une partie de l'assemblée nationale sur le rapport de la procédure du Châtelet . . .*, Paris, 1790.

51 A. Richebé, *Journal d'un Bourgeois de Lille pendant la Révolution*, Lille, 1898, p. 11.

52 *Evènement de Paris et de Versailles par une des Dames qui a eu l'honneur d'être de la Députation à l'Assemblée générale*, slnd, p. 7.

53 *Révolutions de France et de Brabant*, I, pp. 1–2.

54 *L'Ami du Peuple*, 34 and 35, 10–11 November 1789.

chapter eight PETER JONES

Agrarian radicalism during the French Revolution

La Révolution française . . . est une véritable loi agraire mise à exécution par le peuple. Il est rentré dans ses droits. Un pas de plus et il rentrera dans ses biens. [Sylvain Maréchal, *Révolutions de Paris*, 96, 7–14 May 1791]

On 17 July 1793 two plenipotentiaries of the National Convention, Charles Delacroix and Joseph Mathurin Musset, arrived in Versailles. The news of their coming spread tremendous excitement throughout the district for they were empowered to offer a starving population of agricultural labourers the one thing that they most desperately wanted: access to land. Several weeks later, on 7 August, the *représentants* launched an experiment which was probably unique in the history of the Revolution. They instructed local officials to alienate portions of the Royal Domain sufficient to endow every landless family with a plot of arable quality. The first allocation of land occurred on 27 brumaire II (17 November 1793) in the village of Les Loges-en-Josas,[1] where twenty-nine 'pères de famille' who were utterly propertyless and twelve more who owned nothing more than cottages with small gardens each received an *arpent*[2] of best grade land. Similar operations took place in neighbouring villages over the next few months, and they continued even after the recall of the two deputies on 2 pluviôse II (21 January 1794). By the end of the year some 1,568 *arpents* of cultivable land had been distributed between 1,546 poor peasant or artisan households drawn from twenty-five of the eighty-four communes forming the district of Versailles.[3]

This rare encounter between the theory and the practice of social Jacobinism deserves a study in its own right. The surviving documentation is uncommonly plentiful,[4] but few scholars have shown much interest in the material and none has sought to place the episode in a broader context. Nearly a century ago the German historian Boris Minzes[5] examined the files when preparing a monograph on the disposal of *biens nationaux* in the department of the Seine-et-Oise, and Georges Lefebvre[6] extensively footnoted this research in his *Questions agraires au temps de la Terreur*, first published in 1932. Yet even Lefebvre failed to grasp the wider significance of Delacroix's and Musset's activities in the district of Versailles. To judge from his comments, he never weighed up the evidence first hand; had he done so, he might have nuanced his verdict on the ambitions of the poor peasantry during the Revolutionary climacteric. The present chapter offers little more than a synopsis of the events played out in the twenty-five villages of the Versailles *pourtour*: no doubt a fuller account will be written in due course. Rather, it seeks to draw out the implications of those events for the way in which we conceptualise the peasant revolution. Nevertheless, some background information is essential if this purpose is to be achieved.

Versailles and its villages were indelibly associated with the Royal Court, that is to say with the vast complex of palaces, parks, forests, game reserves and farms which Louis XIV began to establish in the 1660s. A century or so later, crown properties entirely dominated the northern half of the future district of Versailles. The Grand Parc of Versailles alone covered nearly 20,000 *arpents*, while the Petit Parc extended to approximately 5,000 *arpents* and the Royal Forest of Marly to 4,400 *arpents*. In addition, the monarch possessed extensive tracts of woodland at La Celle, Viroflay, Sèvres and Chaville, and ornamental gardens in the parish of Louveciennes. Much of the territory was given over to the pleasures of the hunt, but the monarch held arable land as well which was leased out to tenant farmers. By 1789 there existed thirty-six royal farms in the immediate vicinity of Versailles: some were little more than loose collections of fields, but others boasted 200–300 *arpents* of compact plough land. The impact of such a massive concentration of property upon the rural economy and the social structure of the district scarcely needs emphasising. With court nobles vying for the privilege of owning lands adjacent to the Royal Domain (the Marquis de Beuvron possessed 700 *arpents* at Vélizy), peasant tenures had been squeezed almost to oblivion. Whole villages,[7] indeed, had been swallowed up in the Grand Parc, while others suffered a series of encroachments upon their *finage*. A population of some 4,000 souls lived enclaved within the Grand Parc according to an estimate of 1790, but they owned no more than 1,900 *arpents* of land. Moreover, there were clear signs that royal attrition against these inconveniently sited peasant communities was intensifying during the final decades of the *ancien régime*. Afforestation and the enlargement of hunting enclosures deprived villages of their commons and wastes; from about 1770 farm leases began to rise steeply, and in 1780 the management of crown properties in the Versailles area was placed on a more business-like footing. As a result, the yield (from seigneurial perquisites, rentals, sale of timber, etc.) rose substantially during the course of Louis XVI's reign.

The inescapable presence of crown properties, not to mention the plethora of employees whose job was to safeguard the king's hunting rights, gave agrarian tensions a unique complexion in the hinterland of Versailles. But the root cause of the social conflict and political radicalism that welled up in 1789 was an all too familiar condition of village life on the plains around Paris: land hunger. Although less suited to arable husbandry than the neighbouring Beauce, the district of Versailles experienced a comparable process of land concentration and engrossment, and with nearly identical consequences. The shortage of small leaseholds, exacerbated by rapid population growth, resulted in the proletarianisation of a substantial section of the peasantry. In the Beauce perhaps half of the active rural population consisted of agricultural labourers on the eve of the Revolution; but that proportion was comfortably exceeded in most of the Versaillais villages that were to seek redress from *représentants* Delacroix and Musset in the summer of 1793. The parish of Bailly[8] may be regarded as typical. It was dominated by a wealthy *laboureur* named Pierre Augey, who leased a medium-sized farm (150 *arpents* of plough land) from the Royal Domain. Confronting him and several lesser peasant landholders were seventy-two individuals who considered themselves fortunate if they owned the roofs over their heads: nearly all of them made a living from wage labour on the land of others.

Acute socio-economic polarisation, with the bulk of the rural population beholden to crown estate managers or to *coqs de village*, who, more likely than not, were tenants of crown estates, can be regarded as endemic, then. And the tensions which this state of affairs engendered found ample expression in the *cahiers*. Through their elected representatives, the inhabitants of the *bailliages* of Versailles and Meudon expressed near universal hostility towards royal hunting rights which made the sowing, weeding and harvesting of crops a constant nightmare. But they also instanced a series of abuses which went directly to the heart of the problem: the king, or rather his agents, were taken to task for encroaching upon the wastes, for erecting enclosures, for employing *fermiers-généraux* who engrossed peasant tenures, and for failing to respect customary scavenging rights. The most outspoken *cahiers* even ventured to propose a solution to the agrarian problem. 'On demande', declared the inhabitants of Guyancourt, 'qu'il soit distrait 150 arpents de terre des différentes fermes du roi, pour être loués par lots de 4 à 5 arpents, afin de faciliter les paroissiens, et de leur procurer des secours nécessaires pour les aider à vivre.'[9] This was to anticipate the solution of 1793.

The continuing dearth, prolonged by the economic repercussions of the departure of king and court from Versailles in October 1789, worked a rapid politicisation of the rural masses. As the new planting season approached, gangs of agricultural labourers set to work clearing land which they did not own. Reports reached the Constituent Assembly of incursions into the royal sapling nurseries at Rocquencourt, of villagers draining ponds at Bois d'Arcy and of fields being hacked from the edge of the forest at Marly. The leaders of this localised insurgency are difficult to identify, but they were probably members of the newly elected municipalities and, in some instances, parish priests. Certainly it was a priest – the *curé-maire* of Viroflay – who provided the embryonic *partageurs* of the Versaillais with the first theoretical justification of their actions, in August 1790. Ignoring the misgivings of more cautious-minded mayors in neighbouring communes, he issued a thinly veiled call for a general redistribution of the land:

> Vous ne supprimerez pas la pauvreté si vous ne ramenez pas les habitants au premier art, à l'agriculture. Par là, vous les attacherez à la terre; vous en ferez des citoyens. La vraie cause de la pauvreté est l'accumulation de la terre en un petit nombre de mains.[10]

Encouraged, if not yet fired with a vision of the *loi agraire*, the rural poor kept up the pressure on their elected representatives throughout the summer. A volley of petitions loosed off in September left little doubt that the political education of the peasantry was proceeding apace. Whilst they all addressed the monarch in respectful tones, the message contained therein was simple and unambiguous: poverty could be extinguished in the neighbourhood only by hand-outs of land from the Royal Domain.

The petition drawn up by the village of Le Chesnay solicited the creation of plots ranging in size from 1½ to 3 *arpents*; that of Bois d'Arcy mentioned units of 1 *arpent*; while the inhabitants of St Cyr urged the parcelling of territory within the Grand Parc on the principle 'à chacun suivant ce que nécessiterait sa force et sa famille'.[11] Before taking the story any further, though, it is worth trying to put these objectives in a broader context. Calls for a distribution, or rather a redistribution, of land were heard at regular intervals during the Revolution, and legislators were obliged, repeatedly, to rule on what did or did not constitute a legitimate breach of property rights. Broadly speaking, the disposal of church lands was deemed to be legitimate in 1789 and that of *émigré* estates in 1792. However, the alienation of wastes, commons, Civil List and other state-owned landed properties remained controversial in both theory and practice, whereas the chopping up of private property for general distribution (the so-called Agrarian Law) was specifically repudiated by the deputies in March 1793. None the less, these distinctions were often blurred in the minds of agrarian radicals as, indeed, was the concept of the Agrarian Law.[12] Sometimes it was invoked to mean the division and distribution of land in the public domain, and at other times it was invoked as a classical precedent for the division of *all* land, whether public or private. Nor was there much agreement on *how* to partition the soil of France. Some advocates supported a strictly egalitarian or arithmetical distribution on a per capita basis, while others acknowledged the stern laws of agricultural economics and favoured a more flexible arrangement resting on the household. Notions of what represented a sufficient endowment of land varied considerably, too: writing at the outset of the Revolution, Restif de la Bretonne[13] recommended lots of 18–72 *arpents* (7·6–30·4 hectares), with a reallocation every five years; Babeuf,[14] on the other hand, simply divided the number of families into his estimate of the total area of arable land which resulted in a holding of 11 *arpents* per household. Pierre Dolivier,[15] the radical *curé* of Mauchamps (Seine-et-Oise), reached a similar conclusion, albeit by a different route. His vision of the future was peopled with peasant families working farms of 10–12 *arpents*. By contrast, Nicolas de Bonneville,[16] one of the luminaries of the Cercle Social, placed a limit of 5 or 6 *arpents* on the size of properties acquired by inheritance. Solutions involving hand-outs of less than 10 *arpents* (4·2 hectares) were, in reality, little more than palliatives of the social problem in the countryside; nevertheless, the public debate was fuelled with schemes to endow the rural poor with plots or allotments as well. In 1789 Armand Guffroy,[17] the future *conventionnel*, published a pamphlet which sought to popularise the idea of dividing church property into 1-*arpent* plots for purchase by landless 'pères de famille'. Significantly, we find Guffroy assisting the campaign of the Versaillais *partageurs* when he was sent out to expedite recruitment in the area in March 1793.

Actual legislation addressed to the needs of the poor peasantry was slow to materialise, however. Calls for a radical solution to the land question found few sympathisers among deputies raised on the physiocrat authors and persuaded of the superiority of large-scale property. Despite demurrals, they resolved (by the decree of 14–17 May 1790) to place church lands on the market in large blocks with the stipulation that the sales be conducted by auction in the principal town of each district. These arrangements seemed tailor-made to deter peasant purchasers and did nothing to satisfy the land hunger of impoverished wage labourers on the plains around Paris. Not until the burgeoning popular revolution of June–August 1792 forced a change in priorities were the pleas of the landless given greater attention. Swiftly, the deputies moved to liquidate seigneurial dues, judging that it was from this direction that there came the greatest threat to the 1791 constitution. But they made solemn utterances on the subject of the commons and the disposal of *émigré* properties as well. Four days after the uprising of 10 August, a bill was rushed through the Legislative Assembly which positively ordered village communities to divide up their common land. Contained within the same measure was a proposal tabled by François de Neufchâteau to break up *émigré* estates. This proposal constituted a substantial departure from the thinking which had hitherto informed the laws disposing of national assets and it is worth quoting in detail. 'Dans la vue de multiplier les petits propriétaires', the Assembly announced that 'en la présente année et immédiatement après les récoltes, les terres, vignes et prés appartenant ci-devant aux émigrés, seront divisés par petits lots de deux, trois ou au plus quatre arpents, pour être ainsi mis à l'enchère et aliénés à perpétuité par bail à rente, laquelle sera toujours rachetable.'[18]

Copies of the decree of 14 August 1792 were dispatched 'sur le champ' to every department and the news produced a buzz of excitement and anticipation in the villages of Picardy, Champagne and the Ile-de-France. However, it was too good to be true, for neither the clauses relating to the partition of the commons, nor those concerning confiscated *émigré* property were operable without further legislation. This the Convention conspicuously failed to vote; consequently the 'acte de justice'[19] awaited by agricultural labourers throughout the 'pays de grande culture' was postponed for a further growing season. Of course, there were numbers of peasants who refused to wait, although the depth and dimensions of this agrarian radicalism remain poorly understood by historians. Georges Lefebvre[20] cites the case of the villagers of Réau (Seine-et-Marne) who simply seized a farm belonging to the nation and divided it up in the spirit of the decree of 14 August 1792. Impatience bubbled over into illicit action in the Oise department as well, to judge from the researches of Guy Ikni.[21] The events which were nearing a climax in the villages of the district of Versailles form part of the same pattern. An elector of Versailles, Frotié, penned a rousing petition which called for the piecemeal division of ecclesiastical properties as well as *émigré* estates. Moreover, he emphasised that the resultant plots should be attributed directly, either by bill of sale or rental, and not by auction. That was in the late summer of 1792 when the elections to the Convention were in full swing. 'Pense à toi, petite classe, tant des villages que des campagnes', Frotié urged, 'voilà le moment arrivé de ton bonheur ou de ton esclavage.'[22]

By the late autumn of 1792 matters were quite desperate in the district of Versailles. Grave food shortages prompted the local authorities to express fears of a general uprising on the scale of that of the Beauce a short distance to the south, and the spate of petitions calling for the parcelling of crown lands rose to become a veritable flood. The New Year opened with villagers taking matters into their own hands: at Guyancourt the poor and the destitute began to clear portions of the Grand Parc which surrounded them on all sides. Their example was followed by other communes, notably by Ville d'Avray, whose priest led a clearing party of eighty peasants on 18 February 1793. A few days later a general petition from seventeen communities adjoining the Grand Parc reached the Convention, and then another representing no fewer than twenty-eight communes 'des environs de Versailles'.[23] The officials of the district administration of Versailles, if not those of the department, all seem to have been sympathetic to the plight of the agricultural labourers and were lobbying in their interests as well. Louis-Charles Couturier, the superintendant of the royal estates at Versailles and Marly, drafted a long report to his superiors rehearsing the arguments for and against the sub-division of crown properties. Small-scale holdings were economically retrograde, he concluded, but in times of revolution arguments based on political expediency could not be ignored. Admitting the force of this argument, he joined in the hue and cry and, on 7 March 1793, urged the Convention to distribute small plots of uncultivated land at a fixed price, that is to say without recourse to auction.[24]

The Convention finally responded. Clavière, the Minister of Finance, took up the idea of a leasehold partition of sections of the Royal Domain and the relevant committees of government settled down to work out a compromise that would not be too damaging to the Exchequer. The first proposal (emanating from the Comité d'Agriculture and the Comité d'Aliénation) envisaged the dismemberment of selected areas of the Grand Parc into plots of 2–4 *arpents*, which would be offered on one-year leases. This solution seems to have pleased no one in the villages. In so far as we can penetrate the motivations of the agricultural proletariat, they appear to have wanted either a free hand-out of land, direct purchase (at a preferential price) or the cession of land on a perpetual lease with the right of redemption. Since the capital for direct purchase would have to be advanced by the Exchequer, the last two options were pretty much indistinguishable.

With nothing definitive decided and everything still to play for, incursions into the royal forests and parks continued. Guffroy and Chasles, the two *commissaires* of the Convention sent out to speed up recruitment, found themselves subjected to intense lobbying upon their arrival in Versailles, and were induced by Couturier to join the campaign against the auction principle. Meanwhile, as law and order deteriorated in the villages, the pronouncements of the district administrators became ever more shrill and radical. Even the permanent officials of the department were infected by the atmosphere of crisis. On 15 April 1793, amid fresh alarms over food shortages, they offered their own advanced interpretation of property rights: 'Le salut public' commands our primary allegiance and 'toute propriété, de quelque nature qu'elle soit, n'est qu'une délégation du souverain qu'a droit d'en commander, d'en modifier, d'en diriger l'usage, selon que cela est ordonné par l'intérêt public.'[25] Having established a theoretical basis for policy, the administrators met the following day in order to devise a means of parcelling out crown lands in the Versailles area as quickly as possible. However, unilateral action by the combined authorities was forestalled by the promulgation of legislation which had been progressing through the parliamentary pipeline for many months.

On 3 June 1793 the deputies voted to sell off *émigré* estates in lots to the highest bidders. Yet the undertakings given during the preceding summer were not forgotten: provision was made to allocate 1-*arpent* plots to landless families residing in villages which lacked commons. The plots were to be marked out prior to auction and distributed to all qualifying households on a 'hire-purchase' (*arrentement*) basis. A few days later, on 10 June, the vexed issue of the moveable and nonmoveable assets of the crown was sorted out. The latter, with a few exceptions, were to be treated as *biens nationaux*; more specifically, '[ils] seront aliénés conformément aux précédentes lois, et notamment à celle du 3 de ce mois'.[26] So, the dismemberment of the Grand Parc and other royal estates into 1-*arpent* holdings could now go ahead. To cap their handiwork, the deputies gave a final reading to the much delayed law on the commons that same day. It substantially redeemed the promises made on 14 August 1792 by offering peasants a means of acquiring scraps of land on which to grow vegetables or cereals. Unlike the plots to be carved from crown and *émigré* estates, the individual portions of common land were to be ceded gratis and freehold.

In the Versaillais the commons were vestigial and their future failed to ignite the passionate debates which took place in other parts of the country. Instead, all eyes were fixed on the Royal Domain, whose alienation had now become a matter of public policy. Even the decree of 3 June licensing the disposal of *émigré* property was cast into the shadow as the district administration grappled with the technicalities inherent in handing out parcels of crown land to the poor. When, on 13 September 1793, the Convention altered the stipulations of its decree of 3 June, substituting the much less generous facility of a credit note worth 500 *livres* in place of the direct allocation of a 1-*arpent* plot, the district officials took no notice. Not until Prairial of the Year II (May–June 1794) did their preoccupation with the crown estates ease sufficiently to allow thoughts of the unimplemented decree of 13 September and the backlog of *émigré* properties awaiting auction to intrude.

That preoccupation had been kindled by the arrival of Delacroix and Musset in Versailles; tangible evidence that the Montagnard-dominated Convention did have an agrarian policy after all. What Delacroix and Musset thought about the mission entrusted to them is not known in detail. Both, it seems, were staunch Jacobins enjoying the confidence of the Committee of Public Safety, which moved to extend their powers in September 1793. To judge from retrospective sources, they set about the task of parcelling land drawn from the patrimony of the crown with determination and efficiency. According to one sympathetic observer, the two deputies were 'animés d'abord du sentiment de l'humanité, et en même tems du désir d'attacher de nombreuses familles à la révolution en les dédomagent [*sic*] en quelque sorte des longues vexations que leur avoient fait éprouver le régime féodal, et notamment les agents des chasses'.[27] In their own *Compte-Rendu* (dated 30 nivôse II), the envoys expressed evident satisfaction at having stemmed the land hunger of the rural poor in a number of communes. Admittedly, the needs of the proletariat of Versailles remained unanswered: too numerous to settle on the land, they could only be helped by attracting commerce and industry to the town. However, it is instructive to note the way in which Georges Lefebvre[28] interprets the episode. In his writings, he depicts a Montagnard elite which was absent-mindedly anxious about the plight of the poor peasantry, but nothing more. When driven by the thrust of events to take account of the demands of the rural masses, it was torn between humanitarian gestures and the relentless pressure to fill the coffers of the Exchequer. Not surprisingly, therefore, he plays down the magnitude of the social experiment conducted in the district of Versailles in the course of the Year II (1793–94). The decrees of 3 and 10 June 1793 were more significant for what they withheld rather than what they granted; Delacroix and Musset curtailed the scope of the legislation as far as possible; the eventual *partage* benefited 'only' 1,546 poor peasant households, whereas the district contained a vast army of starving agricultural labourers; and the plots were designated in a way that rendered them largely worthless in any case.

Lefebvre's interpretation of agrarian politics during the most radical phase of the Revolution rests on substantial foundations. And so, too, does his interpretation of the whole thrust of the peasant revolution between 1789 and 1795.[29] The case of the Versailles *partageurs* appears to invite a nuancing of those judgements, however. While it is true that the share-out scarcely provided a comprehensive solution to the problem of landlessness in the district, it should be emphasised that Delacroix and Musset were sent out to enforce the decree of 10 June 1793 (and not that of 3 June, as Lefebvre supposed). This measure applied solely to crown properties and could only be implemented to the advantage of communes touched by the Royal Domain. That over 1,500 peasant families were able to benefit under the terms of the law is surely indicative of the good faith of the district authorities and the *représentants*, rather than of any desire to circumscribe the scope of the operation. Perhaps the nub of the story lies elsewhere, though; in the vision of peasant revolution which it conveys. Embedded within the conclusion to Georges Lefebvre's great study of the peasantry of the Nord, we find the following carefully considered verdict: 'la masse rurale', he writes, 'n'était pas hostile au principe de la propriété individuelle, mais elle la limitait étroitement et demeurait très attachée aux conceptions coutumières'.[30] In the district of Versailles, by contrast, the poor peasantry combined an attachment to common rights with an unmistakable enthusiasm for individual plots of land. Was this enthusiasm perhaps the first stirrings inside the rural community of the modern conception of property?

If so, these stirrings were soon nipped in the bud. But not for the reasons which Lefebvre alleged. Most of the plots marked out by the surveyors possessed arable potential, although they often required clearing first. Only occasionally did beneficiaries refuse the portions which had fallen to them in the ballot. The difficulties that subsequently arose derived from other sources. First, the plots were simply too small to support a family: 1 *arpent* represented about 1 acre of land. Usually they were elongated, impossible to enclose and vulnerable to the depredations of game from the nearby forests. Secondly, the plots were permanent 'concessions', strictly speaking; that is to say, they were ceded against a paper-money rent payable annually to the Receiver of National Domains. This arrangement caused untold confusion because it blurred the distinction between leasehold and freehold. In practice, the beneficiaries regarded their plots as private property, and so, it seems, did the Director of National Domains, but other branches of central government did not share such an interpretation, and nor did some of the municipal administrations. When plot-holders defaulted on their ground rents, they placed their status as modest landowners in jeopardy. This was the third difficulty, and it eventually frustrated the Versailles Jacobins' plans to establish a property-owning democracy.

The uprisings of Germinal and Prairial III (April–May 1795) marked the watershed. After this date, even vestigial commitment to the levelling ideals of the Terror evaporated. Instead, there followed a witch-hunt against the petty agents of village and small-town

F

sans-culottism and a determined attempt to remove 'terrorist' legislation from the statute-book. This resulted in the repeal of the decree of 13 September 1793 on 12 prairial III (31 May 1795), the suspension of the law of 10 June 1793 permitting the parcelling of common lands and a general hue and cry against the activities of the *représentants-en-mission* in the departments. In particular, the Minister of the Interior launched an investigation of land 'concessions' on 25 fructidor IV (11 September 1796). While that threat was looming, the more diligent agricultural labourers of the villages around Versailles were gathering in a second, and in some cases a third, harvest from their 1-*arpent* plots. Already, though, the numbers actually cultivating their plots had declined as a consequence of sub-letting, fore-closures by creditors, abandonments and sales. Imperceptibly, the land was being consolidated once more and the deep suspicion with which the new Directorial administration regarded this legacy of the Terror could only hasten the process. An abusive application of the decree of 28 ventôse IV (18 March 1796) on *biens nationaux* resulted in the sale of a number of 'concessions' under the very noses of their owners. Many more appear to have reverted to the state (or to real estate companies which specialised in buying them up), following seizure for non-payment of rent. Of the twenty-one indigent families originally endowed with allotments in the village of La Celle, 'plusieurs d'entre eux sont abandonné [*sic*] dès la seconde année faute de moyens pour les faire valoir', reported the mayor in 1805, 'et d'autres d'années en années, au point qu'aujourd'hui huit seulement sont conservé, encore plusieurs d'entre ces derniers le souloue.'[31] The sharp deflation engineered by Finance Minister Ramel in the Year VI (1797) thinned out the number of plot-holders drastically. With rents (and taxes) payable in metallic currency and with agricultural prices plunging, the commitments entered into during the reign of the *assignat* now exerted an intolerable strain upon the household budgets of the poor.

Bonaparte's accession brought relief from the meanspiritedness of the Directory, in the sense that the law was no longer sharpened against the plot-holders, and on 27 thermidor VIII (15 August 1800) the Consuls upheld the validity of the original 'concessions'. This brought to an end official insinuations that Delacroix and Musset had acted improperly; on the other hand, it betokened a more vigorous enforcement of the law pertaining to contract. On 15 germinal XI (5 April 1803) the Minister of Finance authorised the prefect of the Seine-et-Oise to expropriate the remaining fifty plot-holders of the commune of

Le Chesnay 'dont aucun n'a acquitté la redevance à laquelle il étoit tenu annuellement'.[32] Their allotments, amounting to some 21 hectares in total, were restored to the Grand Parc of Versailles whence they had been drawn. Seizure or foreclosure seems to have been the common fate of the plot-holders of the district. According to a ledger kept in the prefecture which recorded the transactions affecting 336 of the plots, a further spate of writs was served on defaulters in the Year XIV (1805–06). The bulk of the concessions appears to have escaped the clutches of Napoleonic administrators, however. Instead, they were bought up by land speculators: 'il paroît que la compagnie Roulet qui a obtenu le transfert de la rente est devenue propriétaire d'une partie de ces terrains',[33] commented the Intendant of the Civil List to the prefect on 10 February 1816. Indeed, roughly three-quarters of the plots appear to have been ceded in this fashion. The case of Pierre Thibault,[34] a day labourer in the village of Bougival, is typical of many. Owing arrears of rent totalling 96 *livres*, he made over his 1-*arpent* holding to a real estate company in 1802. Six years later he described himself as propertyless and still indigent.

There can be no doubt that the Versailles *partages* represented an experiment in the redistribution of property to the very poor. It was the Agrarian Law in action, although, of course, the actors in the drama carefully refrained from any such analogy. All the beneficiaries, without exception, were either proletarians in the classical sense of the term or modest owners of cottages occupying less than 1 *arpent* of land. Most worked for day wages on the farms of the Royal Domain and other great magnates; the remainder made a living as artisans (stonemasons, smiths, carpenters, etc.), or textile workers. As such they can be described as the menial class of the countryside, and it is worth noting that in a region remarkable for relatively high levels of literacy at the end of the *ancien régime*, only 47 per cent of the beneficiaries proved able to sign the official register of acceptance for their plots.[35] However, the experiment failed. Or rather, it failed as an audacious bid to endow the rural proletariat with land. By the end of the Empire all but a handful of families had abandoned their allotments or had been kicked off for non-payment of ground rent. Traces of this memorable act of social justice survived, most notably in the cadastral plans of several communes which still record places named 'Les Concessions' and 'Les Arpents', but that was all. Delacroix and Musset were not, after all, the unwitting architects of small peasant capitalism in the post-Revolutionary countryside: the Versaillais experience demonstrates, rather, the improbability of the 'voie paysanne' thesis outlined by Anatoli Ado and a number of other historians in recent years.[36] The development of transitional forms of agrarian capitalism based on simple commodity production was hindered by the inability of the peasant masses to secure firm control over adequate plots of land. Yet there is a sense in which the experiment succeeded. By creating a stratum of peasant clients of the Revolution equivalent to the '40 sous' *sans-culottes* of the Paris sections, it bought off popular discontent with the regime at a critical juncture; discontent, moreover, which the ousted Girondin leaders regrouping in the Eure a short distance to the west might have attempted to exploit. Instead, the Mountain nurtured a spirit of village Jacobinism which was to endure beyond the eclipse of Thermidor.

Notes

1   Archives Départementales des Yvelines (henceforth AD Yv) 1 Q 376, file for Les Loges: *division des terres dépendantes de la liste civile en lots d'un arpent*, 27 brumaire II.

2   The *arpent* was an area measurement in common use during the *ancien régime*. However, it varied in value from place to place. In metric terms, the *arpent d'ordonnance* (also known as the *grand arpent*, or the *arpent des eaux-et-forêts*) represented 51 ares 7 centiares; the *arpent commun*, 42 ares 18 centiares and the *arpent de Paris*, 34 ares 19 centiares. Most of the villages of the district of Versailles used the *arpent commun* as their standard. Therefore, a 1-*arpent* plot was equivalent to 0·42 hectares or 1·04 acres. For the sake of comparison, all the area measurements in this chapter relate to the *arpent commun* (and its metric equivalent).

3   The sources vary slightly in their computation of the number of plots, beneficiaries and participating communes. These figures seem likely to be the most accurate and they are compiled from ADYv 1 Q 379; 1 Q 382.

4   See ADYv 1 Q 376–83; 5 Q 1424.

5   B. Minzes, *Die Nationalgüterverausserung während der französichen Revolution mit besonderer Berucksichtigung des Departement Seine und Oise. Ein Betrag zur sozialökonomischen Geschichte der grossen Revolution. Auf Grund ungedruckter Quellen*, Jena, 1892.

6   G. Lefebvre, *Questions agraires au temps de la Terreur*, 2nd edn, La Roche-sur-Yon, 1954, notes to pp. 16–17, 24, 26, 30.

7   Notably Bailly, Bois d'Arcy, Buc, Fontenay-le-Fleury, Guyancourt, Noisy-le-Roi, Rennemoulin and St Cyr.

8   ADYv 1 Q 377, file for Bailly.

9   M. Thénard, *Bailliages de Versailles et de Meudon. Les Cahiers des paroisses avec commentaires accompagnés de quelques cahiers de curés*, Versailles, 1889, p. 61.

10   Lefebvre, *Questions agraires*, p. 17 note 2.

11   Minzes, *Die Nationalgüterverausserung während der französichen Revolution*, p. 12.

12   See R. B. Rose, 'The "Red Scare" of the 1790s: the French Revolution and the "Agrarian Law" ', *Past and Present*, CIII (1984), pp. 113–30 for a thorough airing of the subject.

13   *Ibid.*, p. 120.

14   *Ibid.*, p. 125.

15   *Ibid.*, pp. 114–15.

16   *Ibid.*, p. 123.

17   A.B.–J. Guffroy, *Le Tocsin, sur la permanence de la garde nationale, sur l'organisation des municipalités et des assemblées provinciales, sur l'emploi des biens d'église à l'acquit des dettes de la nation*, Paris, 1789, p. 101.

18   *Lois et actes du gouvernement*, 38 vols, VI, July 1792–March 1793. Paris, 1834, pp. 44–5.

19   The phrase comes from a printed circular of the department authorities of the Lot-et-Garonne promoting the division of the commons (AD Lot-et-Garonne L345).

20   Lefebvre, *Questions agraires*, pp. 23–4.

21   See G.–R. Ikni, 'Documents: sur la loi agraire dans l'Oise pendant la Révolution française', *Annales historiques compiègnoises*, XIX (1982), pp. 19–26.

22   Quoted in Lefebvre, *Questions agraires*, p. 230.

23   A. Defresne and F. Evrard, *Les Subsistances dans le district de Versailles de 1788 à l'an V*, 2 vols, I, Rennes, 1921–22, p. 179.

24   Minzes, *Die Nationalgüterverausserung während der französichen Revolution*, p. 149, appendix 7a; Defresne and Evrard, *Les Subsistances dans le district de Versailles*, I, p. 179 note 4.

25   Minzes, *Die Nationalgüterverausserung während der französichen Revolution*, p. 151, appendix 8.

26   *Lois et actes du gouvernment*, 38 vols, VII, April 1793– vendémiaire an II, Paris, 1834, pp. 130–42.

27   ADYv 1 Q 378, file for Guyancourt: Prunel to prefect of Seine-et-Oise, 2 germinal VIII.

28   Lefebvre, *Questions agraires*, pp. 20–43 and notes.

29   For a succinct statement, see G. Lefebvre, 'La Révolution française et les paysans', in G. Lefebvre, *Etudes sur la Révolution française*, Paris, 1954, pp. 246–68.

30   G. Lefebvre, *Les Paysans du Nord pendant la Révolution française*, condensed version, Bari, 1959, p. 908.

31   ADYv 1 Q 378, file for La Celle: mayor of La Celle to Bureau des Domaines Nationaux, La Celle, 29 nivôse XIII.

32   *Ibid.*, memo of Prefecture of Seine-et-Oise, Versailles, 8 floréal XI.

33   Minzes, *Die Nationalgüterverausserung während der französichen Revolution*, p. 83 note 281.

34   ADYv 1 Q 377, file for Bougival: petition of Pierre Thibault [to prefect of Seine-et-Oise], Bougival, 26 November 1808.

35   Based on a sample of 662 concessionaries.

36   See A. Ado, *The Peasant Movement in France during the Great Bourgeois Revolution of the End of the Eighteenth Century*, Moscow, 1971, 1987. In Russian; F. Gauthier, *La Voie paysanne dans la Révolution française: l'exemple de la Picardie*, Paris, 1977. For a critical assessment, see P. M. Jones, *The Peasantry in the French Revolution*, Cambridge, 1988, pp. 124–7, 147–8.

chapter nine MALCOLM CROOK

'Aux urnes, citoyens!'
Urban and rural electoral behaviour during the French Revolution

The study of elections during the French Revolution remains a badly neglected subject. It has acquired added importance in the light of historians' current preoccupation with Revolutionary politics and culture. Yet, surprisingly, electoral behaviour received little attention in the influential series of conferences recently devoted to *The French Revolution and the Creation of Modern Political Culture*.[1] An explanation for lack of interest in the electoral process is doubtless to be found in the powerful attraction exerted by other forms of political activity, but it also stems from the complexity of the issue itself. The electoral mechanism that was adopted, or rather retained from the *ancien régime*, was a convoluted one which was frequently adjusted during the Revolutionary decade.[2] The relevant documentation is of uneven quality, widely scattered in different archives and far from easy to exploit as a consequence.

In the absence of any comprehensive survey, there has been a tendency to assume that participation in elections, especially parliamentary or legislative ones, was rather higher in towns than in the countryside.[3] This assumption appeared to find confirmation in the seminal work of Paul Bois, *Paysans de l'Ouest*,[4] a study of the department of the Sarthe which highlighted the contrast, indeed the conflict, between rural and urban political attitudes and behaviour during the Revolution. A section of the book was devoted to a comparison of electoral turnout in town and country, the first time that the matter had been subjected to any rigorous historical investigation.

Bois began with an analysis of participation in the 'administrative' elections of May 1790.[5] Primary assemblies in the cantons, the basic electoral unit, chose delegates to attend the departmental college of the Sarthe, which in turn appointed personnel to the newly established district and departmental councils. These were important, inaugural elections, with much local authority at stake, and Bois discovered a high level of rural turnout, frequently in excess of 50 per cent of registered voters (despite some restrictions on the franchise: at this stage of the Revolution, the overwhelming majority of adult males in the countryside could vote, though fewer could do so in towns). The urban attendance at Le Mans, Mamers and La Flèche was, however, significantly lower and only La Flèche reached 42 per cent.

The following year, in June 1791, another round of primary elections took place. This time a 'national' dimension was involved, since delegates sent to the departmental assembly were not only responsible for a partial renewal of district and departmental councils but were also entrusted with the choice of the department's deputies to the Legislative Assembly, created by the constitution of 1791. Participation in the Sarthe plummeted, though while most rural cantons could muster no more than 10–12 per cent, turnout at Le Mans and La Flèche held above 20 per cent.

On the basis of these findings, Bois concluded that *campagnards* took relatively little interest in legislative elections, hence their poor showing in 1791 compared to their strong participation in local elections a year earlier. *Citadins*, by contrast, displayed less enthusiasm in 1790 but exhibited a relatively greater degree of commitment to 'national' elections a year later. It should be noted that Bois's argument ignored the local dimension involved in the renewal of district and departmental councils in 1791. However, he went on to assert that urban voters also turned out more heavily than their rural counterparts in the exclusively 'national' elections of late August 1792 (when delegates from the cantons were solely concerned with the creation of a Convention, which was to draft a new, republican constitution) and again in June 1793 (to deliver a verdict upon the constitution of 1793, via a plebiscite conducted in the same cantonal assemblies).

Bois did not claim that his conclusions for the Sarthe possessed any universal validity but, given the paucity of available electoral studies, it was inevitable that generalisations would be made from them. Yet when

Melvin Edelstein actually brought together the diverse data that had appeared in various local and regional monographs, he was prompted to query a now widely held assumption:

> Nous croyons pouvoir affirmer que les paysans n'étaient pas plus indif- férents que les citadins en matière de vote, et qu'ils furent même parfois plus nombreux que ces derniers à participer aux urnes. On a vu aussi qu'ils n'étaient pas, par nature, détachés de la politique.[6]

The basis of Bois's original hypothesis had been a very narrow one, geographically confined to a single département, chronologically restricted to a short period, 1790–93, and based entirely on primary elections with no reference whatsoever to municipal polls. Yet, while Edelstein is to be congratulated for enlarging the area of debate, his findings rely too heavily upon secondary sources that provide only disparate and often dubious statistics.

Certainly, no scientific precision of the sort derived from the study of more recent elections is feasible where the Revolutionary period is concerned. Regular elections were instituted on a uniform basis during the decade, but the proceedings, or *procès-verbaux*, are invariably incomplete and it is difficult to find registers of voters upon which turnout can be accurately calculated. Even the available lists are all too often deficient; the frank admission by departmental administrators in the Landes that they were employing voter totals from 1790, because in 1795 so many municipalities had failed to submit updated registers, undoubtedly represented a common problem.[7]

Even when the requisite lists can be unearthed and verified a decision must be taken as to which voting figures are chosen for analysis. For the revolutionaries retained the essentials of an electoral procedure with which they were familiar, one that had been employed, albeit with myriad local variations, under the *ancien régime*, and above all in elec- tions to the Estates General in 1789. This entailed a system of assemblies rather than an individual ballot and each assembly, cantonal or municipal (or the sections into which these might be divided accord- ing to numbers), had first to choose its officials (president, secretary and scrutineers) before embarking upon the elections proper. These, too, according to established precedent, were conducted via exhaustive ballots which required three rounds of voting before *pluralité relative*, as opposed to an absolute majority, was finally accepted.

In this chapter the figures cited always refer to the first round of voting for college delegates, in the case of primary elections, and for mayors or leading councillors in the case of municipal contests. These particular *tours de scrutin* did not necessarily attract the greatest participation, which might be higher when assembly officials were chosen or at the initial roll-call.[8] The overall total of individuals who voted at least once during dreadfully protracted proceedings was therefore greater than any single vote, though in most instances there is no means of ascertaining it.

Nor can there be any pretence at a survey covering the whole country. The only *procès-verbaux de canton* collected and evaluated centrally were those emanating from the two plebiscites of 1793 and 1795, when Frenchmen cast a direct vote upon the constitutions of those years.[9] What follows is instead based upon a series of electoral case-studies drawn, for the most part, from half a dozen departments where the remaining evidence is reasonably plentiful. The focus will fall upon larger towns, all *chefs-lieux de département*, in comparison with the rural communities surrounding them which contained a population of less than 2,000 persons. In most instances the *campagnards* under review inhabited the adjacent district, a subdivision of the department abolished in 1795 but an area which will be used here, for analytical purposes, until the turn of the nineteenth century.

Primary elections in the cantons, which in rural areas grouped communes together, will take pride of place, though some reference will also be made to plebiscites and municipal polls. During the Revolutionary decade, direct elections took place only at municipal level while, justices of the peace excepted, the choice of district and departmental personnel, like national deputies, was delegated from the cantons to an electoral college. These *assemblées départementales* comprised between 300 and 900 delegates (*électeurs*), depending upon the number of registered voters in the department, and their papers have been preserved at Paris, but they will not be considered below.[10]

In spite of all the preliminary qualifications which must be entered in a study of this sort, some solid conclusions do emerge that challenge both Bois's description of the contrast between rural and urban voting behaviour and Edelstein's critique of it. There is no doubt that, to begin with, in the primary elections of May/June 1790 the participation of *campagnards* was generally higher than that of *citadins* in the adjacent *chef-lieu*. Vannes, in the Morbihan, represents the only exception to the rule in this sample, which suggests that the larger the urban agglomeration, the greater the propensity towards a low turnout.[11] In the Var, for example, the naval port of Toulon produced one of the

Figure 1 *Primary Elections in the French Revolution*

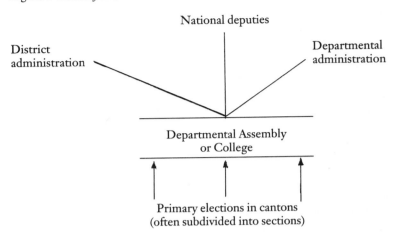

1790 Department and district	1791 Legislative Assembly	1792 National Convention	1795 Legislative Councils	1797, 1798, 1799 Partial renewal of Legislative Councils
	Restricted franchise and eligibility for office	Quasi-universal suffrage and eligibility for office		Restricted franchise and eligibility for office

lowest percentages that has been recovered, while, in the Marne, Châlons fell well below the rural cantons inscribed within its district and the same, relatively poor urban performance was also recorded at Dijon in the Côte-d'Or, together with Carcassonne in the Aude.[12] Paris, the political epicentre of revolutionary France, returned a mere 12 per cent, much at variance with the surrounding countryside in the département of the Seine.[13]

The following year, for primaries held in May or June 1791, the pattern is less clear cut, though, even where the *chef-lieu* failed to overhaul rural turnout, the drop in the participation of urban voters was much less marked. Toulon was the only town in the sample to raise its turnout, but so did many rural cantons in the Var and, overall, they produced an almost identical average.[14] The biggest fall in attendance was recorded at Dijon, yet the average of a dozen rural cantons in the

Table 1 *Primary elections, 1790–92 (turnout in percentages)*

	1790	1791	1792
Carcassonne (Aude)	28·6	25·4	–
Rural cantons in district	35·7	12·2	–
Châlons-sur-Marne (Marne)	24·6	16·1	24·3
Rural cantons in district	66·5	27·5	18·4
Dijon (Côte-d'Or)	36·3	21·0	18·6
Rural cantons in department	72·1	40·4	19·4
Paris (Seine)	12·1	11·4	*c.*10·0
Rural cantons in department	26·4	12·2	15·1
Toulon (Var)	11·7	30·3	17·1
Rural cantons in department	18·4	29·1	11·8
Vannes (Morbihan)	47·0	24·6	22·7
Rural cantons in district	40·0	9·6	2.6

Côte-d'Or reveals a still greater loss, like the *campagnards*' desertion of the assemblies in the district of Vannes.[15] The urban sections of Paris, meanwhile, were frequented by slightly fewer voters in 1791 than a year before, but inhabitants of the hinterland were now exhibiting a similarly high degree of absenteeism.[16]

Data for the primaries of 1792 are still more difficult to evaluate than their predecessors. These elections were held at the end of August, at less than a fortnight's notice and in conditions of acute turmoil caused by the war and the overthrow of the monarchy. In theory, the assemblies were open to all adult males over the age of twenty-one who could support themselves, but there was no time to draft new electoral registers. Whether or not freshly enfranchised individuals were aware of their opportunity to participate is a moot point.[17] In these circumstances calculation of turnout, on the basis of lists compiled later, can only be approximate. In most cases the absolute numbers who took part were superior in the *chefs-lieux* and lower in rural cantons than a year before.

Only Toulon, among the towns in this sample, recorded an absolute and relative decline while, at the other extreme, Châlons-sur-Marne improved in both respects.[18] In rural areas of the Seine the percentage turnout actually rose, though in every case *campagnards* were much less in evidence than they had been in the initial elections of 1790.[19] The collapse of participation in the countryside surrounding the Breton town of Vannes is particularly striking, but wastage in the Var and the

Côte-d-Or was also significant.[20]

This growing rural–urban contrast is reinforced by turnout for the plebiscite of 1793, which, notwithstanding the turmoil of those momentous summer months, attracted almost 30 per cent of the enlarged electorate in the country as a whole.[21] On this occasion Toulon cannot be included in the sample, because the new constitution was rejected without a vote during the federalist revolt which had swept the town and much of the Var. In the Aude, where voting did occur, a low poll revealed little distinction between town and country, but in the districts of Châlons, Dijon and Vannes *citadins* showed much more determination to make their voice heard than *campagnards* in the surrounding areas.[22]

Table 2 *Participation in the plebiscites of 1793 and 1795 (turnout in percentages)*

	1793	1795
Carcassonne	18·7	13·6
Rural cantons in district	17·9	12·5
Châlons-sur-Marne	35·0	47·5
Rural cantons in district	18·3	8·3
Dijon	56·5	48·0
Rural cantons in district	39·8	22·9
Vannes	12·8	18·6
Rural cantons in district	3·9	2·5
National average	c.29·0	c.17·0

There were to be no elections in the cantons over the next two years and precious few in the municipalities, because the constitution of 1793, though overwhelmingly endorsed in the June plebiscite, was suspended *jusqu'à la paix*. In the interim officials were nominated by the government and its representatives on mission until, following the demise of the Montagnard dictatorship, it was decided to draw up yet another constitutional document, that of the Year III. Despite the reintroduction of minimal restrictions on the basic franchise, together with a sweeping reduction of eligibility for office, the scheme was submitted to another plebiscite in which all adult males could vote.

Fewer chose to do so in 1795 and, in France as a whole, only one-sixth of the electorate attended the cantonal assemblies.[23] None the less, to judge by the case studies considered here, *citadins* continued to participate more strongly than their rural neighbours. Once again, there was little difference in the Aude, but in the districts of Châlons,

Dijon and Vannes a huge gap was opened between turnout in the *chef-lieu* and rural areas.

On this occasion, following another hugely favourable response, the new constitution was put into immediate effect. The voters proceeded to choose delegates to attend the *assemblées départementales*, which, as in the past, actually elected departmental personnel and national deputies for the Legislative Councils (but no longer district officials, because this tier of local government was now abolished).[24] Annual primary elections were introduced and operated under the Directory. Departmental administrations, like the parliamentary Legislative Councils, were to be partially renewed each year, and so were the municipalities.

The Directorial period in general is a victim of unjustified historical neglect and its elections are no exception.[25] Frequent comments on electoral apathy notwithstanding, turnout does bear comparison with earlier years of the Revolution, especially where towns are concerned. No information has so far come to light for Paris and, though Toulon is reasonably well served, data on the Var are too disparate to be of real value. However, solid series have been reconstituted for the Aude, Côte-d'Or, Marne and Morbihan, all of which point to a pronounced urban preponderance.

In the Marne, in 1795, 1798 and 1799 (*procès-verbaux* for 1797 have completely disappeared), Châlons consistently polled higher than the average for rural cantons within its former district. Indeed, on all but one occasion turnout in the *chef-lieu* was unequalled by any other single assembly.[26] A similar pattern is evident in the Burgundian department of the Côte-d'Or, where Dijon always attracted at least twice as many of its voters as a sample of rural cantons and even exceeded the countryside by a factor of six in 1795.[27] In the same year Carcassonne, by contrast, polled at a rate not unlike its hinterland, but succeeding years saw the gap widen, especially in 1797.[28] Finally, in the disaffected West, participation was relatively lower all round, though Vannes, departmental citadel of the beleaguered Republic, did stay well ahead of adjacent rural areas.[29]

Finally, some brief reference should be made to comparative figures for turnout in municipal elections. These are extremely difficult to come by in more than fits and starts, since the *procès-verbaux* are badly kept or housed in inaccessible *archives communales*. Nevertheless, it is worth testing Bois's hypothesis that rural interest was more intense where local contests were concerned, even though Bois himself made no attempt to explore this aspect of the electoral system. In fact, rural

Table 3 *Primary elections 1795–99 (Years III–VII) (turnout in percentages)*

	1795	1797	1798	1799
Carcassonne	10·9	44·9	31·5	18·6
Rural cantons in former district	10·6	12·6	22·3	11·2
Châlons-sur-Marne	38·5	–	37·8	13·1
Rural cantons in former district	8·0	–	15·0	6·1
Dijon	58·1	42·1	39·2	18·6
Rural cantons in department	10·3	18·3	16·9	8·7
Vannes	–	25·8	22·9	17·9
Rural cantons in former district	–	8·5	5·4	3·2

participation in the first municipal elections of 1790 was usually strong, or at least more pronounced in villages than in adjacent large towns.[30] Paris, for example, recorded only 18 per cent for its inaugural mayoral election in 1790, while Bourg-la-Reine in the countryside exceeded 50 per cent.[31] Even in the Côte-d'Or, where polls to elect a mayor of Dijon attracted almost two-thirds of registered voters, rural municipalities averaged over 70 per cent and one or two smaller communes managed a full house.[32]

Yet thereafter a similar trajectory to that observed in primary elections became apparent. Diminishing rural returns are to be contrasted with urban participation rates which dropped less drastically or, in some cases, rose significantly. It has been suggested that municipal polls continued to attract more voters than primary assemblies, but this was certainly not always the case and the partial renewal of *conseils municipaux* in November 1790, for instance, aroused a very low level of interest in countryside as well as town.

After a hiatus during the Terror, municipal elections resumed under the Directory, albeit on a different basis from earlier years, without mayors and with councils much reduced in size. The information so far amassed for this later stage in the Revolution is patchy, but turnout was not always as derisory as some historians have imagined. The example of Toulouse and rural communes within its former district, for which a good set of *procès-verbaux* remain, may not prove to be typical but it is indicative.[33] In 1795 the *chef-lieu* recorded a lower turnout than the average calculated for adjacent municipalities (this had been the case in 1790). Thereafter the town polled more strongly, above all in 1797 when a fiercely contested election at Toulouse produced a record attendance of 71 per cent.

Table 4 *Turnout in municipal elections at Toulouse and in rural communes of its former district, 1795–99 (Years IV–VII), in percentages*

	1795	1797	1798	1799
Toulouse	27·7	71·5	50·6	44·2
Average for communes in canton forain de Toulouse	29·6	38·6	48·6	43·1
Average for communes in former district	34·6	43·1	35·9	36·0

As might be expected, particular factors, which varied from one locality to another, could raise or lower participation rates quite substantially. Fluctuations between neighbouring cantons or municipalities, from one election to the next, must be acknowledged, as Edelstein's diverse range of data in a recent synthesis clearly shows.[34] Yet when a continuous series of statistics is compiled and averaged, some patterns, or at least tendencies, can be discerned.

On the whole, urban turnout at both primary and municipal elections was initially lower than in most adjacent rural areas. However, polls at the *chefs-lieux* examined in the sample studied here gradually attracted a higher turnout than neighbouring circumscriptions, or at least lost fewer participants as the Revolution progressed. Both Bois's and Edelstein's conclusions are open to objection as a result: the former was wrong to assert that *campagnards* and *citadins* necessarily differed in their respective attitudes towards local and national elections, which cannot be easily distinguished in any case; while the latter does not allow for the contrast which did develop between urban and rural participation rates.

A more satisfactory explanation for the differences in behaviour than Bois has provided, or Edelstein recognised, remains to be advanced. The best place to begin is by exploring electoral practice under the *ancien régime*, which exerted a more profound influence over the political culture of the Revolution than most historians have realised. Large towns had generally surrendered the principle of election to municipal office or, as in the Midi, restricted participation to a tiny elite of *notables*. By contrast rural communities, like those in Burgundy, had often retained a more 'democratic' tradition via the assembly of all heads of family or, in the case of the *pays d'élection*, had begun an experiment with elected parish councils in the late 1780s.[35]

There was also a dimension of rural solidarity that expressed itself in the smaller village reunions which formed the first tier of voting in elections to the Estates General in 1789, a 'national' election which Bois ignored.[36] Such sentiment was equally apparent in the disputes which occurred in 1790 when, for primary elections in the cantons, neighbouring and rival rural communities were reluctantly brought together to form a single assembly.[37] In the towns, on the other hand, elections to the Estates General had initially been conducted among members of the same artisan corporations or professional bodies. It was only with difficulty that the urban electorate adapted itself to neighbourhood assemblies, or to the sections into which cities were divided to facilitate polling.

This urban apprenticeship was a somehat protracted affair, yet, while rural voters were deserting the assemblies disenchanted, their counterparts in the towns were being encouraged to make their presence felt. The particular case of the Mediterranean naval port of Toulon suggests that political clubs played a major role in mobilising the urban electorate. This town's Jacobin club hand, in fact, entered into conflict with the Municipality precisely over the especially low turnout for a partial renewal of the *conseil municipal* in November 1790. In June the following year the same club requested that dockyard workers be allowed to leave the Arsenal early, so as to attend hard-fought primary elections. As a result of the Jacobins' efforts, electoral participation, which had fallen as low as 6 per cent of registered voters, now climbed above the 30 per cent mark.[38]

A recent survey of Jacobin clubs in Revolutionary France has stressed their involvement in electoral politics and a study of their post-Thermidorian reincarnations, as *Cercles Constitutionnels*, does the same.[39] The press undoubtedly played its part in mobilising voters, too. Its readers seem to have been concentrated in towns, just as political clubs tended to be more active in the cities.[40] Yet it must be admitted that in Provence, even if news-sheets were thinly spread, a high density of Jacobin clubs and the fabled, but perhaps over-exaggerated, *sociabilité méridionale* failed to produce a high level of electoral turnout in any type of community.

On the contrary, it would appear that the strongest participation in elections during the Revolutionary decade, by *campagnards* and *citadins*, is to be found in north-easterly regions of France. This bias is especially evident in departmental turnout for the plebiscite of 1793, which indicates high participation in this area. It is tempting to ascribe this phenomenon to regional features like the high degree of literacy; the greater incidence of Revolutionary journalism; a superior network of road communications; and, finally, an advanced level of economic development.[41]

Even in this area, however, the massive turnout of 1790 rapidly receded and absenteeism became widespread. The contrast between urban and rural electoral behaviour should, therefore, also be explained in terms of factors which inhibited *campagnards* from participating to a greater extent than *citadins*. Contrary to Bois's equation of absence with indifference, it must be emphasised that non-attendance could imply protest, or stem from intimidation. As Charles Tilly commented some time ago:

> 'Paul Bois, in noticing the decline of the rural electorate, has interpreted these changes as a sign of peasant apathy. The election records, however, indicate that at first the two parties (*campagnards* and *citadins*) struggled for control of the political machinery and that the later withdrawal of the peasantry was more in protest than in disinterest [*sic*].[42]

Desertion of the polls as a consequence of disaffection can be illustrated by an incident from the Aveyron, a department in the Massif Central, where at Pont-de-Salars some ninety citizens quit the primary electoral assembly of June 1791 after they were instructed to take an oath of allegiance to the regime in order to vote.[43] As in western France, resistance to the Civil Constitution of the Clergy may have prompted an electoral boycott, though there would not appear to be any automatic correlation between 'refractory' areas, on the one hand, and zones of plummeting participation, on the other.[44] Large towns, after all, recorded a high rate of rejection of the reform of the Church by their parish clergy.[45]

Disappointment with the Revolution could be translated into deliberate abstention, though in some circumstances voters were urged to attend assemblies in order to voice their disapproval. In this case, their determination to do so might well be frustrated by political opponents who set more store by the outcome of elections than by the level of participation. Nobles and their *clientèles* were not infrequently prevented from voting in 1790, while royalists were similarly deterred in 1792 and either faction might come under pressure to absent itself under the Directory, depending on the balance of local forces. Intimidatory tactics ranged from crude assaults to more sophisticated means, which involved the prolongation of proceedings and the postponement of crucial ballots, or the challenging of rival voters' credentials.[46]

In a context of war and civil war it is scarcely surprising that the so-called *apprentissage de la citoyenneté* enjoyed a rather chequered history during the Revolutionary decade. The electoral system itself, inherited from the *ancien régime* with few changes, imposed a tremendous burden upon voters. This was especially true for those in the countryside, where the rhythms of labour and the travelling required to attend primary elections at the *chef-lieu de canton* demanded additional effort. The use of assemblies, which usually lasted for more than a day, instead of an individual ballot; the multiplicity of polls, especially in the early years of the Revolution; the prejudice against declared candidates, which led elected personnel to refuse to serve; and the two-tier procedure for primary elections which vested real power outside the commune, in the hands of an electoral college, all took their toll. It was these factors, rather than the franchise question, which understandably inclined voters to leave the whole business in the hands of local *notables*, especially when a local political consensus existed.[47]

Doubtless, the difficulties that the revolutionaries experienced in operating this system of popular sovereignty were both cause and effect of the crisis of political authority in France. The ruling elites were disconcerted when the people indicated their disaffectation by relatively high levels of absenteeism, yet, in the circumstances, the participation that was recorded amounts to a considerable achievement. In spite of rather than because of the electoral mechanism, a new attitude towards elections was emerging. An apprenticeship in democratic citizenship had commenced, though with uneven results in town and country and from one region to another. This Revolutionary legacy to the longer term process of political acculturation, which resumed in the mid-nineteenth century, remains to be investigated, but a start had at least been made.[48]

Notes

1   K. M. Baker, C. Lucas and F. Furet (eds), *The French Revolution and the Creation of Modern Political Culture*, 3 vols, Oxford, 1987–89. Only two papers, those of Furet and Halévi treating elections to the Estates General, in volume I, make any contribution to the subject of electoral behaviour.

2   J. R. Suratteau, 'Heurs et malheurs de la "sociologie électorale" pour l'époque de la Révolution française', *Annales: Economies, Sociétés, Civilisations*, XXIII (1968), pp. 566–80.

3   E.g., A. Cobban, *Aspects of the French Revolution*, London, 1971, p. 130.

4   P. Bois, *Paysans de l'Ouest: Des structures économiques et sociales aux options politiques depuis l'époque révolutionnaire dans la Sarthe*, Le Mans, 1960.

5 Ibid., p. 261 ff.

6 M. Edelstein, 'Vers une "sociologie électorale" de la Révolution française: la participation des citadins et campagnards (1789–1793)', Revue d'histoire moderne et contemporaine, XXII (1975), pp. 526–7.

7 Archives nationales (AN) F1cIII Landes 1, Département des Landes, 5 ventôse V, 23 February 1797.

8 G. Fournier, 'La participation électorale en Haute-Garonne pendant la Révolution' Annales du Midi, CI (1989), pp. 47–71, uses the highest single total recorded in any vote. The disparities between different tours de scrutin could be substantial. At Saint-Vallier in the Var, for example, 249 electors were present when electoral proceedings began in the primaries of June 1791, but only ninety-one individuals (not necessarily all present at the outset) actually voted in the first scrutin for the canton's nine delegates to the assemblée départementale. At the dernier tour only forty-five voters remained. Archives départementales des Alpes-Maritimes, L547, Procès-verbal (P.–v.) d'élection, 24 June 1791.

9 AN BII 34 and 74, Plébiscites, 1793 and Year III, for a list of returns by department and canton, together with the original P.–v. Some cantons, however, simply recorded 'unanimity', rather than providing a precise figure.

10 I am currently preparing a general survey of elections during the Revolutionary period for future publication.

11 Archives départementales du Morbihan (AD Morbihan), L233, P.–v. d'élection, May 1790.

12 Archives départementales du Var (ADV), 1L218, P.–v. d'élection, June 1790; Archives départementales de la Marne (AD Marne), 1L297, P.–v. d'élection, May 1790; Archives départementales de la Côte-d'Or (ADCO) L225–7, P.–v. d'élection, April 1790; Archives départementales de l'Aude (ADA) L356, P.–v. d'élection, May 1790.

13 AN BI 1 and 2, P.–v. d'élection, November 1790.

14 ADV 1L218, P–v d'élection, June 1791; and see M. Crook, 'Révolution française et comportement électoral: l'exemple de Toulon et le Var de 1789 à 1793', Actes du 112e Congrès national des sociétés savantes, III, Lyon, 1987, p. 299.

15 ADCO, L232–3, P.–v. d'élection, August 1792 and AD Morbihan, L236, P.–v. d'election, June 1791.

16 AN BI 8, P.–v. d'élection, June 1791. R. Monnier 'La politisation des paroisses rurales de la banlieue parisienne', in La Révolution française et le monde rural, Paris, 1989, p. 430.

17 In one canton of the Pyrénées-Orientales, for example, passive citizens were still not admitted to the assembly and those present were reminded of restrictions on eligibility that had in fact just been abolished: Archives départementales des Pyrénées-Orientales, L430, P.–v. du canton de Millas, 26 August 1792.

18 ADV 1L223, P.–v. d'élection, August 1792 and AD Marne 1L297 P.–v. d'élection, August 1792.

19 AN BI 14, P.–v. d'élection, August 1792.

20 ADCO L234 and 235, P.–v. d'élection, August 1792, and AD Morbihan, L237, P.–v. d'élection, August 1792.

21 AN BII 34, Recueil des votes, 1793, and R. Baticle, 'Le plébiscite sur la Constitution de 1793', La Révolution française, 57 (1909), pp. 496–524; 58 (1910), pp. 5–30, 117–55, 193–237, 327–41, 385–410. For the totals of those eligible to vote, see under 'Population' in the series L of the relevant AD, or in AN Series F20, Population.

22 Bois, Paysans de l'Ouest, p. 288, suggests a similar pattern in the Sarthe, but the figures have not been verified.

23 AN BII 74, *Recueil des votes*, 1795, and A. Lajusan, 'Le plébiscite de l'an III', *La Révolution française*, 60 (1911), pp. 5–37, 106–32, 236–63.

24 In the case of one section at Dijon, voters in the plebiscite who were disenfranchised by the new constitution were asked to leave before the primary election began: ADCO L238, *P.–v. d'élection*, 22–3 fructidor III, 8–9 September 1795.

25 One outstanding exception is represented by the work of J. R. Suratteau, above all in *Les élections de l'an VI et le coup d'état du 22 floréal (11 mai 1798)*, Paris, 1971, though this contains few references to participation in the cantons.

26 AD Marne, IL305–11, *P.–v. d'élection, an III–an VII*.

27 ADCO L238–50, *P.–v. d'élection, an III–an VII (1795–99)*.

28 ADA L379, *P.–v. d'élection an V–an VII*.

29 AD Morbihan, L240–46, *P.–v. d'élection, an V–an VII (1797–99)*.

30 R. Marx, *Recherches sur la vie politique de l'Alsace prérévolutionnaire et révolutionnaire*, Strasbourg, 1966, p. 58, suggests that 'partout et toujours les citoyens ont été plus assidus aux élections municipales qu'aux élections ou aux scrutins de caractère législatif'. This was not always the case in the area he has studied if the partial municipal elections of November 1790 are considered, and it is misleading if taken as a general rule for France as a whole.

31 M. Genty, *L'apprentissage de la citoyenneté. Paris, 1789–1795*, Paris, 1987, pp. 74–7.

32 ADCO L258–65, *P.v. d'élection*, January 1790; E. Fortunet, M. Fossier, N. Kozlowski and S. Vienne, *Pouvoir municipal et communauté rurale à l'époque révolutionnaire en Côte-d'Or, 1789 – an IV*, Dijon, 1981.

33 Archives départementales de la Haute-Garonne, L249–56, *P.–v. des élections communales, an IV–VII (1795–99)*, and Archives municipales de Toulouse, IK13–16, *P.–v. des élections municipales, an IV–an VII (1795–99)*.

34 M. Edelstein, 'L'apprentissage de la citoyenneté: participation électorale des campagnards et citadins', in M. Vovelle (ed.), *L'image de la Révolution, Recueil des communications au Congrès mondial*, Paris, 1989, pp. 15–25.

35 M. Bordes, *L'administration provinciale et municipale au XVIIIᵉ siècle*, Paris, 1972, provides the best introduction.

36 Turnout in elections to the Estates General in 1789 is a separate subject, with its different system and particular problems, which has not been treated here. For a good list of available figures on participation see Edelstein, 'L'apprentissage de la citoyenneté', pp. 16–17.

37 G. Fournier, 'Les incidents électoraux dans la Haute-Garonne, l'Aude, l'Hérault, pendant la Révolution', in *Les pratiques politiques en province à l'époque de la Révolution*, Montpellier, 1988, pp. 63–7.

38 M. Crook, 'Rouges et blancs à Toulon: l'essor et la chute du jacobinisme populaire dans le port de guerre de 1790 à 1793', *Provence historique*, XXXVII (1987), pp. 174–6.

39 M. Kennedy, *The Jacobin Clubs in the French Revolution: the first years*, Princeton, 1982, pp. 210–33; I. Woloch, *Jacobin Legacy: the Democratic Movement under the Directory*, Princeton, 1970; and the work of J. Boutier and P. Boutry currently in progress, 'La diffusion des sociétés politiques en France', *Annales historiques de la Révolution française*, CCLXVI (1986), pp. 365–98.

40 See the contribution by H. Gough in this volume and his comments on the electoral role of the provincial press in 'National politics and the provincial Jacobin press during the Directory', *History of European Ideas*, X (1989), pp. 449–50.

41 See the first two volumes in the series of *Atlas de la Révolution française*, which has

recently begun to appear: I: *Routes et communications*, Paris, 1987, pp. 15–16 especially; and II: *L'enseignement 1760–1815*, Paris, 1987, pp. 12 and 23 in particular. For an example of a comparative analysis of regional phenomena, albeit on a different subject, J. Markoff, 'The social geography of rural revolt at the beginning of the French Revolution', *American Sociological Review*, L (1985), pp. 761–81.

42   C. Tilly, 'Some problems in the history of the Vendée', *American Historical Review*, LXVII, (1961), p. 29.

43   Archives départementales de l'Aveyron, IL591, *P.–v. d'election*, Pont-de-Salars, June 1791.

44   J. L. Ormières has recently criticised Bois for ignoring the religious question when considering peasant absenteeism: 'Politique et religion dans l'Ouest', *Annales: Economies, Sociétés, Civilisations*, XL (1985), pp. 1048–50; *ibid.*, 'Les scrutins de 1790 et 1791 et le soulèvement de 1793: interprétation du comportement électoral', in F. Lebrun and R. Dupuy (eds), *Les résistances à la Révolution*, Paris, 1987, pp. 82–6.

45   T. Tackett, *Religion, Revolution and Regional Culture in Eighteenth-Century France: the Écclesiastical Oath of 1791*, Princeton, 1986, pp. 49–56.

46   C. Lucas, 'Le jeu de pouvoir local sous le Directoire', in *Les pratiques politiques en province*, Montpellier, 1988 pp. 285–7.

47   M. Crook, 'Les Français devant le vote: participation et pratique électorale à l'époque de la Révolution', in *Les pratiques politiques en province*, pp. 31–3.

48   P. McPhee, 'Electoral democracy and direct democracy in France, 1789–1851'. *European History Quarterly*, XVI (1986), has posed the question of the relationship between the Revolutionary apprenticeship and nineteenth-century electoral behaviour, but detailed investigation is required.

The volunteers of 1792

On 11 July 1792, following the announcement that the Austrian and Prussian troops were on the offensive, the Legislative Assembly declared 'la patrie en danger'. From 22 July onwards the promulgation of this decree gave rise to a spectacle that would be witnessed in most towns in France. With alarm bells ringing, and drums beating a call to arms, mounted officers – donning their tricoloured sashes – rode through the streets reading out the Assembly's proclamation and made known the extreme danger to the fatherland and the public duty to come to its aid. Town dignitaries took their place on a platform erected in the middle of a main square. The opened enrolment registers were placed in front of them, lying on a plank draped in red, white and blue, and supported by a couple of tambours. Below the platform, members of the National Guard mixed in with detachments from the king's army and the first volunteers climbed the steps to sign the registers and enlist. For the most part, the atmosphere remained restrained. There was less shouting, singing and explosive enthusiasm than certain histories of the Revolution maintain. In reality the mass mobilisation for the struggle against the invading forces, with whom the country had been at war since 20 April 1792, had begun long before, at the time of the king's flight in June 1791. The first volunteers had been levied at that time, when immediate war had seemed inevitable to many. They had been waiting ever since. To true patriots, war did not seem a historical accident, but part of the general course of events dating from 1789, from the outbreak of a revolution which they knew would subvert the whole political and social order of Europe.

This levy of 1792, very different for that of 1791, produced more prospective combatants than anticipated. Not all of these volunteers were willing to give their personal details to the recruiting officers who asked for them. Some feared that in so doing, they would leave themselves open to the designs of ill-intentioned men who would use their identities for dubious purposes. Many saw themselves as citizens offering to give a helping hand to the regular army, rather than as true soldiers. In other words, not all the volunteers of 1792 appear in the *contrôle de troupe* registers transferred to the War Archives at Vincennes. The loss of some of these registers further adds to the problem of making a definitive head count of all those who came forward to defend 'la patrie'. But a survey of local as well as national archives gives an estimated minimum of 200,000 individuals.[1]

We must address a number of questions. How were these volunteers levied and organised? Who were they, and who were their leaders? And, finally what motivation fired them?

Mode of organisation of the 1792 levies

The first difference between the levies of 1792 and those of 1791 concerns their duration. Following the more-or-less spontaneous organisation of a few battalions in June and July, the levies of the preceding year took place over a period of five months. Those of 1792 continued for more than ten months. Even before the 11 July declaration, some departments – the Bouches-du-Rhône, for example – had already set up their own battalions. Most were constituted in the months of August (21), September (62) and October 1792 (56). Others were formed as late as November (19), December (8), and January (11) and February of 1793 (4). Seven waited until the spring of 1793 to be inspected, some being reviewed at the same time as the new battalions formed out of the levy of 300,000 men decreed by the Convention.

The departments providing the first battalions were those close to the combat zones or under threat of invasion, such as the Ain, Meurthe, Moselle and Bas-Rhin, together with departments where active popular societies were numerous – the Bouches-du-Rhône being a prime example. Delays in forming a battalion could not always be blamed on a lack of patriotism; more often than not they were caused by the problems of arming, clothing and equipping the men.

The second difference between the levies of 1791 and those of 1792 was that in the latter case the whole country was affected. In 1791 various departments had not been called upon to 'contribute' – especially those of central France. But in 1792 the Legislative demanded that the departments which had not previously drafted men should now do so. Initially thirty-one battalions had been demanded, but only eleven were asked of the departments concerned – the Cantal, the Aveyron, the Tarn, the Lot, the Lot-et-Garonne, the Ardèche, the Lozère, the Gers, the Dordogne and the Haute-Loire. Other departments were asked to raise numbers in direct proportion to their population, so long as this would not 'be harmful to commerce and industry'. Consequently, a map recording the different sizes of the battalions raised with each levy should not necessarily be seen as reflecting relative levels of patriotic fervour.

Yet another contrast: the voluntary battalions of 1791 were in the main units 571-men strong, whereas those of 1792 varied from a couple of hundred to 800 men. Not all the units raised were the battalions of volunteers which the law required. They were complemented by legions and companies of irregulars levied by foreign patriots, by generals or by municipalities, as well as by members of the *fédéré* battalions who had taken up arms after the events of 10 August. Some volunteers – as provided by law – were sent directly to the front, where their enlistment often contributed greatly to changing the face of the regiments.

The 1791 volunteer battalions were regarded as 'fully operational' only when all their companies had been rallied and passed before a reviewing officer. The situation was quite different for the 1792 battalions. Some left for the front, when they were not even fully formed, whilst the companies which were to reinforce them were gradually put together. The ranks were swollen by men from other departments recruited during the course of their march towards the combat zone.

What were the military consequences of the mode of recruitment of these levies? The role played by these volunteers in the battles of the autumn and winter of 1792 was generally well praised by their contemporaries and remains so today in the historiography of the period. It is true that the generals complained of a mass of men who were badly armed, badly equipped, and undisciplined, and who generally hindered the regular troops rather than helping them to withstand the onslaught of the enemy. The latter did, however, acknowledge that this continual arrival of fresh combatants – this 'active mass' of men who were, on the whole, ready to fight a merciless battle – had a disconcerting effect and damaged the morale of its armies.

As for the precise nature of the volunteers' motivation: some battalions were being created when the constitutional monarchy was still in place and the intensity of protest against it, focused on its leader, the king, differed from department to department. Other battalions reached the front after the proclamation of the Republic, thus leaving the volunteers with a totally different sense of commitment.

The social composition of the rank and file and the officers

The 1791 volunteers were a young body of men. Those of 1792 were even more so: three-quarters of them were twenty-five-years-old or under. The number of men under eighteen rose considerably – 15 per cent of all volunteers, as opposed to 10 per cent in 1791. Alongside these adolescents and those who had only just come of age, the number of men approaching forty was also greater than that of the 1791 levy. In 1791, 3·8 per cent of volunteers were over 36; in 1792 the figure had risen to 6·7 per cent.[2]

Moreover, the physical make-up of the group underwent changes which were not all direct results of extreme youth or advanced age: 62 per cent of volunteers measured 1 metre 67 or less in 1792 as opposed to 52 per cent in 1791. Very few of these had been less than 1 metre 63 tall, yet in 1792 one-third of all the men fell into this category. This can be partly explained by a rising number of contingents of southerners, shorter on average than northerners. The 1792 volunteers were also from more humble origins than their predecessors, their lives of hard labour and poverty often explaining their poor physical development and less-healthy constitutions. Those in charge of examining these troops confirmed as much. For example, the special commission set up at the camp in Châlons revealed that 'we first get rid of the children, the old men and those of an unruly appearance who, governed by their ardour rather than actual physical strength, would only hamper operations and be extra mouths to feed'.[3]

If, as in 1791, the urban population provided numbers exceeding expectations considering its modest size in France at that time, so the rural population should be seen to have made a larger contribution than ever before. Where it is possible to distinguish the social origins and trades of recruits, as it is in the Manche, the Yonne, the Basses-Pyrénées, the Cantal and the Haute-Garonne, we notice that most volunteers had been employed as domestic staff, unskilled labourers or day-labourers finding work as best they could to earn a living.[4] Crippled or infirm, ill or too weak, too puny or incapable of withstanding the strain of long marches – such is the image of the lame-ducks of the 4th battalion of the Basses-Alpes that is revealed to us in the thesis written by Colonel Pélissier using material from the War Archives.[5] Of course, not all the troops corresponded to this image but, as several unpublished theses make clear, it remains a fact that the volunteers of 1792 were less robust than those who came forward at the time of the king's flight.

On the surface, the officers of 1792 and 1791 seem to differ very little. Most were young, 46 per cent of the captains being less than thirty years old and 14 per cent between thirty and thirty-four; one-third of their number had previous military experience, having already served in the regular army. Many were from the bourgeoisie: 43 per cent of the captains and lieutenants, and 32·8 per cent of the sub-lieutenants. Maximilien Guidal, for example, was born in Grasse, the son of a merchant. He decided upon a military career at a very early age and when he was given the command of the 10th battalion of the Var, he had twelve years of practical military experience behind him, both as a soldier in the Artois regiment and as a dragoon in the Deux-Ponts regiment. A better known example is that of Jean-Charles Pichegru, commander of the 3rd battalion of the Gard; a talented petty bourgeois who became a mathematics tutor, he went on to serve in the Metz artillery and take part in the American Campaign, and was made up to sergeant while serving in the royal army. Although less numerous than in 1791, these bourgeois officers were joined by some men of noble origin – or those who aspired to the nobility, such as Honoré Saint-Martin or Vaissière de Saint-Martin, commander of a company of grenadiers from Barcelonnette. He was the son of Louis Vaissière de Saint-Martin, captain in the Vermandois regiment.[6]

If we take a closer look, some differences do appear between these 'cadres' of 1792 and those of 1791. Fewer men in charge of battalions had had substantial military experience than in 1791. The captains and lieutenants rarely had more than six years' soldiering experience, whereas their peers of 1791 had served both longer and better apprenticeships, and had often reached the grade of sergeant in the king's army.

A further difference should be noted: in 1792 bourgeois families were far less willing to send their sons to lead battalions. There were fewer sons of merchants, tradesmen, lawyers or doctors and more sons of self-employed craftsmen, clerks and office-workers, small shopkeepers or modest legal practitioners. In 1792 more volunteers from an agricultural background reached positions of responsibility within the companies, where they accounted for 15 per cent of the officers. Barthélémy Cadar, son of a modest Nîmes ironmonger, who became a major in the 7th Var battalion; Lieutenant Jean-Sylvestre Delaret, who was a shop assistant before joining the 4th company of the 4th battalion of the Hérault; and Lieutenant Durouch, son of a smallholder, who had enlisted in the 1st battalion of the Tarn, are more representative of the body of officers of 1792 than those previously cited.[7]

Whether rank and file, lieutenants or captains, these men did not, however, all revere the cult of the new 'patrie' to the same degree.

The volunteers and the concept of the nation

'Vive la nation!' This rallying-cry first uttered by Kellermann galvanised the troops into action when they were growing despondent as they battled on the slopes of Valmy. Their resistance and their victory were the very foundations of the Republic. Contrary to persistent legend, it was as young recruits joining the regular royal army, that the large number volunteers made their mark on this battle. This is borne out by the troop registers.

What exactly did the nation mean to them? Did they feel solidarity with the Revolution? What is known about the method of recruitment scarcely permits an affirmative answer. Were they nothing more than 'two-penny' soldiers, rather than true volunteers?

Initially, the local authorities drew lots to decide which men should leave to represent the community at the front. But this caused a stir in some assemblies. Was this not the system that had seen used to recruit men to the royal militia, the system which had been denounced in so many *cahiers de doléances* in 1789? So recruitment by election was attempted. But this proved just as unsatisfactory. In some places communities nominated absentees, or those who were unfit for military service. In others, locals proposed men whose 'exaggerated' political opinions, be they for the Revolution or against, meant that no-one voted for them. Recruiting officers, 'young men of intelligence', often out of work or else constitutional priests[8] as in the Ille-et-Vilaine scoured the countryside, fired by patriotism or by the promise of money. But why should such intermediaries be necessary? Why not promise a financial bonus to those from each locality who wanted to enlist as volunteers? It was therefore decided, often after much heart-felt doubt, that volunteers could be bought. Some departments, such as the Puy-de-Dôme,[9] found this repugnant, believing that it 'allowed vipers the honour of being suckled by "la mère patrie" '. Citizens who had enlisted of their own free will would be forced to 'march alongside mercenaries'. The Haute-Marne sought to justify the process[10] by explaining that the money given to the volunteers was an expression of gratitude, a way for the local community to show their solidarity and 'fraternity' with men who were often completely destitute. Such was the case in Saint-Dizier, where Georges Klein volunteered his son, committing himself to provide another volunteer if his son was killed and to leave for the front himself if this second volunteer perished. Knowing he was but a poor shoemaker, the assembly aided his son with 1,700 *livres*. The price which a volunteer could command varied from locality to locality: the villages and towns of the Var offered from 80 to over 200 *livres*, half given in *écus* and half in *assignats*; in Brittany prices varied between 100 and 120 *livres*, and in the Massif Central between 260 and 600 *livres*.

The reason for such a method of recruitment was clear. The volunteers of 1792 were motivated far less by patriotism than those of 1791. Yet in many departments the levies took place amid much civic fervour, as archive sources show for Paris, the Seine-et-Oise and Seine-et-Marne,[11] or for the Bouches-du-Rhône, Gard, Haute-Vienne and Corrèze. These areas were more politically motivated than others. They had seen, amongst other things, peasant revolts against seigneurial rights and the implantation of a comprehensive network of political clubs, as is shown by the maps recently produced by Jean Boutier and Philippe Boutry.[12]

Moreover, on taking a closer look, it becomes evident that unwillingness to volunteer was not always caused by a cold response to patriotic duty or by the rejection of a centralising state, a notion which was alien to the south of the country. People did wish to defend 'la patrie', as the inhabitants of Abriès in the Hautes-Alpes declared, but they meant their small regional homeland, rather than the nation as a whole.[13] Life rarely extended beyond the village which they would defend, even to the death; for to venture far from its confines would be a death in itself. The most frequent, intense and widely spread protests came from the poor. They might not object to helping the national 'patrie en danger' for a while, but who would provide for the elderly, the women, the children and the younger brothers left behind at home? Owners of small plots of land made it clear that if their sons left to defend the frontiers, the greatest danger was that their land would lie fallow for want of manpower; whereas the rich could pay for a *brassier*, they could not. Unskilled labourers were ready to enlist, but if they volunteered their families would become destitute. In many areas, the money given to volunteers was an expression of solidarity rather than evidence that they were trafficking in patriotism.

None the less, those who left to defend France of their own free will did not all have the same level of political consciousness, or the same understanding of the term 'nation'. For after 1789 the meaning of this term was very different from that of pre-Revolutionary times. Before 1789 the nation referred to the local community – both dead and living – who worked on or were at rest under the same soil, under the authority of a king who, although absolute in power, was far from being a tyrant. When the king had called his subjects to arms in 1709, for example, locals everywhere responded by fulfilling their responsibility to defend their cottages, altars and ancestral tombs. As André Corvisier points out,[14] the first couplet of 'La Marseillaise' called for 'an impure blood to drench our furrows', echoing the seventeenth-century war-cry which promised the Spanish that their dead bodies would enrich French soil. This automatic reflex to defend one's home, one's family and one's local community, with which one felt complete solidarity, was just as important in 1792 as it had been in 1791, notably in border regions. The inhabitants of Abriès, as mentioned, made reference in their address to the time when, a hundred years earlier, they had had to defend their lands and the kingdom.

The term 'nation' took on quite a different connotation after 1789. It came to mean a community of free men, possessing equal rights: free in body, mind and free – at least they hoped they soon would be – from seigneurial dues on their land; it meant a community of men equal before the law, subject to an equal system of taxation and equally free to apply for any office. But this nation was more than the simple sum total of all the citizens; it was a superior entity which was henceforth sovereign in the land.

This new concept of the nation, as expressed by the other verses of 'La Marseillaise', was the one transmitted to the 1792 volunteers by their parents, by the local authorities and even by the constitutional clergy. One mother wrote to her son, a volunteer from Saône-et-Loire, to tell him that the state he was fighting for 'is certainly the most beautiful and honourable that you could ever choose, as it stands for humanity and the Rights of Man' and that he should 'pray to the Almighty and obey all your superiors'.[15] The *prêtre-jureur* of Saint-Martin-le-Vieux in the Haute-Vienne preached on 20 August 1792 that the Supreme Being should be continually blessed 'for having broken the monstrous chains cast about us by the *patrie*'s traitors, avid for blood and for carnage', and concluded by saying that 'when we breathe our last, if we can still summon up enough strength, we must use it to repeat the vow engraved so deeply on our hearts – live free or die'.[16] Joseph Serre, a doctor in the Alps and volunteer in a battalion, exhorted his fellow citizens to rise up against 'this horde of armed slaves in the pay of the tyrants of the North' who threatened 'to invade homes, filling them with swords and death, to reinstate ministerial despotism on the ruins of the constitution and, the cruellest blow of all, to extinguish the love of *la patrie* and the love of equality which courses in the veins of all the French'. They were to rise up to defend all that they had gained from the Revolution: 'You have shaken off an odious yoke in order to breathe the fresh air of liberty; you have overcome degrading distinctions to worship equality in their place.'[17]

And yet was this equality, consisting largely of the abolition of privilege, anything more than the civil and political equality won by overthrowing the king on 10th August? The *sans-culottes* of the towns gave a new and different meaning to the word equality which led to a further variation on the concept of the nation. Liberty and equality meant nothing, they said, unless all men were allowed the same basic natural right: the right to exist. It was essential that the poor received, along with a job and some education, their daily bread at an affordable price. The voice of the *sans-culottes* was to be heard with even greater force at the time of the 1792 levies, when many of them stepped forward to volunteer.

A good example is that of the volunteers of the Ponceau Section in Paris, who marched into their sectional assembly on the 8 September 1792.[18] They addressed 'their brothers, friends and fellow citizens', telling them that they were setting out to fight 'for our liberty and for yours'. But they were leaving behind their 'nearest and dearest – fathers, mothers, wives and children' – and fearing that their families would suffer by their departure, they called for the local community to assist them. Another example is that of *citoyenne* Lamare, wife of a paver who had left for the front: she explained to the Roule Section that she was penniless and about to give birth. She was counting on the humanity and public-spiritedness of her fellow citizens to help her. Yet another example is this list of gunners who were leaving for the front and who were demanding that the nation provide the necessary aid to keep their families alive: Cordier, who left behind a wife; Janjey, whose wife was expecting a baby; Terrier, a widower with two children to support and La Coquery, with a wife and two children, numbered among those who signed the petition. The sections appointed commissioners to establish the extent of need, to provide essential aid and to canvass the deputies with the aim of broadening the base of the nation so that the poor should not be left out, taxing the rich, if necessary, to make them contribute to national defence. This echoes the cry of the 'two-penny' soldiers demanding financial aid for themselves and their families.

As Isser Woloch has emphasised, this was the precondition for an innovative system of social security for servicemen and was to underpin the system of state 'bienfaisance' proposed in the Year II.[19]

A nation which undertook to recognise the right to public aid and the duty of solidarity led many men of 'courageous poverty' to volunteer to face the enemy. The Prussian Laukhard noted in 1792, that:

> the volunteers were not as straight as a die, as were the Prussians, and were not as polished, well-trained or skilled in handling a gun or marching in step; nor did they know how to tighten their belts around their tunics as the Prussians did, yet they were devoted to the cause they served in body and in soul. Nearly all those I encountered at that time knew for whom and for what they were fighting and declared that they were ready to die for the good of their *patrie*. The only alternatives they knew were liberty or death.[20]

This was echoed by the prophetic words pronounced by Goethe on the evening of the battle of Valmy. 'From here and from this day', he declared 'begins a new era in the history of the world', an era in which among other things, an army expressing solidarity with the nation was ready to assume its rights and its independence.

Notes

1   Enquiry carried out by the history seminar at University of Paris I, 'Guerre et société', see *Annales historiques de la Révolution française*, 272 (1988), pp. 151–69.

2   J.–P. Bertaud, *The Army of the French Revolution, from Citizen Soldiers to Instrument of Power*, Princeton, 1988, pp. 66–74.

3   A. Chuquet, *Lettres de 1792*, Paris, 1911, p. 176.

4   Archives de la Guerre, Xw 109, 10, 39, 17.

5   Col. H. Pélissier, 'Volontaires des Basses-Alpes, des Hautes-Alpes et du Var', M.A. thesis, University of Paris I, 1987.

6   For the Gard department, see the M.A. thesis of Olivier Plancke, University of Paris I, 1985. For the Vaissière, see Col. Pélissier, 'Volontaires des Basses-Alpes'.

7   See the theses of Col. Pélissier and O. Plancke, as above.

8   J. Melloul, 'Les Volontaires du Morbihan, de l'Ille-et-Vilaine et des Côtes-du-Nord', M.A. thesis, University of Paris I, 1987.

9   O. Siffrrin, 'Les Volontaires du Massif Central', thesis, University of Paris I, 1987.

10   P. Jacquot, 'Les Volontaires en Haute-Marne (1791–1799)', 3 vols, thesis, University of Dijon, 1979.

11   A. Crépin, 'Armée de la Révolution, armée nouvelle? L'exemple de la Seine-et-Marne', Ph.D. thesis, University of Paris I, 1979.

12   See special number of *Annales historiques de la Révolution française*, 226 (1986).

13   Col. Pélissier, 'Volontaires des Basses-Alpes'.

14   A. Corvisier, *La France de Louis XIV, 1643–1715. Ordre intérieur et place en Europe*, Paris, 1979, p. 50.

15   Archives de la Guerre, Xw 91.

16   Archives de la Guerre, Xw 43.

17   Archives de la Guerre, Xw 43.

18   F. Régnier, 'L'assistance aux militaires et aux familles de militaires sous la Convention', M.A. thesis, University of Paris I, 1987.

19   I. Woloch, 'War-widows' pensions: social policy in revolutionary and Napoleonic France', *Societas*, VI (1976).

20   W. Baver, *Un Allemand en France sous la Terreur*, Paris, 1915, p. 89.

NB Proof of the presence of *aumôniers* in the battalions of national volunteers can be found in C. Epaulard, 'L'aumônerie militaire de la Révolution à la Restauration', M.A. thesis, University of Paris I, 1987.

Regionalism and linguistic conformity in the French Revolution

An extract from Pierre-Jakez Hélias's *Le Cheval d'Orgueil* may serve to introduce the main subject of this chapter: namely, the relationship between the nationalist and integrating ideology of the French Republic and the actual diversity of the country at the most funda-mental level of cultural expression – language. Hélias, recalling his own childhood near Plozevet, in the Finistère, towards the beginning of the twentieth century, told us that the *Vie des Saints* had been part of his mother's trousseau, and he went on to write:

> A la maison, outre le paroissien de ma mère et quelques recueils de cantiques, il y a deux livres importants. L'un qui reste à demeurer sur l'appui de la fenêtre, est le dictionnaire français de Monsieur Larousse . . . l'autre est enfermé dans l'armoire des noces de ma mère, que nous appelons la presse. C'est la Vie des Saints, rédigée en breton.[1]

A series of cultural dichotomies are linked in this account. The *Vie des Saints* was, first, a specifically female preserve; and, secondly, the maternal wedding chest was a hoard of religious knowledge, in opposi-tion to the famous Larousse, a treasury of lay wisdom. The *Vie des Saints* (or *Buhez ar Zent*) represented catholic France, while Larousse was a product and an emblem of secular republicanism. Hélias's mother's chest, finally, was Breton-speaking territory, while the window-sill supporting Larousse was a kind of altar devoted to the French language.

Many revolutionary Jacobins, and their nineteenth-century heirs, came to identify this breton world as catholic, archaic and reactionary. It seemed a hostile and impenetrable *foyer* of counter-revolution. Widespread ignorance of French in the provinces undoubtedly obstructed the spread of the Revolution's message. But exactly how much of a threat was linguistic diversity to the Revolution's nationalist ideology? How firmly could Revolutionary propaganda take root in non-Francophone France?

According to the *abbé* Grégoire in the Year II, at least 6 million Frenchmen were ignorant of the French language, and as many again could not sustain a conversation in it.[2] Only a minority of Frenchmen and women were exclusively Francophone at the end of the eighteenth century. According to statistics compiled in 1806, the French Empire included almost 1 million Breton-speakers and about 100,000 Basque-speakers.[3] Even without Imperial conquests, there were still about 1 million German-speakers, and perhaps a smaller number of Flemish- and Italian-speakers within France. Even these figures do not account for France's *patois*-speakers in the Centre, South and South-west, described by Pierre Chaunu as 'un Midi profond imperméable au français'.[4]

For millions of French citizens, therefore, the French Revolution, like the affairs of the *ancien-régime* monarchy, was conducted in a foreign language. The events and legislation of the Revolution were perceived through intermediaries, like the parish priest, who announced news from the pulpit. In the Quercy, peasants who felt the Revolution was failing to deliver all the benefits it had promised turned against their priests, accusing them of distorting political news, and of not telling them the full story.[5] The impact of the French Revolution cannot be appreciated without an awareness of the linguistic medium through which its message was articulated, and of the role played by non-French languages in popular life.

Grégoire's attempts to eliminate *patois*, which culminated in a report to the Convention in the Year II, are a valuable source for the history of non-Francophone France in the eighteenth century. The circular Grégoire issued in 1790 to correspondents all over France on the use of *patois* invited them to consider their local uses, their philological derivations, and the use of French or *patois* by the clergy and rural schools. For Grégoire, the priest and the schoolteacher could both be key figures in the struggle against peasant ignorance, and for the spread of the French language.

Grégoire wrote to his personal acquaintances, some colleagues from the Constituent Assembly, and he also sent his questionnaire to several *Sociétés des Amis de la Constitution*. It was also published by Brissot in *Le Patriote français*, in August 1790.[6] Grégoire's geographical coverage was not systematic. He had many replies from the East, where he had several personal contacts, but he also received many replies from Languedoc, where linguistic diversity was probably more of a problem.

Nineteen of Grégoire's correspondents were ecclesiastics, and fourteen replies came from the *Sociétés des Amis de la Constitution*. Another seventeen were sent in by lawyers, teachers and public functionaries. These members of the enlightened provincial bourgeoisie viewed the *patois*-speaking countryside as alien territory, ready and waiting to be civilised by new political ideas. In De Certeau's phrase, they saw the peasants beyond the gates as the nineteenth-century bourgeoisie viewed Africa: as an immobile continent, to be exploited, cultivated and moulded by the forces of history and progress.[7] Its inhabitants had to be introduced to the *patrie*, and to its language.

Grégoire invited his correspondents to define *patois* as dialects which fitted the everyday needs of rural life and work. According to the notables and clerics who supplied him with information, *patois* specialised in words for plants and agricultural tools. It was used for place-names and common diseases, animals and the stars. Some correspondents also agreed with Grégoire that *patois* was the natural language to adopt in moments of anger, hatred or passionate love.[8] For agricultural labourers, on the other hand, French was the language of formal occasions, and the language of social superiors. It could not define the rural universe with the rich resources of local dialect.

Patois could be perceived by Grégoire's followers as expressions of ignorance, archaic prejudice and obscenity; but for some it also expressed a pastoral simplicity and closeness to nature. 'Le patois est abondant', wrote one correspondent, 'pour toutes choses qui tiennent à la simplicité, à la décence et à la tranquillité.'[9] The labourer spoke *patois* to his oxen, and the shepherd to his dog.[10] The French language penetrated this rustic world very slowly, being confined, according to another correspondent, to the main towns, the chief communications routes and the châteaux.[11] One writer from Poitou told Grégoire quite bluntly that if he wanted to get rid of *patois*, he had only to open up more side roads to link up remote villages. This emphasis on roads is reminiscent of Eugen Weber's theories of the assimilation of the peasantry, but Grégoire had other ideas. He was obsessed with the notion of an educational crusade to wipe out peasant prejudice.

Patois was a familiar and familial language; French was a more deferential one. French was the official language of law and administration, needed to write a will, sell some property or get married. Bureaucratic expansion created a demand at the level of the small town for a class of local *notaires* and functionaries using French. To these people, and to all one's social superiors, one might expect to speak French. It was said in 1789 that the delegates of the villages of the Comté de Foix knew only three words of French: 'Avis de Monseigneur'.[12] *Patois*-speaking France cannot, therefore, be defined solely in geographical terms, nor simply in terms of a division between literate towns and a non-Francophone countryside. There was an important social demarcation line, too, between *patois*-speaking labourers and artisans; and the educated clergy and bourgeoisie, who were Francophone or bilingual. The Camisards had been reportedly so inspired that they would speak French in moments of religious ecstasy, which one observer regarded as quite miraculous for ordinary peasants.[13] At the very summit of the social scale, God spoke French. In popular Christmas carols in the Midi, the angels would speak French, but the shepherds replied in Provençal.[14]

Although God spoke in French, his representatives on earth were more versatile. Just as a shepherd might address his flock in *patois*, so *curés* often preached in local dialects. One of Grégoire's correspondents from Auch told him sourly that *patois* 'n'est bon que pour piétiser ou pour prier', and recommended the re-education of the priesthood.[15] This advice would have been appreciated by Grégoire, as a liberal intellectual and future leader of the constitutional church. Not everyone in the congregation wanted to hear sermons in *patois*. At Capbreton, in the Landes, the local bourgeoisie complained that the clergy were treating them like peasants. The Bishop of Dax replied:

> Je n'ai trouvé l'ignorance la plus grossière des plus essentielles verités de notre sainte religion que dans certaines paroisses où l'on n'instruisait qu'en français.[16]

In Perpignan, priests were still preaching in Catalan in 1874.[17]

The clergy was often bilingual, and in the Midi even trilingual, fluent in Latin, French and *patois*. Fournier, a deputy from the Périgord, described the role of each language thus:

> Grâces à Dieu, nos curés prêchent peu. Quand ils arrivent du seminaire, c'est en français; ils citent même du latin, et on les admire; mais quand ils veulent être entendus, ils parlent périgourdin.[18]

A French-speaking priest could have an important role as a cultural intermediary in a non-Francophone world. In 1794 a French-speaking suspect was arrested in Châteauneuf-du-Faou in Finistère because it was thought he must be a priest in disguise.[19] (This constitutes an interesting inversion of the catholic and breton/republican and French dichotomy outlined above by Hélias.)

The question of who spoke *patois* cannot be divorced from questions of social structure. It was the middle classes everywhere, the local *notables* who replied to Grégoire, who were the chief agents of the spread of the French language, and therefore of the nationalist ideology of the Revolution.

This fact was temporarily disguised by the phenomenon of bourgeois bilingualism. While the urban bourgeoisie of the South-west in the eighteenth century used French in their business transactions, they would often speak *patois* in everyday conversation.[20] Lorain *fils* reported from the Jura that 'les gros' used to speak *patois*, in order to 'se familiariser avec les petits'.[21] According to Yves Castan, the judges of the criminal courts of Languedoc knew *patois*.[22] Wealthy Toulousain bourgeois would converse in *patois* in the mid-eighteenth century, but this does not alter the fact that only a narrow social elite had effective access to French written culture. Husbands and wives, Castan writes, who wanted to send messages to their spouses in the jails of Languedoc had to pay a third party to compose a letter in French. On receipt, the jailer would re-translate into Occitan for the prisoner. In Bordeaux, aspiring artisans would use French whenever possible, as a sign of status, to distinguish themselves from the Gascon populace.[23]

In the eighteenth century, the ability to use French in speech or writing was a trait which distinguished the bourgeois from the labourer or artisan, and this was true in both town and country. In the Aveyron, Grégoire was informed, the French-speakers were retired soldiers, doctors, clergymen, nobles and *négociants*, and in Agen labourers did not get beyond learning a smattering of Latin for use in church.[24] In Bordeaux market, Gascon could often be heard, but it was mainly spoken by fishwives, for

Il y a cinquante ans que les négociants parlaient volontiers gascon. Plusieurs anciens richards aiment encore à le parler. Maintenant il n'est dans la bouche que [des] harengères, des portefaix et des chambrières.[25]

In Provence in the 1830s, the story goes, a highway robber had a dismal career until a Toulon bourgeois passed and he ordered him to stand and deliver in French instead of Provençal.[26] The bourgeoisie took the lead in the spread of the French language. Fournier told Grégoire:

> Il n'y a pas vingt ans que c'était ridicule de parler français, on appelait ça francimander; aujourd'hui, au moins dans les villes, les bourgeois ne parlent que cet idiome.[27]

The transition from *patois* to French usage was a transition from a predominantly oral language and culture to a written language and culture. The illiterate, of necessity, recognised the increasing power of the written word over their lives. The burning of the *terriers* (feudal title deeds) by the peasantry in revolt in 1789 may be seen as the vengeance of rural illiterates against the power of written culture. The written word took some time to penetrate the oral cultures of the French peasantry. In 1848, some Périgourdin peasants had heard of Lamartine (or 'La Martine'), but they were under the impression that she was the mistress of Ledru-Rollin – a mistake they would probably not have made if they had been accustomed to reading Lamartine's name in print.[28]

The French Revolution considered, in theory at least, that access to written culture was essential for the formation of the citizen and the acculturation of the masses. Grégoire wanted to adapt the traditional forms of *colportage* literature for revolutionary purposes. He recommended the use of dialogue and moral anecdote. Revolutionary propaganda also adopted another form of popular oral literature: the catechism. In 1791 the Jacobin club offered a prize for the best almanac for the rural masses, won, incidentally, by Collot d'Herbois's *Almanach du Père Gérard*. It was the Revolution, too, which invented the presentation of primary school book prizes.[29] The Revolution invested the printed word with a consciously militant function.

So, too, did its enemies. Under the Bourbon Restoration, catholic missionaries organised *autodafés* of harmful literature during Lent, at Bourges in 1817, Avignon in 1819 and elsewhere. In the Massif Central in the 1830s, Peter Jones reports, some clergy even forced children to recite in *patois* the catechisms they had first learned in French.[30]

Eventually, the coming of universal literacy in French created the conditions for cultural homogeneity, and made nationalism a real possibility for the first time. At the same time, written culture was the medium through which the Revolutionary bourgeoisie attempted to establish its supremacy, in the name of the indivisible Republic.

Fernand Braudel, in his last, unfinished work, stressed the diversity of

France, which he saw as a country of 'micro-pays', an archipelago of microeconomies and microdialects.[31] Grégoire himself counted thirty different *patois*, but an outsider could not hope for an exhaustive enumeration of local variations. In 1792 the department administration of the Corrèze questioned the point of translating political texts into *patois*, in these terms:

> Le traducteur qui s'est trouvé du canton de Juillac n'a point pris l'accent des autres cantons, qui présente des différences plus ou moins sensibles, mais qui deviennent considérables à la distance de 7 ou 8 lieues.[32]

Here it is apparently only a question of an oral translation.

The Revolution found it difficult to alter this situation. The expansion of the press, and the mass of official literature, laws and decrees issued by Revolutionary authorities, all contributed to the spread of French. The sound of respected orators making speeches in French at local *sociétés populaires* must also have encouraged a rudimentary knowledge of the national language. This is only to say, however, that the Revolution accelerated a trend already begun in the eighteenth century, which witnessed a great expansion in literacy. An imperial official from the Bouches-du-Rhône recognised the impact of the Revolution when he reported that

> Le provençal s'y réfugie désormais dans les vieux quartiers. . . . Quant au peuple des campagnes, il parle provençal, mais on y sait le français, et si le conservatisme paysan maintient sa langue, une tendance se dessine, celle que la Révolution a mise en branle, et un auteur peut dire: le provençal s'en va.[33]

The Revolutionary and Napoleonic armies broke down local exclusiveness, in widening the geographical horizons of the peasantry, and in demanding a comprehension of French from illiterate and non-Francophone conscripts. However, in the Army of the Moselle, in Egypt, and later in the Army of the Alps, Marcel Reinhard encountered veritable epidemics of homesickness, nostalgia or 'mal du pays'.[34] Bretons and the 'gens de l'ouest' were among those particularly affected by what was a pathological state, whose symptoms included fever, headaches, loss of appetite and occasionally delirium.

Linguistic unity, however, could not be forged overnight. In 1864 the Minister for Education, Duruy, found that there were still eighteen mainland departments where over 60 per cent of the population could not speak French.[35] These lay principally in Brittany, the Alps and the Var, the Massif Central and, above all, in the South-west.

The Revolution had nevertheless launched an aggressive attack on *patois* and non-French languages. Grégoire seems to have regarded *patois* as oral corruptions of an old written norm, and here he echoed the *Encyclopédie*, which described *patois* as a 'language corrompu tel qu'il se parle presque dans toutes les provinces . . . On ne parle la langue que dans la capitale.'[36] In Barère's eyes, French was 'la plus belle langue de l'Europe'. It was the language of enlightenment and democracy, and the medium through which the rest of the world was privileged to learn of these advanced concepts.[37] While Italian was the language of voluptuous and indolent poetry, English the language of banking and mercenary trade, German appropriate to a feudal, militaristic society, French was the language of the Rights of Man. As such, it ought to be intelligible to every citizen. Unfortunately, Barère's argument ran, the Bourbon monarchy had made the French language an instrument of social division. The court had affected a distinctive accent and manner of speech to define its superiority. Linguistic diversity was thus part of the monarchical ploy to 'divide and rule'.

Behind the rhetoric lay an awareness that linguistic conformity was a political necessity. Citizens could not be expected to obey the law unless they understood it. This was a hard lesson for the inhabitants of Allassac in the Corrèze in January 1790, when they burned the local seigneur's church pew after Mass. Martial law was proclaimed in the village – but in French. The *maréchaussée* eventually dispersed the crowd by force, but fatal casualties were reported.[38]

Bourgeois notions of equality demanded a universal knowledge of French, for the equal access to office could not become a reality until all could read and write the same language. Linguistic barriers, as Grégoire also realised, were barriers to the free development of commerce. He tried to eliminate *patois* from the services of his constitutional church.

Unless the rural population knew French, wrote a *curé* from Bergerac to Grégoire, they would not know their rights 'pour ne plus se laisser fouler comme on l'avait fouler jusques ici sans qu'il [le peuple] ose faire entendre ses gémissements et ses sanglots.'[39] Knowledge of French was thus fundamental to the workings of a liberal–democratic society.

Barère directed his attacks against a dozen peripheral departments where non-French languages were current. These were the four Breton departments, Corsica and the Alpes-Maritimes, the German area of the

Haut-Rhin, Bas-Rhin, Moselle and Mont-Terrible, the Flemish areas
of the Nord, and the Basque region of the Basses-Pyrénées. His speech
of Pluviôse, often quoted, and often out of context, defined these areas
as centres of counter-revolution:

> Le fédéralisme et la superstition parlent bas-breton; l'émigration et la
> haine de la République parlent allemand; la contre-révolution parle
> italien, et le fanatisme parle le basque. Cassons ces instruments de
> dommage et d'erreur.[40]

Other revolutionaries were more circumspect and more practical.
Roland, as Minister of the Interior, politely invited priests to use the
vernacular.[41] Merlin de Douai passed a decree at the end of the Year II
ordering that all legal documents should be drawn up in French, on
pain of six months' imprisonment.[42] This was as much an attack on
Latin usage as on German or Flemish, and Merlin the jurist charac-
teristically cited decrees of François I and Charles IX banning Latin
from public documents.

Many of the Revolution's educational schemes, like that of Lan-
thenas in 1792, proclaimed the need to destroy patois, but little was done
to achieve this. French made slow headway in the educational system,
except perhaps in the Directory's écoles centrales, where French
completely ousted Latin as a medium of instruction. These failures
were ironic, for Barère and Grégoire firmly believed in the power of
education and the state to achieve the linguistic conformity they
desired.

Barère, it should be stressed, had not attacked patois as such in his
speech to the Convention quoted above ('Le fédéralisme et la superstition parlent bas–breton'). He selected the peripheral areas of the
Republic as his targets, and he carefully distinguished a threefold
hierarchy of non-French languages. First, he condemned the 'langues',
or foreign languages, particularly German and Italian. Secondly, he
attacked the 'idiomes', by which he meant Breton and Basque,
associated with the counter-revolution. Thirdly, patois remained relatively immune from political opprobrium.

It has been shown, in support of Barère, that frontier areas where
non-French languages were spoken tended to resist the oath to the
Civil Constitution of the Clergy in 1791. In the East, the German-
speaking parishes of the bilingual district of Belfort were only half as
inclined to accept the oath as the French-speaking areas. Similarly, in

the Moselle department, only 19 per cent of the clergy in German-speaking areas took the oath, compared to an acceptance rate of 69 per cent in French parishes.[43] The oath to the Civil Constitution was also strongly rejected in Flanders and Roussillon, where non-French languages were common.

Patois, on the other hand, as Barère acknowledged, were not exclusive tongues, and many *patois*-speakers could understand French. There was nothing intrinsically counter-revolutionary about *patois*. There were *sociétés populaires* in the Midi, such as the one at St Cyprien in the Dordogne, where the minutes were read in *patois*.[44] In Toulouse, the *cahiers de doléances* were drawn up in French, but commentaries (and also parodies) circulated in Occitan.[45] In Toulouse again, the federated National Guardsmen of the South-west were addressed in *patois* by the constitutional bishop Sermet, in apparent contradiction of the policy of the *abbé* Grégoire.[46] Dugas, editor of *Le Point du Jour*, translated the decrees of the Revolutionary assemblies, in 1791 and 1792, for the *patois*-speakers of the South-west, the Massif Central and the Mediterranean departments.[47] Clearly, one could be a good patriot and republican without speaking French. After all, the republican martyr Viala cried out in *patois* when shot.[48]

The Revolution had to make its decrees intelligible, and sometimes that made it necessary to compromise with linguistic differences, and even with the 'langues' and 'idiomes' that Barère was to identify with the counter-revolution, in Brittany, the Bas-Rhin and Paoli's Corsica. In January 1790 the National Assembly adopted a suggestion to translate its decrees into Flemish and German.[49] A student in Plouagot-Guervaud won his school prize in the Year VI by reciting the Rights of Man in Breton.[50] Grégoire had envisaged the *sociétés populaires* as agents in the spread of the French language, but in Strasbourg at least, the *société* was bilingual.[51] The vigour of Barère's rhetoric should not lead us to ignore the *lack* of fervour with which Revolutionary administrations pursued the policy of linguistic nationalism. Patrice Higonnet has overlooked this, and his insistence on the concept of 'linguistic terrorism' seems to me very inappropriate.[52] The threatening language of Barère's report, it should be remembered, simply culminated in a motion to appoint more Francophone school-teachers. Revolutionary governments did not usually support their rhetoric on this theme with any coercive measures.

Some regional and regionalist historians have sometimes assumed that they did. Mary-Lafon, in 1842, saw the triumph of the

Montagnards over the Girondins as a victory for the North over the true revolutionaries of the Midi.[53] The Midi, and particularly Languedoc, was in fact well represented in the Montagnard Committee of General Security.[54] Armengaud and Lafont's history of Occitania is a more general story of alleged linguistic marginalisation, and ethnocide at the hands of the French state.[55] Jules Ferry is singled out in this account, cast in the role of the matador whose educational reforms delivered the death-blow to independent Occitania. This is also at times a contradictory story: the authors describe protestantism as a 'religion du Midi', and yet Calvinism paradoxically spread through the medium of the French language. If Languedoc experienced the expansion of the French language as foreign domination and oppression, the least one can suggest is that there were plenty of willing collaborators among the local protestant, and generally pro-Revolutionary, bourgeoisie. One was perhaps the school inspector from the Tarn who had lost patience with romantic regionalism and complained in 1856 about 'cette prétendue langue des troubadours, dont on me vante inutilement la richesse, la douceur, la variété des tons et une harmonie qui ne parvient pas jusqu'à moi'.[56]

Instead of lamenting the 'betrayal' of regional cultures by bourgeois elites and their followers, who adopted French and rejected *patois*, we might try to understand the positive choices they were making. They clearly saw advantages for themselves in terms of education and career opportunities, and these rewards perhaps seemed even more worth while in the light of the economic underdevelopment of Brittany or the South-west. If we return to Hélias, we cannot ignore the advice given by his grandfather, a man fluent in French and Breton, a rarity for a nineteenth-century clog-maker. Grandfather warned Pierre-Jakez:

> Avec le français on peut aller partout. Avec le breton seulement, on est attaché de court comme la vache à son pieu. Il faut toujours brouter autour de la longe. Et l'herbe du pré n'est jamais grasse.[57]

The Jacobin thesis, and the argument of Soboul, was that local 'idiomes' were potentially counter-revolutionary, and that the forces of provincialism were manipulated by a counter-revolutionary elite. Yet, recent work on the federalist revolt by Alan Forrest and Bill Edmonds, among others, has done little to bear out this centralist argument.[58] These historians have looked in vain for a genuinely separatist component to the federalism of 1793.

The promotion of the French language was essential to the ideals of national unity, equal access to office and bourgeois leadership. In practice, however, Jacobins were deflected by the power of localism. If they wanted to neutralise clerical influence, then they had to compete for popular attention on the clergy's own terms; like *ancien-régime* preachers, they were obliged to use the languages of their audience.

Patois, finally, did not necessarily threaten or exclude republicanism. Republican ideas frequently borrowed the most traditional means of communication. Republican almanacs and Revolutionary catechisms were just two ways in which popular literary culture could be adapted to carry a revolutionary message. The Second Republic, too, offers many examples of the transformation and politicisation of folk culture in support of republicanism. Maurice Agulhon noted that the radicalisation of the 'Midi rouge' coincided with the apogee of collective celebrations, fêtes and carnivals in Provence in the 1820s and 1830s.[59] Roger Magraw has also argued that these manifestations of popular culture were not archaic remnants of a 'pre-political' era, acting as a barrier to modernity. They could themselves become media of protest, and vehicles of a new political consciousness.[60] French Revolutionary Jacobinism, like any other form of political authority, ignored the pluralism of French culture at its peril.

Notes

*This chapter draws on material previously published in the *Australian Journal of French Studies*, 18 (3) (1981), pp. 264–81.

1   P. J. Hélias, *Le Cheval d'Orgueil: mémoires d'un Breton au pays bigouden*, 2 vols, I, Geneva, 1979, p. 167.

2   *Abbé* Grégoire, *Rapport sur la nécessité et les moyens d'anéantir les patois et d'universaliser l'usage de la langue française*, presented to National Convention, 16 Prairial Year II.

3   F. Brunot, *Histoire de la langue française des origines à 1900*, 10 vols, IX, Paris, 1924–39, p. 598.

4   P. Chaunu, *La Civilisation de l'Europe des Lumières*, Paris, 1971, p. 144.

5   J. Boutier, 'Jacqueries en pays croquant: les révoltes paysannes en Aquitaine (déc. 1789–mars 1790)', *Annales: économies, sociétés, civilisations*, 34 (1979), p. 767.

6   M. de Certeau, D. Julia and J. Revel, *Une politique de la langue: la Révolution française et les patois – l'enquête de Grégoire*, Paris, 1975, pp. 22–30.

7   *Ibid.*, p. 121.

8   A. Gazier (ed.), *Lettres à Grégoire sur les patois de France, 1790–94*, Geneva, 1969 (Slatkine reprint of Paris edn of 1880), pp. 55–6, 111–12 and 201.

9   De Certeau, *Une politique de la langue*, p. 188, Bernadau to Grégoire, Bordeaux, 14 December 1790.

10   Gazier, *Lettres à Grégoire*, p. 166, reply from *Sociéte des Amis de la Constitution* of Limoges, 6 November 1790.

11 *Ibid.*, p. 166.

12 A. Brun, *Recherches historiques sur l'introduction du français dans les provinces du Midi*, Geneva, 1973, p. 473.

13 Cited by F. Braudel, *L'Identité de la France*, I, *Espace et Histoire*, Paris, 1986, p. 74.

14 *Ibid.*, p. 479; M. Agulhon, *La République au Village: les populations du Var de la Révolution à la Seconde République*, Paris, 1970, p. 192 note 8.

15 Gazier, *Lettres à Grégoire*, p. 89, reply from *Amis de la Constitution* of Auch.

16 A. Armengaud and R. Lafont (eds), *Histoire d'Occitanie*, Paris, 1979, p. 571.

17 P. McPhee, 'A case-study of internal colonisation: the *francisation* of Northern Catalonia', *Review*, 3 (1980), p. 403.

18 Gazier, *Lettres à Grégoire*, p. 155.

19 Brunot, *Histoire de la langue française*, VII, p. 267.

20 Brun, *Recherches historiques sur l'introduction du français*, p. 472.

21 Gazier, *Lettres à Grégoire*, p. 203, reply from mayor of St–Claude, 14 September 1790.

22 Y. Castan, 'Les languedociens du 18e siècle et l'obstacle de la langue écrite', *96e Congrès national des sociétés savantes, Toulouse, 1971: section d'histoire moderne et contemporaine*, I, Paris, 1976, pp. 73–84.

23 Gazier, *Lettres à Grégoire*, Bernadau to Grégoire, 14 December 1790.

24 *Ibid.*, p. 53, Chabot to Grégoire, 4 September, 1791, and pp. 119–20, reply from *Amis de la Constitution* of Agen.

25 De Certeau, *Une politique de la langue*, p. 186, Bernadau to Grégoire, Bordeaux, December 1790.

26 Agulhon, *La République au Village*, p. 193 note 10.

27 Gazier, *Lettres à Grégoire*, p. 155.

28 E. LeRoy, *Le Moulin du Frau*, Paris, 1905, p. 147 – a fictional source, but one which is a miniature encyclopaedia of folk culture.

29 N. Richter, *La lecture et ses institutions: la lecture populaire, 1700–1918*, Le Mans, 1987, pp. 53 and 69.

30 P. M. Jones, *Politics and Rural Society: the Southern Massif Central, c. 1750–1880*, Cambridge, 1985, pp. 118–27.

31 Braudel, *L'Identité de la France*, I.

32 De Certeau, *Une politique de la langue*, p. 162.

33 Brunot, *Histoire de la langue française*, VIII, p. 417.

34 M. Reinhard, 'Nostalgie et service militaire pendant la Révolution', *Annales historiques de la Révolution française*, 150 (1958), pp. 1–15.

35 De Certeau, *Une politique de la langue*, pp. 270–2.

36 Cited by Braudel, *L'Identité de la France*, I, p. 81.

37 B. Barère, speech to National Convention, 8 Pluviôse Year II, *Le Moniteur Unversel (ré-impression de l'ancien Moniteur)*, 32 vols, XIX, Paris, 1861, pp. 317–20.

38 Brunot, *Histoire de la langue française*, IX, p. 79.

39 De Certeau, *Une politique de la langue*, p. 207, Fonvielhe to Grégoire.

40 *Moniteur*, XIX, pp. 317–20.

41 Brunot, *Histoire de la langue française* IX, p. 133.

42 *Moniteur*, XXI, p. 273, speech to Convention on 4 Thermidor Year II.

43 T. Tackett, *Religion, Revolution, and Regional Culture in 18th Century France: the Ecclesiastical Oath of 1791*, Princeton, 1986, pp. 201–2.

44 P. Butel and G. Mandon, 'Alphabétisation et scolarisation en Aquitaine au 18e siècle et au début du 19e siècle', in F. Furet and J. Ozouf (eds), *Lire et Ecrire: l'alphabétisation des Français de Calvin à Jules Ferry*, 2 vols, II, Paris, 1977, pp. 32–3.

45   J. Godechot and J.–B. Palustran, 'Discussions en occitan sur les doléances de Toulouse en 1789', *Annales du Midi*, XCIV (1982), pp. 301–18. There was also at least one Catalan *cahier* (J. N. Farreras and P. Wolff, *Histoire de la Catalogne*, Toulouse, 1982, p. 536).

46   Brunot, *Histoire de la langue française*, IX, pp. 56–7.

47   Archives Nationales AA 32.

48   Brunot, *Histoire de la langue française* IX, p. 258.

49   *Moniteur*, III, p. 132.

50   Furet and Ozouf, *Livre et Ecrire*, I, pp. 336–7.

51   Brunot, *Histoire de la langue française*, IX, p. 67.

52   P. Higonnet, 'The politics of linguistic terrorism and grammatical hegemony during the French Revolution', *Social History*, V (1980), pp. 41–69.

53   Mary-Lafon, *Histoire politique, religieuse et littéraire du Midi de la France*, Paris, 1842.

54   M. Eude, 'Les députés méridionaux membres des comités de gouvernement en 1793–1794', *96e Congrès national, etc.*, pp. 113–24.

55   Armengaud and Lafont, *Histoire d'Occitanie*, see Chs 5 and 6.

56   *Ibid.*, pp. 777–8.

57   Hélias, *Le Cheval d'Orgueil*, p. 221; Emmanuel Le Roy Ladurie, 'Occitania in historical perspective', *Review*, 1 (1977), pp. 21–30.

58   A. Forrest, 'Le mouvement fédéraliste dans le Midi de la France: réaction anti-jacobine ou croisade méridionale?', *Provence historique*, XXXVI (1987), pp. 183–92.

59   Agulhon, *La République au Village*.

60   R. Magraw, *France 1815–1914: the Bourgeois Century*, London, 1987, pp. 146–8.

The provincial press in the French Revolution

Recent trends in the historiography of the French Revolution have laid great stress on the role of political culture and ideology in creating its dynamism. Whatever the strengths and weaknesses of such an approach, it does serve to draw attention to the mechanisms of political communication. The printed word was one of these mechanisms, and political journalism one of its principal components. Newspapers played a significant role in the dissemination of ideas and of information throughout the Revolution, and while that role has been extensively studied at the Parisian end, much less is known about its workings in the provinces. This chapter therefore sets out to explore some aspects of the provincial press during the Revolution. In particular, it attempts to examine its size and geographical distribution; the factors that encouraged and facilitated its growth; and the kind of people who became Revolutionary journalists.

There is no national inventory of the provincial press during the Revolution. However, my own research suggests that just under 600 provincial newspapers were published between 1789 and 1799. This is an aggregate figure which includes titles that went no further than their prospectus, as well as those which lasted for several years or the whole decade. On the other hand, it omits those which were mere name changes for existing newspapers, unless that name change came as a result of new ownership, or a distinctive alteration of format or of editorial policy. The total of almost 600 contrasts with almost 2,000 titles published in Paris over the same period.[1] Unlike the heyday of the provincial press during the Third Republic, therefore, Paris still dominated newspaper production during the Revolution. Yet it nevertheless represents a sharp growth over the levels of the *ancien régime*. At the beginning of 1789 there were some forty-three newspapers in provincial France, the vast majority of them devoted largely to advertisements and literature and launched since the mid-eighteenth century.[2] During the course of 1789, as Figure 1 shows, some forty-five new titles appeared; over ninety were launched in 1790, forty-eight in 1791, sixty-two in 1792, sixty-eight in 1793, and so on. The rhythm of new titles appears to correspond to the ebb and flow of political life. So the peak years were 1790, when the new departmental and municipal administrations were being put into place: 1792, which saw the outbreak of war and surge of popular radicalism: 1793, which was marked by the federalist crisis and the beginnings of the Terror: and 1797, when the spring elections and the Fructidor *coup* were crisis points in the political life of the Directory.

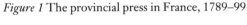

Figure 1 The provincial press in France, 1789–99

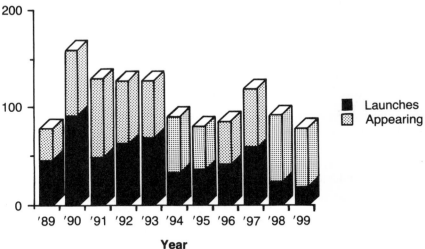

The number of new titles is only part of the story, however. Of equal interest is the number of provincial newspapers appearing in any one year, a figure which combines that year's launches with newspapers still in production from previous years. Here, again, the figures are given in

Figure 1, and they reinforce the view that the first four years of the Revolution (1790–93), along with the crucial year of 1797, were the years of peak production. These were the only years when the number of newspapers appearing exceeded 100. Conversely, apart from 1797, the Directory saw fewer newspapers in circulation, even before the police controls installed by the Fructidor *coup d'état* became effective. Political and economic factors probably explain this decline. The experience of the Terror, when several provincial journalists had been arrested or guillotined, certainly reminded the others that liberty might be less eternal than political rhetoric suggested. Profits were, too, for many of the titles launched earlier in the Revolution had closed down after failing to attract sufficient sales. The optimism of the early years had faded and prudence had become the order of the day.

These figures suggest that there were approximately 100 newspapers appearing every year in provincial France, or an average of one per department. However, the average distorts the true picture as some departments inevitably produced more than others. Sixteen departments had more than ten titles: ten of these were in the North (Calvados, Loire-Inférieure, Maine-et-Loire, Marne, Meurthe, Moselle, Nord, Bas-Rhin, Sarthe and Seine-Inférieure) and six of them in the South (Bouches-du-Rhône, Haute-Garonne, Gironde, Isère, Rhône and Vaucluse). All sixteen were departments with the strong urban base, the economic infrastructure of printshops and postal services, the active political life and the sizeable readership necessary for successful journalism. All of them, significantly enough, had already produced journals under the *ancien régime*. Several departments, on the other hand, produced no newspapers at all during the Revolution. They tended to be remote and sparsely populated ones with low levels of urbanisation and poor communications: the Aude, for example, the Lozère and the Haute-Marne. There are exceptions to this, for the Var had no newspaper despite the size of Toulon, with close to 20,000 inhabitants. Nîmes too, with some 40,000 inhabitants, produced only a handful of short-lived titles; while Avignon, which had a thriving press between 1789 and 1794, had no newspaper at all after 1795. Nevertheless, the overall picture of production reveals a pattern similar to that of the map of literacy in eighteenth-century France, with distinct areas of weakness in the Massif Central, the South-west and much of the western coastal region.[3]

But these production figures need to be analysed more closely for they overstate the size of the provincial press. In sheer numbers the departments of the Gironde, the Rhône and the Seine-Inférieure produced the most newspapers, chiefly because of the size and regional importance of Bordeaux, Lyon and Rouen, respectively. In Bordeaux there were at least fifty-seven newspapers between 1789 and 1799, including well-organised and durable dailies such as the *Journal patriotique et de commerce*, the *Journal de Bordeaux* and the *Courrier de la Gironde*. Yet, of that total of fifty-seven titles, only one-third lasted for more than a month, and only twelve survived for longer than a year. Moreover, of those twelve, only eight were political newspapers; two more were medical journals and two exclusively commercial.[4] In Lyon there were approximately forty-one titles during the Revolution, and again they included important journals such as the *Journal de Lyon* of Mathon de la Cour and the *Moniteur du département de Rhône-et-Loire* of Prudhomme and Carrier. Yet only eight lasted more than a year: moreover, two of these were *ancien régime* journals that had continued production during the Revolution, and two others were medical journals with no political content at all. Of the remaining thirty-three, over a half appear not to have progressed beyond the prospectus stage, or their first edition, while two-thirds lasted for less than a month.[5] To complete the picture with Rouen, here nine out of at least thirty-one newspapers remained in production for more than a year, a tribute to Norman stability. Yet, once again, over two-thirds collapsed within a year of their launch.[6]

High numbers, therefore, often conceal the fact that only a small percentage of newspapers managed to find a foothold in the market. Not all of them were intended to, for, as in Paris, many were published as speculative ventures, or were brochures masquerading under the form of a journal. This means that the number of reasonably durable newspapers appearing in a city at any one time, namely those which lasted for more than a year, rarely exceeded three or four. Lyon, for example, supported three newspapers at any one time between 1789 and 1792: the apolitical *Affiches de Lyon* and the conservative *Journal de Lyon* remained in production for all three years, rivalled successively by the *Courrier de Lyon* (September 1789–February 1791) and the *Moniteur du département de Rhône-et-Loire* (April 1791–August 1793). After the closure of the *Journal de Lyon* in July 1792, the *Moniteur* provided continuity until its discredit with federalism in the spring of 1793. The Terror saw a very ephemeral semi-official press, sponsored by the representatives on mission, but after Thermidor only two durable journals existed. The first was the *Journal de Lyon*, edited by Alexandre-Michel Pelzin, which lasted from February 1795 until September 1797 when it was banned at the time of the Fructidor *coup*. The second, *le Petit Tachygraphe*, then took over its conservative role, in a more muted form. From the autumn of 1792 onwards, therefore, only one stable journal flourished in Lyon at any one time. Political factors certainly played a part in this, for, although there was a sufficient radical audience to sustain the locally produced *Courrier de Lyon* and the *Moniteur* before the summer of 1792, the *Moniteur* subsequently trimmed its sails to a more moderate course during the winter of 1792–93 because that audience diminished rapidly. After the trauma of the Terror the city was too small to sustain a radical newspaper at all. Lyonnais Jacobins still appear to have read the Parisian radical press, but their own local press was conservative.[7]

Marseille is a city where one newspaper, the *Journal de Marseille*, dominated the market, except during the Terror, when it was forced to suspend publication, and after the Fructidor *coup*, when it was closed down altogether. Its only rivals were short-lived Jacobin papers, some supported by the club, others by representatives on mission, none of which was able to last as long as a year.[8] Yet at the other end of the country Rouen was able to sustain a much larger number, probably helped by proximity to the capital, which enabled its papers to provide accounts of National Assembly debates for local readers well ahead of the Paris press. From late 1789 onwards it usually had three, and often four, newspapers at any one time – all of them dailies and all conservative except for the republican *Vedette Normande* during the Directory.[9] Bordeaux, too, had at least three papers running concurrently for much of the decade, and during 1796–97 was able to support five. Strasbourg often had three, too, helped by sales of its predominantly German-language press to the other side of the Rhine.[10]

If large cities could support only a handful of durable titles, what of the smaller towns? Here, too, the picture is variable. In many of them, elevated to the status of a departmental *chef-lieu* by the Revolution, newspapers proved short lived, probably for financial reasons. In Guéret, for example, the *Journal de la Creuse* lasted only six months: in Tulle, the *Journal du département de la Corrèze* probably lasted no longer: neither did the *Feuille hebdomadaire de Lorient* in the Morbihan nor the *Journal de Seine-et-Marne* in Melun. Yet there were exceptions: La Flèche, a small town in the Sarthe with a population of some 7,000, was one – the *Affiches de la Flèche*, launched in January 1790, was to last for almost two years.[11] Angers was another, with at least three news-papers vying with each other between 1789 and 1792, and two during the Directory between 1795 and 1798. Yet here the longest lasting newspaper of the Revolution was the *Affiches d'Angers*, owned by the wealthy printer Mame, which certainly covered political affairs but concentrated mainly on commercial information and advertisements.[12] This survival of the *ancien régime Affiches* was typical of what occurred in many other medium-sized cities. Some survived by ignoring politics almost completely – the *Affiches du Maine* is an example – while others covered political news but were careful to reduce their coverage when issues became contentious. The few which became heavily involved in the politics of the Revolution suffered as a result: Giroud *fils* in Grenoble was forced to close down in the summer of 1792: Pipaud Desgranges in Périgueux was executed during the autumn of 1794; Broulhiet in Toulouse and Beaugeard in Marseille were forced into hiding after the Fructidor *coup*. If the economics of provincial jour-nalism were difficult during the Revolution, the politics were too.

Despite these difficulties, a new political press did emerge in prov-incial France in the years after 1789 and several factors encouraged its growth. Legal changes, with the abolition of the necessity for prior permission and censorship, were important. Some legal control on press activity remained after 1789, for charges of libel or sedition could always be brought before the courts by individuals or administrative authorities. During the Terror legislation forbidding support for the monarchy and the Law of Suspects of September 1793 led to the arrest and execution of many journalists and after the Fructidor *coup* in 1797 the Directory was also empowered to ban any title which it considered a threat to political stability. Yet during both these periods, the number of journalists affected was quite slight and many were able to escape arrest and prosecution. Attempts to pass an effective press law, made repeatedly from 1791 onwards, also ended in relative failure because of the reluctance of juries to convict, so that for almost the entire ten years there were few legal distincentives for anyone wishing to take up journalism.[13]

A second factor in the growth of the provincial press was the politicisation of daily life created by the Revolution. Freedom to publish coincided with a flood of political news, argument and commentary which provided editors with ample copy. The provincial press in particular benefited from the administrative reforms of 1790 which replaced the old provinces with departments, districts and municipalities. Dozens of newspapers sprang up to cater for the needs of these new administrative units, just as the *Affiches* had tried to forge a collective identity for the pre-Revolutionary provinces.[14] As a result, provincial newspapers now provided their readers, not just with the national news featured by the Parisian press, nor merely with the commercial and literary information covered by the *ancien régime* *Affiches*, but with local news as well, including the decisions of local administrations, the debates of Jacobin clubs and the decisions of local courts. They also drew readers into political debate through the publication of their letters and – in some cases – by running question-and-answer columns on the details and implications of new legislation.[14] This politicisation of local life brought divisions, too, which benefited the press as rival newspapers were launched to defend conflicting viewpoints. In Grenoble the *monarchien* views of the *Affiches du Dauphiné* prompted the launch of the *Vedette patriotique*; in Caen the conservatism of the *Affiches de la Basse-Normandie* encouraged the appearance of the *Courrier des Cinq Jours*; in Limoges the *Extrait des journaux patriotes* was a reply to the *Feuille hebdomadaire*. This kind of press war was common from 1789 onwards, but became particularly significant during the Directory, when conservative and neo-Jacobin titles vied for influence in several towns, from Marseille to Angers and Périgueux to Le Mans.[15]

If legal changes and politicisation were both important stimuli to the growth of the provincial press, so, too, were changes in the printing trade. The Parisian printing trade has recently found its historian: provincial printers as a group have not, and yet their part in the growth of the press throughout the country was fundamental.[16] It was less a question of technical innovations – for there were none in printing techniques until the early years of the nineteenth century – than of a rapid expansion in size, caused by the abolition of controls and the massive demand for the printed word. The French Revolution generated printed paper on a staggering scale, and newspapers were far from being the only beneficiary of this demand, for brochures, pamphlets and posters were produced in great numbers, too. There was a rapid growth in administrative printing in particular, generated by the needs of administrative authorities and of political clubs to transmit legal changes and political propaganda. This had two effects on the newspaper press. In some cases printers rapidly found themselves overburdened with work, or else found that administrative work was more profitable, and consequently withdrew from journalism. In Agen, for example, Raymond Noubel closed down his *Journal patriotique de l'Agenais* in the spring of 1792 after the departure of some of his printing workers as army volunteers because official contracts from the departmental administration, worth 20,000 *francs* per year, provided more profitable business. In Rouen, too, the three established printers who went into newspaper publishing in 1789 had all withdrawn three years later, attracted by the better profits available elsewhere. And the profits could be large, for the departmental administration alone paid out 219, 119 *livres* on printing in the five months between mid-October 1791 and late March 1793.[17]

On the other hand, the abolition of controls on the printing trade also meant that anyone could now set up a printshop, and many were indeed established to meet the expanding demand. In Le Mans, for example, the number of printing establishments trebled between 1789 and 1799; in Montpellier it doubled. In the department of the Nord five towns possessed a total of twelve printshops in 1789: by the end of the decade seven towns owned twenty-eight. In the Deux-Sèvres, Niort had a single printshop in 1789; ten years later it had three, and five other towns in the department had one too. A recent study of six departments in the West of France shows that the number of towns there with printers increased from three to twenty-one.[18] Similar examples could be drawn from many other parts of France, but the essential importance of it was that, while journalism was very rarely the cause of a new printshop, it was often one of its results, as printers sought to maximise their output and to use their presses at off-peak hours. In 1799 the printer Duval, writing to the Ministry of Police from Rouen, argued that he had recently purchased a press and 'to put it to work I resolved to print a newspaper, with myself as publisher and editor'. His case is just one of many.[19]

So much for the newspapers themselves, but they needed journalists to produce them. Any analysis of their backgrounds and motives is, however, a potentially enormous subject which permits of few easy answers because of the numbers involved and the variety, or obscurity, of many of their careers. Only a broad picture can therefore be drawn. From the outset, several were literary figures or printers who had worked as editors and owners of provincial newspapers before 1789 and proved well capable of adapting to political journalism. They include controversial figures such as Sabin Tournal in Avignon, Ferréol Beaugeard in Marseille, Jean-Baptiste Broulhiet in Toulouse and Paris de

Lespinard in Lille. However, as in Paris, the great majority of journalists were new to the business. A great many of them came, naturally enough, from the world of letters, and had been authors or teachers before the Revolution. There is little evidence in provincial journalism of the Grub Street style analysed so brilliantly for Paris by Robert Darnton, as most provincial towns had too restricted an intellectual life to cater for a literary underground of any size.[20] Paris was the centre of publishing and patronage before 1789 and the undisputed mecca for the ambitious provincial writer. Nevertheless, most towns of any size had some kind of literary group, whether an academy, a college, a school, a private salon, masonic club or simple *cabinet de lecture*, and most of them attracted minor writers or poets, local historians and agronomists, several of whom switched their talent to journalism when the opportunity arose. They included men such as Pierre Chantreau in Auch, Du Planier de La Sablière in Guéret, Pagès Vixouse in Aurillac, Pierre Bernadau in Bordeaux and Noel de la Morinière in Rouen.[21]

Many newly established printers also became involved, as much out of political commitment as commercial interest. In Libourne, for example, Joseph Puynesge launched the *Sentinelle du district de Libourne* in September 1792. In Niort, Louis Averti, the son of a merchant from La Flèche, opened a bookshop in 1790, bought himself a press and launched the *Journal des Deux-Sèvres* the following year. By this date he had already founded the town's Jacobin club and, under the adopted name of Brutus, was to play an important political role during the Terror.[22] In the town of Vire in the Calvados, Jacques Malo was a former *frère questeur* in the Cordeliers order who returned to lay life in 1790 and in association with a local surgeon founded the Société typographique de Vire. In January 1791 they launched the *Courrier des Campagnes*.[23] Other printer-journalists included Tubeuf in Beauvais, Bazin in Le Mans, Jahyer in Angers and Treuttel in Strasbourg.

Catholic priests were frequently journalists, too, most notably the constitutional priests of the early years of the Revolution, many of whom were politically active. Euloge Schneider owned and edited the German-language *Argos* in Strasbourg in 1792–93, and his clerical colleague Jean-Jacques Kaemmerer produced the *Rheinische Chronik*. The *abbé* Laussel was responsible for a string of short-lived publications in Lyons between 1791 and 1793; the *abbé* Jumel edited a local version of the *Père Duchesne* in Tulle; while in Besançon the Lazarist priest Claude Ignace Dormoy launched and controlled the highly influential

Vedette.[24] During the Directory professors in the *écoles centrales*, the new lay 'churches' of the Revolution, played a similar role. In towns such as Châlons-sur-Marne, Nevers, Bordeaux, Grenoble and Angers, the editors of republican and neo-Jacobin journals were almost all drawn from their ranks. Other lay professions also featured prominently, including doctors, such as Benjamin Bablot in Châlons-sur-Marne; lawyers, such as Jean-Joseph Lagarde in Lille or the irrepressible François Robert in Fécamp and Rouen: engineers, such as Du Planier de la Sablière in Guéret: and Lutheran pastors, such as Jean Ehrmann in Strasbourg.[25]

No doubt one day there will be sufficient biographical information on provincial journalists to construct a prosopographical study of their social backgrounds. Yet it may not be worth the effort, for they will certainly emerge as being from predominantly bourgeois and petit bourgeois backgrounds. Three other characteristics of journalists are, however, worth noting. The first is that provincial journalism was almost exclusively a male occupation. Not entirely so, for some women were involved as printers or publishers, and after the Fructidor *coup* wives such as Angélique Lefebvre in Rouen or Françoise Lawalle in Bordeaux played an important role in keeping their husbands' newspapers afloat while they were in hiding, avoiding arrest.[26] Nevertheless, they were exceptions, and there is no example, to my knowledge, of a provincial paper which was launched and controlled by a woman. A second characteristic is that provincial journalists enjoyed a great deal of geographical mobility. Half the journalists in the Nord were born outside the department; in Normandy the proportion was closer to a third; while in the Mayenne, where admittedly the numbers were small, the only journalists were outsiders.[27] Similar proportions can be found in cities such as Marseille or Lyon, where during the Terror journalists were mainly Parisians brought in by the representative on mission to educate the recalcitrant local population, and they reflect both the demographic importance of urban migration in eighteenth-century France, and the role that journalism could play in providing outsiders with a path to political influence.

One final feature – and this applies to Paris as much as to the provinces – is that journalism was as often a group activity as the work of a lone writer. Certainly, there were many individualists, such as Ferréol Beaugeard in Marseille or Joseph Paris de Lespinard in Lille; yet they were more than counterbalanced by the teamwork involved in many other newspapers, often indicated by the terms 'par une société d'hommes de lettres' or 'par une société d'hommes de loi' in a journal's title. Jean-Charles Laveaux, for example, was editor of the *Courrier de Strasbourg*, but he had editorial assistants, and a four-man team appointed by the city's Jacobin club took over the paper while he was away on business in Paris. In Marseille most of the Jacobin newspapers that appeared between 1790 and 1798 were team efforts, as were several of the Jacobin journals of the Directory, such as the *Chronique de la Sarthe* in Le Mans or the *Ami des Principes* in Angers. Provincial journalism was as much a social as a solitary activity, frequently linked to the activity of political groups or clubs, and it was this wider involvement which gave it much of its strength.[28]

The provincial press could never rival the Parisian press as a source for national news, nor could it enjoy the same national circulation and influence. Its readership was predominantly local, restricted often to the town or city where it was published, or more frequently to the wider ranges of a department or province. Yet these limitations were also its strength, for it was able to provide coverage of local news and political activity in a way that the Parisian press could not, and integrate this news and opinion into a national pattern. Thus, it became an integral part of political life until the Fructidor *coup* gave the government powers of censorship which enabled it to eliminate independent political comment completely. Anaesthetised by the Fructidor *coup*, then entombed by Napoleonic authoritarianism, the political role of the provincial press was to re-emerge only during the July Monarchy. Yet its first faltering steps after 1789 had made an important contribution to the political life of the Revolution.

Notes

1   A. Martin and G. Walter, *Catalogue de l'histoire de la Révolution française, tome V: Ecrits de la période révolutionnaire. Journaux et almanacs*, Paris, 1943; see the diagram produced from the data in this volume in C. Bellanger, J. Godechot *et al.* (eds), *Histoire générale de la presse française, tome I: Des origines à 1814*, Paris, 1969, p. 436.
2   G. Feyel, 'La presse provinciale au XVIIIe siècle: géographie d'un réseau', *Revue historique*, CCLXXII (1984), p. 359. Feyel lists forty-four journals, but includes the *Journal de Besançon* which had ceased publication by 1789 (see M. Vogne, *La presse périodique en Franche-Comté des origines à 1870*, I, Besançon, 1977–78, pp. 25–6).
3   D. Julia (ed.), *Atlas de la Révolution française, tome II: l'enseignement 1760–1815*, Paris, 1987, pp. 12 and 30; F. Furet, *Lire et écrire, l'alphabétisation des Français de Calvin à Jules Ferry*, Paris, 1977, Ch. 1.
4   *Journal de santé et d'histoire naturelle*, 20 pluviôse V–6 messidor VI: *Journal des*

mères de famille, January 1797–December 1798; *Journal maritime des opérations commerciales*, floréal III–vendémiaire VIII; *l'Echo du commerce*, December 1797–March 1811. Although old, the most reliable inventory of Bordeaux newspapers remains that of E. Labadie, *La presse à Bordeaux pendant la Révolution*, Bordeaux, 1910.

5   M. Loche, 'Journaux imprimés à Lyon 1633–1794', *Bulletin de la société archéologique, historique et critique. Le Vieux Papier*, 29, (1968), pp. 10–28.

6   E. Wauters, 'La presse à Rouen pendant la Revolution (1789–1800)', *Mémoire de DEA, Université de Rouen*, June 1988.

7   L. Trénard, *Lyon de l'Encyclopédie au préromantisme*, 2 vols, Paris, 1958, *passim*; M. Fajn, 'The circulation of the French press during the French Revolution: the case of R. F. Lebois. L'Ami du peuple and the royalist Gazette française', *English Historical Review*, LXXXVII (1972), pp. 100–5.

8   For information on some of these, see M. Kennedy, 'Some journals of the Jacobin club of Marseille, 1790–1794', *French Historical Studies*, VII, 1972, pp. 607–12; *Les Bouches-du-Rhône. Encyclopédie départementale*, tome VI, Marseille, 1914, pp. 550ff.

9   Wauters, 'La presse à Rouen', p. 8.

10   For the sales of Strasbourg newspapers into Germany, see *Archives municipales de Strasbourg, Registre du corps municipal*, 18 July 1791, 23 September 1791, 3 November 1791, 17 October 1792.

11   C. Peyrard, 'Le journalisme politique dans l'Ouest en Révolution', *History of European Ideas*, vol. 10, no. 4 (1989), p. 461.

12   E. Queruau-Lamerie, 'Notice sur les journaux d'Angers pendant la Révolution', *Revue de l'Anjou*, new series, XXIV (1892), pp. 113–56.

13   M. Lanfranci, *Le régime de presse sous la Revolution*, Paris, 1908.

14   For a good example of the use of readers' letters, see *Journal du département de Maine et Loire, par les amis de la constitution d'Angers*, Bibliothèque municipale d'Angers, H5427.

15   H. Gough, 'The provincial Jacobin press during the Directory', *History of European Ideas*, x (1989), pp. 443–54.

16   C. Hesse, 'Res Publicata: the Printed Word in Paris, 1789–1810', Ph.D. thesis, Princeton University, 1986; see also C. Hesse. 'Economic upheavals of publishing', in R. Darnton and D. Roche (eds), *Revolution in Print. The Press in France 1775–1800* Berkeley, 1988, pp. 69–97.

17   R. Marquant, *Aux origines de la presse agenaise: le 'Journal patriotique de l'Agenais', (1789–1792)*. Agen. n.d. [1947], p. 43; Wauters, 'La presse à Rouen', pp. 15–16, 25. For the surge in official printing, see A. Patrick. 'Papers, posters and people: official communications in France, 1789–1794', *Historical Studies*, XVIII (1978), pp. 1–23.

18   Peyrard, 'Le journalisme politique', pp. 456–7; R. Andréani, 'Jalons pour une approche de la presse de la France méridionale à l'époque révolutionnaire', *History of European Ideas*, vol. 10, no. 4 (1989), p. 474; X. Maeght, 'La presse dans le département du Nord sous la révolution française (1789–1799)', Ph.D. thesis, University of Lille, 1971, pp. 12–17; H. Clouzot, *Notes pour servir à l'histoire de l'imprimerie à Niort et dans les Deux-Sèvres*, Niort, 1891, pp. 120–3.

19   Archives Nationales F^7 3451, letter of 10 pluviôse VIII.

20   R. Darnton, 'The high Enlightenment and the low life of literature in pre-Revolutionary France', *Past and Present*, LI (1971), pp. 81–115.

21   For Bernadau, see M. Lhéritier, *Les débuts de la Révolution à Bordeaux d'après les tablettes manuscrites de Pierre Bernadau*, Paris, 1919, intro.; for Chantreau, G. Brégail, 'Un apôtre jacobin, Pierre-Nicolas Chantreau. Professeur, journaliste, agent secret (1746–1808)', *Bulletin de la société archéologique du Gers*, XXIV (1923), pp. 213–34; for

Noel de la Morinière, see Wauters, 'La presse à Rouen', pp. 26–9.

22   Clouzot, *Notes*, pp. 118–20.

23   Peyrard, 'Le journalisme politique, p. 465'.

24   R. Jaquel, 'Euloge Schneider an Alsace', *Annales historiques de la Révolution française*, IX (1932), pp. 21–7; E. Barth, 'Notes biographiques', *Revue d'Alsace*. 2nd series, XXXI (1880), pp. 270–2; W. Edmonds, 'A Jacobin débâcle: the losing of Lyons in spring 1793'. *History*, LXIX (1984), pp. 2–3; F. Braesch, *Le Père Duchesne d'Hébert. Réimpression avec notes*, Paris, 1922–38, p. 57; C. Fohlen, *Histoire de Besançon*, II Paris, 1965, pp. 261–2.

25   G. Clause, 'Le journalisme à Châlons-sur-Marne en 1790 et 1791', *Mémoires de la société d'agriculture, commerce, sciences et arts du département de la Marne*, LXXXIX (1974) pp. 291–4; Maeght, *La presse dans le département du Nord*, pp. 132–9; Wauters, 'La presse à Rouen', pp. 94ff.; J. Levron, *La presse creusoise au XIXe siècle*, Limoges, 1931, pp. 9–10; E. Barth, 'Notes biographiques', *Revue d'Alsace*, 2nd series, XXVIII (1877), p. 267.

26   H. Gough, *The Newspaper Press in the French Revolution*, London, 1988, pp. 145–8.

27   Peyrard, 'Le journalisme politique', *passim*; A. Angot, *Dictionnaire historique, topographique et biographique de la Mayenne*, 3 vols, Mayenne, 1975.

28   *Courrier de Strasbourg*, 6 June 1792, p. 525, 13 July p. 656; M. Kennedy, 'Some journals', pp. 607–11; M. Reinhard, *Le département de la Sarthe sous le régime directorial*, St Brieuc, 1935, pp. 246–7; *Archives municipales d'Angers, Registre des délibérations de la municipalité d'Angers, 2e jour sans-culottide, an V*; Queruau-Lamerie, 'Notice sur les journaux d'Angers pendant la Révolution', *Revue de l'Anjou*, new series, XXIV (1892), pp. 304–12.

The Revolutionary and royalist traditions in southern village society: the Vaucluse Comtadin, 1789–1851

The debate about the rate and degree of political awakening in village society during the nineteenth century has been raging for many years now. Whilst the political intelligence and sophistication of urban society has been taken very much for granted, French country dwellers appeared in many studies to have languished in naivety and backwardness for several decades longer than the average town dweller. Some commentators, like Eugen Weber, have found little evidence of political awareness until the 1870s.[1] However, more recently consensus has focused on the Second Republic as the decisive watershed when rural inhabitants for the first time became aware of their political role in the life of the nation. Ted Margadant has demonstrated that agricultural producers and artisans who had become integrated into national markets were prodded as a result of the crisis of over-production in the late 1840s into an understanding of national politics.[2] Peter McPhee has described how the seeds of republicanism were sown in the Pyrénées-Orientales as a result of a shift to wine monoculture; the peasantry was consequently transformed into a rural proletariat receptive to the advanced ideas of the towns.[3] The radicalism exhibited during the insurrection of December 1851 has been pointed to as palpable proof of this discovery of rural political consciousness.

None the less, in the majority of nineteenth-century studies to date, the Revolutionary era of the 1790s counts for little, and the Restoration and July Monarchy have come to be regarded as dark ages of rural

political inactivity. The importance of Revolutionary political traditions is considered negligible, and any factional allegiances to which the
peasantry may have succumbed during the First Republic were, it is
claimed, totally erased. Such is the belief of Maurice Agulhon, who
detects 'une véritable conversion' amongst the peasantry of the Var
from royalist conformity in 1815 to red radicalism by 1851.[4] Before the
gradual slide into electoral democracy after 1830, peasants appear to
have been lost in a timeless universe of political sterility governed only
by the monotonous routine of changing moons, tides and seasons. Was
the Revolution of 1789 really, as Eugen Weber has claimed, 'a magnificent irrelevance', affecting only the towns and 'passing above the
villages, hamlets and farms without affecting economic life and the
everyday routine of life'?[5] It is the intention of this chapter to cast light
on to the rural shadows of the early nineteenth century and to question
such assumptions. By taking the example of the Comtat Venaissin,
which roughly formed the western half of the department of the
Vaucluse, I should like to point to the continued existence of Revolutionary affiliations as the principal determinant of political options in
the French countryside during the period 1789 to 1851.

The Comtat Venaissin had an unfortunate and gory Revolutionary
experience.[6] Rivalry between the two papal capitals of Avignon and
Carpentras led to bitter confrontations over annexation, culminating in
civil war in April 1791. The excesses of the *braves brigands d'Avignon* led
by the notorious Jourdan *Coupe-Tête* alienated the vast majority of
Comtadins; in the majority of villages Patriot extremists clashed violently with local people who were regarded as counter-revolutionary
aristocrates. In 1793 the 'aristocratic' groups sided wholeheartedly with
the Marseille sections as a means of removing the depised Patriot
extremists. This allegedly counter-revolutionary stance was decisively
punished in the Year II. Mass executions became the order of the day in
Messidor and Thermidor; more than 300 Comtadins were guillotined
after having faced the Commission Populaire at Orange. Some villages
lost as many as forty inhabitants, whilst the roving commission which
visited Bédoin in Prairial executed sixty-three inhabitants and ordered
the destruction of the commune. Not surprisingly the Counter-Terror
of the Directory was particularly bloody in the region. The bands of
Pastour (based at Lagnes near L'Isle) and St Christol (based at St
Paul-Trois-Châteaux in the Drôme), embarked on co-ordinated plans
of revenge which claimed at least ninety victims. If more remote
communes in the Ventoux foothills were almost entirely purged of

republicans, small groups continued to maintain a tenuous foothold in the villages of the Comtat plain. The nineteenth century was to witness the never-weakening confrontation between the conservative majorities and the republican minorities of this rural society.

The first symptoms of political continuity become poignantly apparent during the flashpoint of violence in 1815.[7] In the Comtat, Napoleon's Hundred-Day regime was supported by precisely the same men who had implemented the Terror in the Year II. For instance, Bonapartist *fédérés* who reared their ugly heads in the village of Courthézon included the Terrorist Michel Louis, described as 'un de nos plus forcenés révolutionnaires', André Gauthier 'dénonciateur à gage' during the Revolution and the appropriately named Marat Bertrand whose father had been assassinated in Floréal Year III. At Malaucène five men arrested in August 1815 included the arch-Terrorist Edouard Bergier, who during the Hundred Days sent a printed address to the Emperor 'où il jure haine à la royauté'. Another leading *fédéré* was Michel Fabre. Arrested in 1815 for 'propos injurieux' against the Bourbon family, he too was a former Terrorist, responsible for smashing statues of saints and for having forced a nun to set a church on fire in Provence. Jean Adam, a captain of a company of *fédérés* in 1815, was accused of being a member of the cannibalistic breed of revolutionary: 'On lui reproche d'avoir été un de ceux qui après avoir assassiné le sieur Vitalis dans le temps du siège de Carpentras, mangèrent sur le gril le foie de la victime.'[8] At Vedène, the disturbances of 1815 were regarded as no more than a continuation of the outrages which the Patriots had committed since the beginning of the Revolutionary era. The supporters of Napoleon were the same men who had previously distinguished themselves in the art of assassination and pillage at Cavaillon, Sarrians, L'Isle, and at the Château d'Aiguille in Vedène itself. It was reported that 'une sorte de terreur règne encore dans cette commune pour nous tous qui depuis vingt-cinq ans avons tout souffert – de persécution, d'outrage et de perte de bien – et qui n'avons échappé à la mort que par une espèce de miracle.'[9]

Many of the supporters of the Emperor had scarcely moderated their bloodthirsty views since Robespierre's day. Throughout the department it was reported that 'les chansons d'alors et les mêmes injures qu'on se permettait en 1793' had been heard on many occasions; in Lapalud, for instance, a hardened Terrorist threatened the mayor, saying that 'il voulait tuer douze royalistes avant de se coucher'.[10] In Caderousse the 'hommes de sang' who supported Napoleon uttered 'propos révoltants', such as 'A bas les royalistes, il faut leur couper le col, on n'avait pas encore répandu assez de sang.'[11] In Gadagne the 'patriotes de quatre-vingt-neuf' urged people to support Napoleon, holding out promises of land acquisition which would follow the imminent sequestration of royalist property. One Patriot appeared determined to mete out to Gadagne the fate which Bédoin had suffered in the Year II: 'Gadagne ne renfermait que de jean foutre de royalistes et que s'il était Empereur il ordonnerait d'y mettre le feu.'[12] The Hundred Days revealed that extreme republicanism had survived the Counter-Terror in certain communes of the Vaucluse, and demonstrated that, even after a period of quiescence, Terrorists could suddenly reassert themselves and maybe even implement the policies of the Year II which they so obviously still worshipped. Henceforth, the conservative majorities of the Comtat remained on their guard against the awful possibility of a resurrection of Terrorist extremism.

The *faits divers* of the Restoration continued to reflect this obsessive horror of radicalism. Numerous outbursts of sedition (be it songs, shouts, emblems, notices, signs or symbols) were reported to administrators by sensitive villagers. Shouts of 'Merde pour le Roi', 'Vive l'Empéreur' and renditions of 'La Marseillaise' uttered by itinerant travellers, former soldiers and local drunks were enthusiastically denounced by local people and severely dealt with by zealous officials. The courts distributed draconian punishments for crimes of sedition, which normally entailed a three-month prison sentence, a fine and a period of surveillance.[13]

The manœuvres of revolutionaries were carefully supervised. For example, an inhabitant of Bollène who had professed 'principes dangereux' since 1791 was monitored by police, despite the fact that he lived a quiet life 'en marge de la société'.[14] A man who had recently taken up residence in Cairanne similarly received the authorities' attentions; his father had been 'un des plus fougueux partisans de l'anarchie que l'interrègne ait produit'.[15] Die-hard republicans who failed to conform to the new order became outcasts, like a former Terrorist of Gadagne who refused to accept a coin bearing the king's head 'car je ne puis voir cette face sans avoir mal au coeur', and an inhabitant of Lapalud who continued to create anxiety with his incessant references to the 'bonnet rouge'.[16]

Restoration authorities clamped down heavily on republican meetings. Cafés, which after the demise of the club movement had become the most obvious location for political activism, were shut down on the slightest suspicion of republicanism. Roubaud of Bédarrides, whose café was reputed to be the meeting-place of 'les partisans de l'anarchie', was one of many proprietors to be forced out of business.[17] Republican meetings in private houses were equally frowned upon, for example in Carpentras, where the arrondissement's hardened republicans were believed to be plotting at the house of Jacques Escoffier. The members of this clique had all been involved in 'l'époque de quatre-vingt-treize et n'ont pas peu contribué au sang qui a coulé sur les échafauds'; their shady past continued to arouse the most intense suspicion.[18] Such fears were increased further following rumours that republicans had armed themselves. The inhabitants of Caumont were quick to protest about such a possibility and denounced thirty-seven republicans as the enemies of the king's government in July 1815: 'La tranquillité de cette commune sera toujours exposée à ête troublée tant que ces personnes auront des armes en leur pouvoir.' In the same way, villagers at Bollène, Courthézon and Carpentras insisted upon the disarmament of revolutionaries, fearing that they might re-attempt to dominate their communes by means of armed force as they had done in 1791–93.[19]

It was not unusual for republican trouble-makers to be expelled from communes as a result of popular protest. A resident of Visan, for instance, who had supported Napoleon during the Hundred Days, was ordered to withdraw to his native Valréas in February 1816.[20] The village of Caromb, which had lost thirty-seven inhabitants at the Commission Populaire d'Orange in the Year II remained understandably jittery about Terrorists. When one of them returned to the village in 1816, protests ensued. It was reported that 'personne n'a dormi tranquille dans la commune tant sa présence a excité d'inquiétude depuis vingt-cinq ans. On le nomme le commandant parce qu'il était toujours à la tête des persécutions exercées contre le pays. Il est soupçonné de toutes sortes de forfaits révolutionnaires, de commissions, de dénonciations, d'avoir contribué à l'assassinat de M. Gaudibert et nombre d'autres délits, dont tout le monde l'avoue, sans pouvoir le prouver.'[21] Gilles, the republican in question, was barred from returning to the village but this did not prevent his twelve-year-old son from being involved in a scuffle with three villagers who were singing 'Vive le Roi'. This incident poignantly reveals both the enduring vivacity of anti-republican paranoia and the way in which Terrorists' politics were frequently adopted by their sons.

Despite all the measures implemented to combat extremism, republican militancy continued to flourish in the rural communes of the

Comtat plain. Courthézon witnessed numerous clashes between the young men of the two opposing factions, despite sporadic truces, like that of March 1816, when they united during the annual carnival to dance a *farandole*.[22] At Bédarrides the royalist rallying-call of 'Vive le Roi' was riposted by taunts of 'Vive le Rat', after which republicans attempted to extinguish bonfires lit in honour of the king by urinating on them.[23] In Caumont, black *fleurs de lys* were affixed to the doors of royalist houses, including those of the mayor and the *adjoint*.[24] In February 1817 a *farandole* was mounted by 'malintentionnés' from Caumont and the neighbouring radical village of Velleron, and in the resultant brawl there was a royalist fatality.[25] Throughout the Comtat plain it was not uncommon for tricolour flags to appear above village fountains during the night, much to the annoyance of the largely royalist population.

The villagers of Sainte Cécile, meanwhile, were split by a dispute over the division of the *garrigues*, a move opposed by the royalist faction of François Saussac. It was Joseph Clément Mauric (of Revolutionary stock) who headed the popular protest against this reactionary decision. Several clashes ensued between 'les amis du roi et ceux de l'ancien gouvernement'.[26] The opposition between the Mauric and Saussac clans, which originated in the Revolution, continued to divide the population of this village under the same political banners. The overall impression is clear. During the Restoration dominantly royalist villagers of the former Comtat continued to clash with republican minorities on the battle-lines inherited from the Revolutionary period.

The arrival of a *roi citoyen* preaching a doctrine of *Union et Oubli* seemed to hail an era of conciliation in July 1830. Such hopes remained unfulfilled in the department of the Vaucluse where the Orleanist years were characterised by a hardening of rural differences. Far from defusing factional strife, the July Monarchy exacerbated it by restoring the symbols and trappings of the Revolution and Empire. The return of the tricolour, like a red rag to a bull, incensed the conservative inhabitants of the Comtat Venaissin. The flag – inextricably associated with Robespierre, the *braves brigands* of Avignon and the Terrorists of the Hundred Days – continued to be stigmatised by those who had been nurtured on myths about *mangeurs de foie* and *buveurs de sang*. And when the Orleanist regime was greeted with patriotic songs, liberty-trees, the language of the Terror and the replacement of Legitimist *notables* with Liberals of Revolutionary stock, understandable shivers of alarm ran down many a royalist backbone. The July Monarchy was for many a regime which could not be trusted and Legitimist agents had little difficulty enlisting the support of a population fearful of war, conscription, Terror and religious persecution, with which republicanism was synonymous.

Symbolic protest against the Orleanist regime was widespread in the Comtat, and tricolours were frequently ripped down, degraded, burned and replaced with the beloved white flag of the Restoration. Events in Le Thor typify this situation. Conflict arose when Legitimists were removed from the municipal council and when the National Guard unit was filled with revolutionaries. Arguments concerning the composition of the National Guard led to a duel between the Legitimist mayor and his Liberal *adjoint*. The former was dismissed and subsequently led popular opposition to the new Liberal administration, whose apparent favouritism towards men of its own faction only further fuelled Legitimist wrath. Whilst the Liberals could parade the provocative tricolour through the village streets and sing patriotic songs in their cafés, Legitimist *farandoles* were broken up, their rallying-calls were treated as seditious and their cafés were closed down. Not surprisingly *rixes* were forever livening up the sleepy rural routine of this and other villages throughout the southern Comtat as Whites attempted to combat the threat of radicalism.[27]

From the earliest years of the July Monarchy, Legitimists built up an impressive party organisation.[28] A network of *cercles* was established in the major communes and villages and these received spasmodic visits from Legitimist emissaries from Avignon and L'Isle. Local agents brought song-sheets and newspapers like *Le Drapeau Blanc* back to their villages from the departmental *chef-lieu*. However, most symptomatic of Legitimist anxiety about the increasingly Liberal climate of the July monarchy was the way in which the White groups in Le Thor, Caderousse and Cavaillon armed themselves and bought consignments of gunpowder. They were prepared for any possible republican *coup*.

If republicanism was very much the minor political force in the region, it none the less prospered in Velleron, a commune whose idiosyncratic dedication to the Revolutionary cause in this land of dominant conservatism can be traced back to the First Republic. In 1834 the village continued to attract the authorities' attentions when it was reported that a secret republican association existed. It subscribed to the *Progrès* newspaper and was presided over by Pierre Grillet, a former Terrorist and son of a victim of the Counter-Terror in the Year VII. The persecutions of the Directory and Restoration remained prominent in his thoughts for he was forever reporting the existence of royalist plots, the aim of which was reputedly 'l'extermination de tous les patriotes'.[29] The village itself was besmirched with unrest during the July Monarchy. Disturbances in Velleron in April 1834 coinciding with unrest in Lyon necessitated the arrival of a force of police. Velleron youths were continually clashing with Whites from surrounding communes. In August 1835, for example, they marched into Pernes with a tricolour and a drum, only to be chased away by the Pernois who shouted 'A bas les gueux, les brigands de velleronais! Nous ne voulons pas de leur drapeau! A bas le drapeau tricolore!'[30] It is typical of the era that the men from Velleron continued to be referred to by Whites with the Revolutionary epithet of *brigand*, a legacy from the Jourdan era.

The example of the villages of the Vaucluse conclusively demonstrates the impinging pressure of Revolutionary traditions during the 1815–48 period. Polemical argument remained embroidered with quarrels that had originated during the Revolution, as the prefect reported in March 1835:

> Dans un grand nombre de communes ces divisions remontent aux premiers temps de nos orages politiques et en conservent l'empreinte. La révolution de '91 a son drapeau et ses adeptes. La réaction de 1815 a les siens. La lutte des principes a dégénéré en lutte de personnes et de familles; ce sont pour ainsi dire des haines et des oppositions traditionelles qui dominent la conduite des individus, lors même qu'il s'agit d'intérêts administratifs complètement étrangers par leur nature à cette politique de vieille date.[31]

Amongst the peasantry, political change was exceptional and it was the accepted norm that affiliations were dependent upon one's Revolutionary experience. Consider, for instance, the rebuke hurled at an inhabitant of Monteux who had taken the side of the Liberal group in a *rixe* in February 1833: 'Tu ne devrais pas être libéral parce qu'en '89 on t'a arraché les dents et traîné dans la Rigale. De ce temps-là tu étais avec les braves gens. A présent tu t'es tourné avec la canaille.'[32]

Mentalities remained impregnated with hazy, impressionistic prejudices born of widows' tales during fire-side *veillées* and of idle *chambrée* gossip. The Liberals of the Restoration and the July Monarchy continued to be called Patriots, brigands, Jacobins and even Terrorists. The symbols of the republic which had been adopted in 1830 continued to be associated with Revolutionary excess, and in the words of one individual from Monteux: 'les libéraux sont tous des brigands, tous ceux qui ont planté l'arbre de la liberté sont des voleurs'.[33] There is little doubt that, in the minds of many, the republic continued to be synonymous with anarchy and violence.

It was against this backcloth that the Second Republic was installed in February 1848. The peasantry of the arrondissements of Avignon, Carpentras and Orange did not hesitate to manifest their disapproval. Revolutionary stigmas had not been effaced, and, in the words of one official, the Comtat was still affected by 'les bruits qui dans notre pays portent un grand préjudice à la République, empêchant l'adhésion d'un grand nombre de citoyens ainsi que leur confiance.'[34]

If villages initially remained passive and impervious to the change of regime at national level in February 1848, there was considerable protest when republicans were nominated to key posts in the municipal administration and in the National Guard. In Châteauneuf-de-Gadagne villagers complained that 'le conseil municipal de Gadagne a été organisé sous la pression de la démagogie. La saine majorité des habitants se voient ainsi forcés de plier devant une minorité turbulente.'[35] There were also complaints in Monteux and Pernes, where zealously republican *commissaires de police* discriminated in favour of their faction. Whites were prosecuted for seditious rallying-calls in favour of Henri V and were denounced to superior officials as 'les hommes de 1815'. Whites reacted angrily against such republican officials. When the police in Monteux closed down the Whites' café in March 1849, several hundred Whites besieged the Reds' café and threw the despised *brigadier de police* into a pile of manure. Republican mayors were also the butt of public anger; at Caumont, for instance, the front door of the despised mayor was covered with muck in June 1849.[36]

At Le Thor, where residents still clearly lived in the shadow of the Terror, the Second Republic was particularly turbulent. As a petition sent to the prefect revealed, the root of the problem was a republican municipality whose excesses paralleled those of the early 1790s. The mayor had filled the National Guard with 'une minorité audacieuse et insultante', many of whom were outsiders:

> Vieillards, enfants, étrangers de la commune portés plus ou moins vers le mal, ne possédant rien pour la plupart, toujours prêts à semer la discorde, se partageant d'avance les propriétés, courant avec enthousiasme à tous les banquets socialistes, leur commandant en tête et suivis de porteurs de bannières plus ou moins terroristes, voilà notre garde nationale.[37]

The Reds had embarked upon a campaign of violence which included denunciations, lists of suspects, *sommations* and arbitrary imprisonments. Furthermore, it was claimed that, when the Whites came to vote on 30 July 1848, the National Guard commander threatened to open fire on them unless they withdrew. As in other villages of the Comtat, the Reds showed scant regard for the mechanisms of democracy and threatened to annul the results of elections, should they go against the Red candidate.[38] Local people in the Comtat did not disguise their hostility to the new regime, a hostility born of suspicions dating back to the Revolution of 1789.

The return of hated symbols which republican mayors encouraged also provoked hostility. In many communes liberty-trees bedecked with Phrygian bonnets were planted, the tricolour floated proudly above the municipal building and busts of the *déesse de la liberté* adorned the *mairie*. Worse still, 'La Marseillaise' and other Patriotic songs became the official anthems of the government of the day.

White villagers objected to the proliferation of symbols which continued to be associated with the slaughter of the Year II. The red bonnet, for instance, provoked particular anger and was described by the prefect who outlawed it in November 1848 as 'un emblème qui rappelle les souvenirs les plus pénibles de notre première Révolution'. For the conservative villagers of the Comtat, it was little more than 'un symbole de la Terreur' which summoned up macabre images of that age.

Other trappings of the Republic were equally resented. As they had done during the July Monarchy, White youths continued to rip up tricolours. Marianne, the goddess of liberty, was also disliked in villages where busts had been installed by republican committees in the heated excitement of February 1848. At Jonquerettes the *instituteur* had to run a gauntlet of abuse from parents and pupils alike 'parce que dans la salle qui sert tout à la fois et aux séances de la mairie et à la réunion des écoliers se trouve le buste de la liberté'. Liberty-trees were particularly disliked and were chopped down in Cabrières d'Avignon in January 1849, Vedène in February 1849 and Bollène in February 1850. At Mondragon fifteen children disfigured the tree which had been ornately painted in the national colours and covered it with 'matières fécales'.[39] Meanwhile, the *conseil municipal* of Courthézon – despite protests from local republicans – refused to buy a liberty-tree, deciding that the money would be far more wisely spent on the needs of the poor.[40] In a similar fashion Caumont's municipality rejected the liberty-tree, and significantly celebrated the advent of the Second

Republic with the erection of a cross, the symbol which during the Revolution had been one of anti-Jacobin revolt.[41]

Such was the innate hostility to republicanism in the Comtat that Red activists made little impression and converted few villagers to the cause of social-democracy. Their doctrines were quite simply repugnant in this part of the Vaucluse. Toasts to Robespierre and shouts of 'Vive la guillotine' which punctuated speeches were obtusely insensitive in villages which had seen many inhabitants executed in the Year II, and where the audience may have contained the children, friends and relatives of these victims. Lectures which advocated massacre, pillage and the division of property were frowned upon in an area which had experienced the consequences of Jourdan's army and the iniquities of the Terror. The inhabitants of L'Isle who attended an electoral meeting were singularly unimpressed with a speech by Dupuy of Cavaillon on the theme of 'le pauvre contre le riche'.[42] At a banquet in Malaucène in May 1850 not only was the local populace offended by a particularly threatening version of the Carmagnole but a speech attacking the right to property and calling for 'la destruction des machines' proved to be equally inflammatory. This 'pays d'industrie' welcomed the jobs and prosperity which outside investment created and was not at all enamoured of this misplaced Luddite programme. Remarks about property only generated stereo-typed images of revolutionaries unscrupulously taking le bien des autres.[43]

Colporteurs dealing in republican wares found business particularly slack in the Comtat once the small number of local Montagnards had been kitted out with their obligatory red belts and ties. Villagers were often offended by the merchandise on show, and traders were frequently being reported to officials. Thus, a hawker in Cavaillon was arrested after attempting to sell 'des hymnes abominables à l'honneur de Robespierre, de Marat et de leur système'.[44] A similar fate befell a trader from the department of the Ardèche who wandered into a café in Vaison and told an embarrassed clientele that he was in favour of 'une république comme celle que Barbès avait désirée, pareille à celle de quatre-vingt-treize, suivie d'une guillotine à purger les riches'.[45] It was clearly not the case that the villages perchés near Mont Ventoux were lethargic about radical politics during the Second Republic because they lay beyond the reach of the most intrepid Red pro-pagandist. These communes, like many others in the Comtat, found the democratic-socialist programme abhorrent because of its references to the Revolutionary maelstrom of the 1790s under whose shadow they continued to live.

The extravagant behaviour of local Reds hardened White opposition further still. Quite understandably, the squeamish villagers of Malaucène objected to a republican mayor who encouraged *farandoles*, the singing of Patriotic songs and the display of the Phrygian bonnet. Whilst *procès-verbaux* were drawn up against those who voiced support for Henri V, the mayor himself encouraged shouts of 'Vive la guillotine! A bas les riches! Qu'ils viennent les riches; que je les embroche tous!'[46] Needless to say, stony silences met Montagnard projects for a massacre like that proposed by a Red in Robion who believed that 'il y a trop de monde en France, il fallait en faire périr la moitié.'[47] In Aubignan villagers were left particularly queasy when the following conversation between four local Montagnards was overheard: 'Il était question d'incendier les maisons des riches pour les mettre ensuite au pillage. Un massacre général devait être organisé et il était question de tuer jusqu'aux enfants.'[48] In this village, midway between the villages of Sarrians and Bédoin, both of which had been put to flame during the Revolution of 1789, such projects were regarded as shocking in the extreme.

Songs, many of which originated in the bloodthirsty Revolutionary era, were equally abhorrent. In Cavaillon it was reported that Whites 'ici comme partout tremblent au chant seul de la Marseillaise'.[49] Songs like *Ça Ira*, *Les carlistes à la lanterne* and *Fêtons Marat et Robespierre* offended the sensitive ears of many in the region. *Le Vrai Montagnard*, a song which was frequently heard in the arrondissement of Orange, was particularly threatening:

> C'est le temps de porter nos coups,
> Sur tous les carlistes de France,
> Jurons donc tous francs Montagnards,
> Vrais descendants de Robespierre,
> D'anéantir tous ces cafards,
> De les mettre tous en poussière.[50]

The villagers of Bédarrides objected to songs 'où on parlait de sang et de guillotine et où on disait qu'ils feraient couler le sang à pleines rues'.[51] In this commune, which had suffered as much as any other during Jourdan's rampages of 1791, the language of pillage was violently disliked.

When Montagnards, forced underground by the Bonapartist

repression, organised their secret societies, traditional fears of associations were aroused. Inevitably comparisons were made with the Revolutionary clubs; few people believed that the objectives of these new *sociétés secrètes* would be any different from those of the *sociétés populaires* of the 1790s which were deemed responsible for sending innocent villagers to the scaffold at Orange. Few youths consequently were initiated into these societies.

The Montagnards' adoption of the colour red also drummed fear into the rural folk of the arrondissements of Avignon, Carpentras and Orange. Red, the colour of the Phrygian bonnet worn by the Terrorists and the colour of the tunic worn by convicted murderers on the way to the gallows, automatically associated the Montagnard movement with violent crime. Red, the colour of blood, summoned up images of the guillotine and the mythical *buveur de sang*. In short, the Reds' violent and bloodthirsty language, their secret associations and their adopted symbolism confirmed the veracity of folkloric tales of Terrorist violence.

By 1851 republicans had come to be regarded as little less than the men of 1793 reincarnate. Those who continued to attempt to put forward constructive plans of sensible reform were faced with a wall of hostility. As one bitter moderate complained, the Republic was automatically regarded as an evil that was to be combatted: 'Démocratie signifie désordre, vol, pillage; démocrate est synonyme de malhonnête homme.'[52] The same response was evoked in village after village. In Vedène, after the Reds had danced a *farandole* shouting 'Vive la guillotine! Vive Robespierre! Il faut pendre les modérés! A bas les aristocrates!', they were described as 'hommes qui n'ont que les mots de sang et de pillage dans la bouche et qui n'aspirent qu'à voir revenir les jours néfastes de quatre-vingt-treize.'[53] In Sorgues it was commonly believed that 'les républicains étaient tous de la canaille et que la vraie République ne désirait que le pillage', whilst the somewhat naive *commissaire de police* of Jonquières believed that it was White agents who had led the credulous country dwellers to believe that 'la République n'a pour objet que le pillage, le meurtre et la dévastation'.[54] It was, on the contrary, the excessive behaviour of his own party, which, by confirming Revolutionary myths, had established these convictions.

So strong were such *idées reçues* that in Cavaillon during Midnight Mass on Christmas Eve 1848 the congregation feared that the Reds intended to lock the church doors and pillage the town.[55] Similarly, in Monteux, the Party of Order mobilised its forces in May 1849 because of a rumour that the Reds were about to start their pillaging.[56] In March 1849 reports of a massacre (later proved unfounded) led the communes of Bédoin and Mazan to send a force of 600 men to crush the Red assassins.[57] The radicalism of Red supporters provoked very real anxieties which had been moulded by Revolutionary folklore.

From this evidence one can conclude that the Revolutionary heritage played a far larger role in rural politics during the first half of the nineteenth century than has previously been imagined. In the Vaucluse factional disputes originating in the 1790s pervaded every aspect of village-pump politics. The spectre of the Red peril clearly played a significant part in determining the long-term conservatism of this and other regions of the French countryside, and it is with reference to fears dating back to the 1790s that the unhappy fate of the Second Republic is to be best explained. Furthermore, the vivacity and sensitivity of the rural inhabitants in the post-Revolutionary era demonstrate that they were not – as they have sometimes been depicted – a spineless mass possessing as little intelligence as the average beast of burden, prone to ill-reasoned outbursts of *jacquerie* and easily manipulated by the politics of the highest urban bidder. On the contrary, the rural inhabitant of France possessed – like his better mannered counterpart in the urban setting – his very own firmly held political beliefs and prejudices. Despite the conspicuous absence of electoral democracy before 1848, the peasantry did not remain impervious to political matters, and, as the proponents of Red politics discovered during the Second Republic, the countryside remained a stumbling-block to ambition over which one could not easily ride roughshod.

Notes

1 E. Weber, *Peasants into Frenchmen*, London, 1979, *passim*.
2 T. Margadant, *French Peasants in revolt*, Princeton, 1979, *passim*.
3 P. McPhee, 'The seed-time of the Republic', *Australian Journal of Politics and History*, XXII (1976), pp. 196–213.
4 M. Agulhon, *La République au Village*, Paris, 1970, *passim*.
5 Weber, *Frenchmen*, p. 247.
6 Works on the Revolution in the Vaucluse include: C. Soullier, *Histoire de la Révolution d'Avignon et du Compté Venaissin*, 2 vols., Paris, 1844; R. Moulinas, *Histoire de la Révolution d'Avignon*, Aubanel, 1986.
7 Similar continuities have already been discovered in the neighbouring department of the Gard. See G. Lewis, *The Second Vendée*, Oxford, 1978, *passim*.
8 Archives Départementales du Vaucluse (henceforth ADV) 1M 744.
9 ADV 1M 744.

10 ADV 1M 744.
11 ADV 1M 742.
12 ADV 1M 744.
13 ADV 1M 745.
14 ADV 1M 745.
15 ADV 1M 745.
16 ADV 1M 746.
17 ADV 1M 745.
18 ADV 1M 746.
19 ADV 1M 744, 745, 746.
20 ADV 1M 745.
21 ADV 1M 745.
22 ADV 1M 745.
23 ADV 1M 744.
24 ADV 1M 745.
25 ADV 1M 737.
26 ADV 1M 746.
27 ADV 1M 747.
28 ADV 1M 747, 748.
29 ADV 2M 57.
30 ADV 1M 748.
31 ADV 2M 57.
32 ADV 1M 747.
33 ADV 1M 747.
34 ADV 1M 750.
35 ADV 1M 751.
36 ADV 1M 750.
37 ADV 3M 26.
38 ADV 3U 3/635.
39 ADV 1M 750.
40 ADV 1M 750.
41 ADV 1M 752.
42 ADV 1M 750.
43 ADV 1M 751.
44 ADV 1M 751.
45 ADV 1M 750.
46 ADV 1M 750.
47 ADV 1M 776.
48 ADV 3U 3/635.
49 ADV 1M 750.
50 ADV 1M 751.
51 ADV 1M 776.
52 *Le Mémorial de Vaucluse*, ADV 10 per 5, 17 September 1848.
53 *L'Union Nationale*, ADV 10 per 8, 28 February 1849.
54 ADV 1M 750.
55 ADV, unclassified document, dated 26 December 1848.
56 ADV 1M 750.
57 *L'Union Nationale*, ADV 10 per 8, 31 March 1849.

The state and the villages in Revolutionary France

When the National Assembly fashioned the nation's new civic geography in 1789, it recognised as autonomous 'communes' not only all towns and bourgs but a seemingly boundless number of rural entities. From the largest city to the smallest village – 'in each town, bourg, parish, or rural community' – every commune was to have a similar form of elected local government consisting of a mayor, procurator and council. The Assembly's own Committee on the Constitution opposed this prodigality, proposing instead that rural communities be grouped into a smaller number of *municipalités* or *grandes communes*. They did not see anything sacred or definitive about the civic fragmentation of the countryside. As a Napoleonic prefect later expressed it, they regarded many rural communes as mere products of circumstances 'created by feudalism, by the ecclesiastical order, or by the caprice of the inhabitants', and therefore unsuited for political and administrative autonomy.[1] The Assembly felt otherwise, evidently sensing, as Marc Bloch has argued, that the villages were veritable 'rural communities' linked by economic and sentimental ties. Though overshadowed historically by seigneurial institutions, 'they were de facto associations long before they acquired a legal personality'.[2] The revolutionaries built on whatever legal personality the villages had developed since the sixteenth century. They certified as a commune any rural collectivity which had a parish church *or* elected, co-opted or appointed officers (*consuls, jurats, syndics* or *échevins*). As a prefect in Haute-Garonne later recalled: 'In 1790 it was necessary to erect all the hamlets which had a consul into municipalities.[3]

This use of the term 'hamlet' was actually misleading in relation to certain regions of France. In areas of dispersed settlement – in mountainous pasturing regions, in the *bocage* country, in the *pays de grande culture* – tiny hamlets never had and never would have autonomous status. Rural communities in such regions often consisted of a dozen or even several dozen hamlets and isolated households. Thus, the commune of Anthully (Saône-et-Loire), population 1,189, comprised thirteen hamlets, some more than 3 kilometers from the communal *chef-lieu*.[4] In at least one-third of France's departments, especially in the West and Centre, more rural inhabitants probably lived in such dispersed settlements than in nucleated villages.[5] That dispersed pattern of settlement, however, did not pose the most serious civic problem. It was in the areas of agglomerated rural settlement, especially the classic regions of *petite culture*, that the Assembly's controversial policy actually produced 'as many municipalities as there were villages' – thousands of miniscule communes whose civic viability remained very much in doubt.[6]

The National Assembly understandably took the easiest, most liberal and most popular course by simply consolidating the status quo of rural communal identity. After all, it was courting enough trouble in obliterating the provinces and calling into question the traditional status and privileges of hundreds of towns. Warnings by some deputies that this system was too cumbersome were ignored for the time being but soon proved prophetic.

It is not easy to draw a statistical portrait of this situation. One can drown in a sea of numbers without finding exactly the right ones. The first difficulty that the new regime confronted is obvious enough: the sheer number of communes, the surfeit of 44,000 'spokes' in the chain of responsibility and authority. The size and viability of these communes are harder to get at systematically. We can turn for help, however, to the *Description topographique et statistique de la France*, a 2,500-page compendium published in 1810 by Peuchet and Chanlaire, though this product of the regime's obsession with statistics covers only about half of France's indigenous departments. Of singular value is the method used by their informants; they separated distinctly urban communes, noting their number (anywhere from twenty to fifty-five per department) and their combined population. By subtracting the urban population, and dividing the remaining rural population by the number of rural communes, we can determine an *average* population of rural communes per department (see Appendix).[7]

The median of these averages is 509, and the combined weighted average in the forty-three departments comes to 499. If a population of 500 can be taken as a likely threshold of civic viability, then these figures point to the government's dilemma, and confirm an impression derived from a number of departmental almanachs as to the large proportion of communes with a population under 500. These figures, of course, subsume but do not explicitly reveal the specific problem posed by the bottom tier of miniscule communes. Comprehensive statistics on that question are not to be had, as far as I can tell, but there are indications enough. Peuchet and Chanlaire's informants, and Napoleon's prefects, sometimes provided detail on their departments' least-substantial communes. To take but four reported examples from different regions: the Haute-Garonne had 131 communes with a population of under 200; the Corrèze had 292 communes with a population of under 150; the Moselle had sixty-five communes with a population of under 100; and the Calvados had eighty-one communes with fewer than fifty inhabitants.[8]

The three-tiered system of local administration – departments, districts and communes – survived the fall of the monarchy but not the Revolutionary crisis of 1793. Triumphant Montagnards shouldered aside the departmental administrations – half of which were tainted by flirtations with federalism – and turned the districts into the fulcrum of Revolutionary government. But the Mountain simply left existing municipalities in place so as 'not to deprive their citizens of the consolation of administering themselves fraternally',[9] though, in fact, the regular authorities in the countryside were often superseded by Revolutionary committees, popular societies and itinerant commissars. When the Mountain fell from power, politics and practical considerations shaped the Thermidorians' approach to the future of local government. Predictably, it was a belated victory for the Girondins. In the constitution of the Year III (1795) the Convention restored primacy to elected departmental directorates and jettisoned completely those instruments of Revolutionary government and the Terror, the districts. It also addressed the problem of civic fragmentation in the countryside. Having cut out the middle tier of jurisdiction in the districts, the Thermidorians embraced the once-spurned idea of joining together rural communes for administrative purposes. While towns with over 5,000 inhabitants continued to elect independent municipalities under the Directory regime, smaller communes were grouped into *municipalités cantonales*, which to all intents and purposes became the lowest level of local government and administration. A new civic experiment was launched.[10]

Territorial units ordinarily taking in between six to twelve communes, cantons had existed since 1790 to serve two functions: a canton was the circumscription for a primary assembly which named electors for departmental electoral assemblies, and each constituted the bailiwick for a justice of the peace and his assistants. Now the 5,250 cantons became the locus of the civic order in the countryside. They would replace 'the 44,000 [communal] municipalities . . . that immensity of administrations all acting at the same time, too often in contrary directions, and almost always without subordination.'[11] Though villages retained their identity as independent entities called *communes* they lost most of their governmental roles. Rural communes virtually disappeared from the official administrative hierarchy.

The cantonal municipality, known as the *administration municipale*, was in its way an ingenious contrivance. During their primary assembly the canton's voters, after choosing their justice of the peace, now elected a president to head their municipality. Subsequently, voters in each commune, who had elected their mayor and municipal council under the constitution of 1791, designated instead one person for a two-year term as their *agent municipal* and another as his deputy (*adjoint*). The *agent* represented his commune in the periodic meetings of the municipal administration at the canton's *chef-lieu*. That is, the canton president and the *agents* from the individual communes together constituted the *administration municipale* of the canton, which in turn hired a secretary paid from local funds.[12]

As if they had read Tocqueville before the fact, the architects of this system then added an official appointed by Paris to represent the national state in each canton. Like the commissioners of the Executive Directory attached to each departmental administration and court, the cantonal commissioners were paid by Paris (though at the far more modest rate of 300 *livres*), in contrast to the locally elected men who were unpaid. In theory, the cantonal commissioner did not have the power to act but only to monitor the administration's compliance with laws and decrees coming down from Paris or the departmental administration. In reality, he advised, goaded and shared the work of the part-time amateurs of the administration, and in extreme cases did most of it himself. The commissioners were also the eyes and ears of the government, reporting to their immediate superiors, the departmental commissioners, who distilled their information and passed it along to the Ministry of Interior in Paris. For the first time in French history, these canton commissioners brought a quasi-bureaucratic presence to the grass-roots.

Under this new system the *agent municipal* had minimal responsibilities. Within the precincts of his commune his main functions were to maintain the *état civil* (registers of births, deaths and marriages), to serve as a kind of police officer linked to the justice of the peace, and to participate in the allocation of the commune's share of property taxes among its citizens. Tax rolls, requisitions, budgets and reports were fashioned collectively at the cantonal level. Cantons also became the repositories of the law. The *Bulletin des Lois* – that ultimate artefact of state-building and centralisation – no longer went out to each commune but only to the *chef-lieu de canton*, which was required to maintain three subscriptions: for the president, the commissioner and the secretary.[13] Except for the *état civil*, all archives were also regrouped at the cantonal seat. Under the constitution of 1795, each cantonal seat was supposed to maintain an elementary school, while other communes need not. When the *fête décadaire* became obligatory in 1798, celebrations were required only in the *chef-lieu* and not in each commune. Likewise, civil marriage ceremonies were to be performed only by the president at the cantonal seat on the *décadi*. All told, the canton figured very heavily in the civic agenda of the Directory.

Unlike the former mayor, the *agent municipal* was not obliged to correspond with superior authorities, nor was he responsible for the budget and expenditures of his commune. He merely supplied information to his colleagues on the cantonal municipality. All decisions, correspondence and accounting were handled collectively at its meetings. Instead of anywhere from 200 to 950 separate sets of instructions, reports and accounts per department, formal administration now required only thirty to ninety. Moreover, the system was stronger than its weakest links, for it could tolerate a number of incompetent or absentee *agents*, while the abler ones shouldered the paperwork with the president and secretary.

According to the few local studies we have, it is true that it was extremely difficult to get these cantonal administrations off the ground. Rural voters were initially indifferent to the whole business and could scarcely be bothered to choose their *agent municipal*. When they finally did, that citizen as often as not declined the dubious honour. Reluctant to haul themselves periodically to the cantonal seat, tired of Revolutionary politics, often hostile to the Republic and (especially in the West) fearful of anti-republican violence, their responses amounted to a *grève des élus*. Pleading inability, infirmities or the need to tend to their own affairs, many declined to accept or immediately resigned. An expense allowance would likely have increased the acceptance rate, since these unpaid posts required an outlay of cash for food and drink on meeting days, but the government never offered this simple inducement.[14]

Though it took as long as a year in certain departments, enough *agents* were eventually recruited to get these cantonal administrations functioning. Admittedly, their participation was usually grudging, and if threatened with dismissal by the department for indifference or lassitude, they were likely to depart with a smile. 'Almost all the *agents* lack capacity and talent; they do not bother to read the laws. Insouciance is at its height,' complained one departmental commissioner. 'If the department orders rigorous measures, they produce resignations', warned another. Unfortunately the *agents* were frequently called on to implement distasteful measures of several kinds, even if they seemed mild by the standards of the Terror: allocating the detested forced loan of 1796; implementing the military draft of 1798–99; and, above all, complying with or evading the Directory's relentless demands in 1798–99 to enforce the republican calendar.[15]

Meanwhile, in return for their modest salary, the cantonal commissioners were supposed to maintain 'a regular, constant, and habitual correspondence' with the departmental commissioner. No such thing could have been expected from unsalaried and often barely literate mayors or *agents* in each village. But even on the cantonal level it proved endlessly difficult to achieve the desired standard of reporting. Initially demanding a *compte décadaire* from its commissioners, in June 1798 the Directory agreed to settle for one report per month. Even so, the results were unsatisfactory: 'silences, inexactitude, pusillanimous wariness', complained the departmental commissioners, especially in regard to enforcing the republican calendar. Elaborate model forms provided by some departmental commissioners did not necessarily help since it was just as easy to be perfunctory or dilatory with them as without.[16]

Ostensibly, the cantonal commissioners were the lowest echelon of the central government's apparatus. They were chosen by the Directory upon recommendations from the department's legislative deputation and central administration. But unlike the departmental commissioners, who belonged to the Revolution's national political class, most were local men without significant experience or ambition who were likely to respond as much to local interests or inertia as to pressure from above. Most seem to have been petit-bourgeois types minimally familiar with the world of public affairs and the art of the pen (modest country lawyers, notaries, low-level public employees and the odd constitutional priest), along with a scattering of rural proprietors, cultivators, tradesmen and artisans.[17] The Directory was, of course, free to recruit its commissioners from the cities, but few capable men would accept underpaid postings to small rural bourgs. During the near-anarchy and anti-republican violence that engulfed certain departments in 1796, it was understandable that these commissioners were 'paralysed by terror and persecutions'. But even after the violence abated most were unable to energise their administrations or even to convey information honestly and efficiently. 'The commissioners attached to the municipal administrations', complained one departmental commissioner, 'are isolated and without force.' In the eyes of some observers, the old districts regained their allure as reasonable outposts for the state's functionaries. A correspondent of Director Merlin de Douai thus wrote from Vienne: 'I again propose suspending the cantonal commissioners, almost all imbeciles, and turning over their functions to the commissioners in the former district capitals, who are generally better educated and more detached from individual passions.'[18] It appeared as if the Thermidorians had overreached themselves.

It would be premature, however, to take this as a conclusive argument that the cantonal administrations were artificial creations doomed to fail. From an ecological and social perspective, the cantonal municipalities were a promising basis on which to aggregate rural citizens and nurture civic life in the countryside while leaving each commune its residual autonomy. In the first place, the great majority of cantonal seats had periodic markets which attracted peasants from surrounding villages. In addition to their justice of the peace and primary school, many had a local notary, a post office or a local registry bureau as well. To its citizens the canton was likely to be a meaningful entity, far closer and less forbidding than the old district capitals. The majority of *chefs-lieux* were already a locus of rural life. Small, isolated villages did not after all constitute self-contained worlds. Peasants and rural artisans required wider communities for marriage, hiring, credit, purchasing and selling – communities likely to form around market villages or bourgs. Anthropologist William Skinner has charted such communities in traditional China, which he calls 'standard marketing areas'. His Chinese market villages served an average of eighteen smaller villages with total populations of around 7,000; the average population of a French rural canton was slightly over 6,000.[19]

From the beginning the revolutionaries in France set out to create uniform administrative mechanisms in the most basic units or cells of their society. When their three-tiered, decentralised, scheme collapsed, they seemed in 1795 to back up one step by withdrawing almost all administrative responsibility from the rural commune. Yet in reality they were extending bureaucracy further down by organising cantonal municipalities in the equivalent of 'standard marketing areas' and stationing a commissioner in each one. Finding several thousand commissioners for these rural bourgs may have stretched the nation's administrative capital too thinly, but for good reason it seemed a preferable alternative to relying on 40,000 unpaid mayors. Given time, cantonal government might have reduced the isolation of rural communes by building on the existing relationships that their citizens had with the market villages.

One type of evidence for the social and ecological viability of the cantons comes in a paradoxically negative form, in petitions from rural communes to be included in a different canton (*distraction*) and in petitions by an *administration municipale* or some of its members to transfer the canton's *chef-lieu* from one commune to another. Virtually all such petitions claimed that the original circumscriptions drawn by the Constituent Assembly in 1790 were faulty. But the petitions usually provide a counter-image of what a soundly-designed cantonal circumscription would entail – the situation in the vast majority of places that did not find it necessary to initiate such demands.

The petitions for *distraction* complained of the distance and inaccessibility of the *chef-lieu* in contrast to that of the neighbouring canton in which they wished to be included. As the inhabitants of Salès (Haute-Garonne) explained, 'everything calls us to Carbonne which is our common centre. All our affairs bring us to that place, whether for the market or by virtue of its river-borne commerce . . . whereas nature has placed often insurmountable obstacles in the way of going to Rieux.'[20] In requesting the transfer of their communes into the nearby canton of Montflanquin instead of Montfiguer, the inhabitants of three villages in Lot-et-Garonne depicted an almost ideal cantonal seat where, among other things, they could make their quarterly tax payments while taking care of other business:

> They have their relations and their affairs at Montflanquin. There they find frequent markets and fairs for the sale of their produce and livestock; merchants and artisans who provide necessary goods; workers to repair their broken implements; lawyers and notaries to assist them in their civil transactions . . . In a word, the communes in question can be considered so to speak as faubourgs of Montflanquin.[21]

The elements determining a canton's social or ecological viability are apparent, too, in the more numerous requests for transfer of the *chef-lieu* within a canton. These demands note the haste of the Assembly in drawing cantonal circumscriptions in 1790, its occasional ignorance of local topography and the apparent influence of special-interest pleading. That is not to say that even with sufficient time and knowledge the task would have been simple. Should the centrality of a cantonal seat, for example, be reckoned relative to the number of communes it served or to those with the most inhabitants? What if it were comfortably accessible for seven or eight villages but excessively remote from one or two? (While the great majority of communes clustered in reasonable proximity to each other, the veritable isolation of some threatened to contravene the constitutional principle that no commune should be more than a *myriamètre* (10 kilometres) away from the *chef-lieu*.) Nor was mere distance necessarily a useful guide, since topography could alter its meaning: did a swollen river surge through the canton? What were the roads like leading into it? Other considerations could loom equally large: did the *chef-lieu* have facilities for meetings and archives, and amenities like an inn for the *agents* and for voters in the annual primary assemblies? Petitions for a shift of the *chef-lieu* – for a reconfiguration of the canton – suggest that siting the *chef-lieu* could be a difficult zero-sum game. But, like the petitions for *distraction*, they also present a counter-image of a properly ordered canton.

In 1790 the siting of the cantonal *chef-lieu* was a matter of local pride and rivalry, but scarcely a great moment in the daily life of the rural community. Once administration and taxation devolved on the canton in 1796, favouritism or ignorance by the National Assembly in 1790 in establishing an inaccessible cantonal seat had grave results. A few prior errors were blatant and easily rectified. The 'vicious organisation' of the cantons of Seranon and Mujoulx in the Var, for example, had the citizens of the six northern communes in Seranon up in arms. The legislature eventually performed the radical surgery that was indicated by reorganising a canton centred in Gars. It was also hard to understand how Fontenay (Meurthe) had ever been designated as a cantonal seat, but under the new system it was insupportable. With a population of only about 200, it had no locale for the authorities or for convening the primary assemblies and no facilities for lodging or feeding them. Gonderville, on the contrary, had about 1,000 inhabitants, was in the centre of the canton on the main road from Paris to Strasbourg, and had buildings for the administration's meetings and the primary assemblies. In 1796 the departmental administration authorised the provisional transfer of the *chef-lieu* to Gonderville, and the Legislature ratified that decision in 1798.[23]

Distance, topography and inconvenience were the most likely causes of protests. The cantonal municipality of Candes (Indre-et-Loire) wished to move the *chef-lieu* to Lerne because 'the extreme remoteness of Candes puts off the inhabitants of the other five communes which constitute the canton so much that their primary assemblies are too often incomplete and the sessions of the administration lose prodigiously of their majesty and utility'. Similarly, six of the seven communes in the canton of Gault (Loir-et-Cher) demanded the transfer of the *chef-lieu* to more centrally located Arville 'because the refusal of the *agents* to travel to Gault obstructs the administrative service'.[24] Lack of facilities sometimes loomed larger than topography in prompting municipalities or villagers to demand the relocation of the cantonal *chef-lieu*. The hapless *agents* in the administration of St Just (Aveyron) wanted to relocate in St Martial, a central and commodious bourg with 'a town hall that is offered free of charge', whereas at St Just 'there is no locale for our sessions other than the tumult of a tavern'.[25] Another motive for transferring the cantonal seat was the political environment. The departmental administration of the Manche provisionally transferred a cantonal seat from St Poix because the newly elected *agents* refused to be sworn in there, 'where their safety was compromised since the renewal of chouannerie'. A legislative report concluded that Biez (Pas-de-Calais) was more centrally located, endowed with better facilities and more patriotic than Fressin, an allegedly royalist commune where republicans felt threatened.[26]

In disputed cases, fate did not always combine central location, adequate facilities and a patriotic ambience so neatly. In about two dozen cases it proved exceptionally difficult and contentious to settle on the proper configuration of a canton.[27] In the vast majority of cases, however, the pieces came together and cantons were superimposed on existing patterns of interaction among rural villages without such dissension.

In the Interior Ministry's view, however, after two years the anticipated advantages of cantonal municipalities had not materialised. In a circular of 27 November 1797, it proposed to reduce the number of cantons substantially and called upon the departmental administrations to devise new and larger circumscriptions:

> Undoubtedly none of you have failed to sense how much the multiplicity of cantons has weakened the impetus coming from the central point of the department by dividing it excessively; how much the large number of spokes [*rouages*] undermines the selection process, the uniformity of measures, the activeness of correspondence, the rapidity of execution; finally how much that superfluity of municipal administrations causes useless expenses.[28]

As a corollary to reducing the number of cantons, the Ministry also asked the departments rather offhandedly to prepare lists of small communes that might be merged with others – in reality, a far more fundamental and difficult operation.

Encouraged by the generally enthusiastic responses it received from thirty-four departments as of August 1798, the Ministry pushed ahead. Since the 1,886 cantons in those departments might be reduced to 1,081, it expected that altogether about 1,750 cantons could be suppressed. The Ministry anticipated the arguments that this project would face in the Legislature, which had deferred the question a few months earlier on the grounds that any discussion of such a delicate matter would be ill advised on the eve of the primary assemblies. Article 50 of the constitution read: 'The cantons are to retain their present circumscriptions. None the less their boundaries can be modified and corrected by the Legislature; but in that case no commune can be more than a *myriamètre* (10 kilometres) distant from the canton seat.' In the Ministry's view this did not permanently fix the number of cantons. The wording ('les cantons conservent leurs circonscriptions actuelles') 'had no other purpose than to avoid inserting into the constitution a lengthy nomenclature'. Constitutional scruples need not prevent a drastic reform. The inevitable protests and complaints by the individual cantons marked for suppression were dismissed as 'petty rivalries' that should not concern policy-makers.[29]

The project moved through the Council of 500 where a committee presented a bill. The debate began on 22 November 1798 and revealed a host of reservations about the plan, in addition to the anticipated constitutional objections which the Directory considered specious. According to Duplantier, the biggest problem in cantonal administration was getting a quorum of *agents*, with the result that municipalities often went two or three months without being able to deliberate properly. 'That inaction which is attributed to the multiplicity of cantons is due on the contrary to their excessive size. In augmenting their territory you will therefore exacerbate the problem.' In defending the current size and distribution of the cantons, Duplantier argued that a massive redeployment of primary assemblies and municipal administrations would force a useless change in 'the habits and interactions of the citizens'. Moreover, citizens already found trips to the *chef-lieu* for a *fête décadaire* or a marriage ceremony long enough; the new plan would necessitate far more arduous journeys. Delbrel, even more positive about the existing cantons, believed that the closer an administration was to its citizens the more willingly they would support its expenses. 'I am convinced', he added, 'that the multiplicity of *rouages* works, up to a certain point, for the maintenance of public liberty by making it possible for a larger number of citizens to participate in governmental activity. . . . A municipal administration whose sessions are public is a kind of school, a source of emulation for the inhabitants of the countryside.'[30]

Defenders of the Directory's reduction project focused not on the citizens' relations to the canton but on administrative and financial problems – 'the costly nullity . . . the inexecution of the laws . . . the despair of the superior administrations' caused by the present arrangements. Barra contended that the success or failure of the system really depended on the capacity of the commissioners. Since the Directory simply could not find enough competent men, it preferred to rely on a smaller number and pay them better. The other expenses of cantonal administration, such as the salaries of secretaries, postal courriers, supplies and maintenance – which he estimated to average 1,400 *livres* a year – could be significantly reduced by abolishing a third of the cantons. These arguments proved unavailing, however. After two days of debate the Council of 500 left the project on the table, effectively giving the cantonal municipalities a vote of confidence.[31]

Brumaire overturned that status quo completely. Bonaparte's Local Government Act of February 1800 jettisoned the cantons (except as judicial and electoral circumscriptions) and reverted to a three-tiered system parallel to the original concept of 1790. Instead of authorising elections for departmental, district and communal administrations, however, the Consulate appointed prefects, sub-prefects and mayors. Under this model, communes again became the lowest level of active administration, the base point in the chain of responsibility and official communication. In that sense, the state seemed to move closer to the grass-roots. As a sign of this change, the government redirected the *Bulletin des Lois*. Under the Directory subscriptions had been maintained only at the cantonal seat; now each and every mayor was obliged to maintain a subscription paid for from his communal budget.[32] But the abandonment of cantonal municipalities and the re-establishment of the mayors was also a retreat by the state bureaucracy to the level of the district (now called the *arrondissement* or sub-prefecture), a step back from the Directory's insertion of salaried functionaries in rural bourgs.

Altogether, administrative penetration of the countryside took a giant leap forward with the Revolution and then stalled. Two solutions were advanced to neutralise the surfeit of communes inherited in 1789, but neither succeeded. The cantonal municipalities of the Directory attempted to build a civic community parallel to the wider socio-economic universe that most peasants already inhabited. But impatient – as the Directory itself had become – with the costliness, sluggishness and problematic electoral basis of these cantonal municipalities, the Consulate discarded them before the case against them had really been proved – even if ordinary rural citizens, zealous of their communal autonomy, could only applaud the cantons' demise.[33] The Napoleonic regime intended to govern the countryside with a streamlined hierarchy of appointed officials whose work was to be facilitated by the merger of small communes. But that essential element of their design proved in the main unachievable. Even if Napoleonic and Restoration prefects managed to amalgamate a small number of the least-viable communes, they did not carry the process far enough to make a significant difference. Local resistance, playing off official scruples and ambivalence, thwarted the drive for consolidation of rural communes in all but a handful of departments. Predictably, some officials began to regard the old cantonal municipalities in a more favourable light. And Napoleon himself, in effect, resuscitated the cantonal circumscriptions in 1804 for the purpose of conscription, having despaired at the 'insouciance', incompetence and communal self-interest of rural mayors acting on their own in this all-important matter.[34] In other respects, however, prefects of the nineteenth century had to deal with the surfeit of rural communes that they inherited. Over these villages they held great leverage but not nearly as much as they would have wished.

Notes

1   Archives Nationales (hereafter AN). F^2 II Aveyron 1: prefect to Minister of Interior (hereafter MI), 5 vendémiaire X. For an overview see A. Cobban, 'Local government during the French Revolution', in his *Aspects of the French Revolution*, New York, 1968; L. Gauthier, 'Les Municipalités cantonales et la tradition révolutionnaire', *La Révolution française*, LXIX (1916), pp. 243–55; A. Patrick, 'French Revolutionary local government, 1789–1792', in C. Lucas (ed.), *The Political Culture of the French Revolution*, Oxford, 1988, pp. 399–420.

2   See M. Bloch, *French Rural History: an Essay on its Basic Characteristics*, Berkeley, 1966, pp. 167–70.

3   AN F^2 II Haute-Garonne 1: prefect to MI, 21 September 1805. On the variety of elected and co-opted village officers, see M. Bordes, *L'Administration provinciale et municipale en France au XVIIIᵉ siècle*, Paris, 1972, pp. 175–98.

4   AN AF III 105: *Plan topographique de l'étendue du canton d'Antully et des différents communes et hameaux le composant; Plan du canton de Plouha* (Côtes-du-Nord) showing its four communes with numerous hamlets. See also AN F^2 II Indre-et-Loire 1: communal maps for Assay et Grazay and Chenusson et St Laurent-en-Gatine.

5   J. Peuchet and P. G. Chanlaire, *Description topographique et statistique de la France*, 1810, reproduced on microfiche by Clearwater Publishing Co. in 'Statistical Sources on the History of France: Prefect Studies Under the Empire,' edited by J.-C. Perrot. I have extracted population statistics from forty-three of the indigenous departments treated in this compendium. See also some of the correspondence in AN F^2 I 840–841 *Nomenclature des communes*, 1820–21.

6   This point was raised even during the perfunctory debate over Bonaparte's Local Government Act: *Tribunat: Opinion de Ganilh sur les administrations locales, 25 pluviôse VIII* in AN, AD I 61. Another deputy later called this the 'fundamental error' of the Constituent Assembly (AN F^2 I 444 Dastorq to MI, 30 May 1811).

7   See note 5. In addition to this compendium, the Perrot microfiche collection includes separate volumes on fifty-seven indigenous departments.

8   Peuchet and Chanlaire, *Description topographique*; also F^2 II Haute-Garonne 1 prefect to MI, 30 October 1810; F^2 II Corrèze 2 *Compte administratif*, 1806.

9   Gauthier, 'Les Municipalités, pp. 249–53.

10   The thorough debate may be followed in the *Moniteur* (réimpression), XXV (An III), pp. 106, 173–6, 189–92, 195.

11   *Ibid.*, p. 106.

12   See especially the *Manuel des Agents Municipaux* (an VII), BN F 39474, and its *Supplément* (published in year VIII just before the demise of the regime); J. Godechot, *Les Institutions de la France sous la Révolution et l'Empire*, Paris, 1968, pp. 472–6.

13   For criticism of this restriction see, e.g., AN F^{1a} 422 (Meurthe) *Mémoire sur les*

inconvénients de l'art. XI de la loi du 12 vendémiaire IV qui détermine un mode pour l'envoi et la publication des loix (fructidor V); AN., F^{1a} 408. Commissioner to the canton of Carlux (Dordogne), 30 vendémiaire V; Departmental Commissioner Côtes du Nord to MI, 28 germinal IV; AN F^{1c} III Yonne 7 *Compte*, nivôse VII.

14 M. Reinhard, *Le Département de la Sarthe sous le régime directorial*, St Brieuc, 1935, pp. 37–57 and 161–4; C. Bloch, 'Le Recrutement du personnel municipal de l'an IV', *La Révolution française*, XLVI (1904), pp. 153–68 on the Loiret; and L. Gauthier, 'L'Organisation des municipalités cantonales dans le département de la Vienne', *La Révolution française*, LXVI (1914), pp. 427–40.

15 AN F^{1c} III Somme 7 *Compte*, messidor VI; F^{1c} III Nord 7 *Comptes*, germinal and fructidor VII; F^{1c} III Vosges 7 *Comptes* brumaire and frimaire VII. See also E. Desgranges, *La centralisation républicaine sous le Directoire: les municipalités de canton dans le département de la Vienne*, Poitiers, 1954, Ch. 1, especially pp. 19–20.

16 AN F^{1a} 50 MI circular to central commissioners, 23 prairial VI; F^{1c} III Jura 7 central commissioner's circular to cantonal commissioners, 8 messidor VI. Similar circulars to the cantonal commissioners may be found in F^{1c} III Aude 5; F^{1c} III Calvados 8; F^{1c} III Gironde 5; F^{1c} III Lot-et-Garonne 7; and F^{2}C III Marne 6 (messidor VI), which included a printed model form: *Compte de la situation morale et politique du canton d'——— pendant le mois de ———*. The rubrics included 'Esprit public' (with special attention to observance of the *décadi*); 'Instruction publique'; 'Police générale et champêtre'; 'Police des cultes'; 'Subsistances;' Hospices et bienfaisance'; 'Epidemies et epizooties'; 'Maisons d'arrêt et prisons'; 'Contributions et biens nationaux'; 'Grandes routes et chemins vicinaux'; 'Agriculture et plantations'; 'Eaux et forêts'; 'Commerce et industrie'; and 'Force Armée'. See also Desgranges, *Vienne*, pp. 17–19, and Mona Ozouf, 'Passé, présent, avenir à travers les textes administratifs de l'époque révolutionnaire', in *L'Ecole de la France: essais sur la Révolution, l'utopie, et l'enseignement*, Paris, 1984, pp. 56–61, for a good discussion of the *comptes* prepared by the departmental commissioners.

17 See, e.g., AN F^{1C} III Seine et Marne 6 *Tableau politique des commissaires du Directoire près les administrations municipales*, prairial–messidor VI; Reinhard, *Sarthe*, pp. 57–63, 161–8, 176–8; and Desgranges, *Vienne*, who concludes that for all their deficiencies 'les commissaires du Directoire furent bien supérieurs aux agents des cantons' (p. 47).

18 AN F^{1c} I 43 Bauvinay to Merlin, 3 frimaire VII.

19 W. Skinner, 'Marketing and social structure in rural China', *Journal of Asian Studies*, XXIV (1964), pp. 3–43.

20 AN AF III 104, doss. 466 petition from inhabitants of Salès to Council 500, prairial VI; also petition from Lentille to Council 500, vendémiaire VI; petition from Peyrussevieille (Gers), frimaire VII; F^{2} II Loir-et-Cher 1 petition from Mur, brumaire VI. Some of the requests dealt with by the Directorial Legislature are collected in AN AD I 61.

21 AF III 104, doss. 466 to Council 500, 24 vendémiaire VI. Also petitions from Paches and Marmont, nivôse VI.

22 AN AF III 105 Two of the most interesting cases involved rivalry between Autricourt and Belan in the Côte-d'Or, and between Perthe and Villiers in the Haute-Marne. Also the rival petitions of *Les Républicains de St Bonnet (Gard)* and *Les Citoyens de Montfrin, chef-lieu du canton*, 20–22 messidor VI.

23 AF III 105 Petition from citizens of Ufaix to Dept. Admin., pluviôse VI, and *Message du Directoire, 3 germinal VI*. AF III 104 *Conseil des Anciens: Rapport fait part Gastin, 13 fructidor VII* (on Seranon); Dept. Admin. of the Meurthe, 24 fructidor VI.

Other cases include *Council 500: Rapport par Souilhé, 6 ventôse VII* on Cabrerits (Lot); *Rapport par Benard-Lagrave, 8 floréal VII* on Oppy (Pas-de-Calais); *Rapport par Guillard, 3 prairial VII* on St Lubin (Eure-et-Loire); *Conseil des Anciens: Rapport par Simon, 23 prairial VII* on Val Fleuru (Loire), all in AN AD I 61.

24   AF III 105 Admin. Municip. de Candes, 20 floréal VI; *plan topographique*; and Dept. Admin., 17 messidor VII. AF III 105 Admin. Municip. de Gault to Council 500, 13 frimaire VII; petitions from six communes in the canton; and *Message du Directoire*, 28 thermidor VII. See also Admin. Municip. de Meuvi (Haute-Marne), 29 brumaire IV, and Dept Admin, 16 brumaire VI.

25   AF III 105 Admin. Municip. de St Just, 23 pluviôse V, and *procès-verbaux* of its session of 27 messidor VI; Admin. Municip. d'Allene, 2 germinal VII.

26   AF III 104, doss. 466 petition from inhabitants of Roussillon, 15 brumaire VI; petition from Manon (Bouches-du-Rhône), 26 frimaire VI; AF III 105: Dept. Admin. Manche, 13 prairial VII; *Les citoyens d'Eperluques* (Pas de Calais), ventôse VI (with four pages of signatures!). Also AD I 61 Council 500: *Rapport par Gourlay, 29 messidor VI* on Fressin (Pas-de-Calais).

27   E.g. AF III 105 Admin. Municip. de Frasne (Doubs), 15 pluviôse VII and other petitions against transferring the *chef-lieu* permanently to the more centrally located Dampierre. Frasne was said to be larger, to have better facilities, 'et jamais n'a formé de Vendée comme Dampierre'. The municipal administration of Bouisse (Aude), 7 ventôse VI, wanted to shift its *chef-lieu* to Lanet: 'Bouisse est située sur une des montagnes les plus élevées des Corbières, chemins presque toujours impracticables . . . il se trouve sur la ligne circulaire formée par les dites [neuf] communes du canton', whereas Lanet, with a similar population and the necessary facilities, was at the centre of the canton. But, according to the cantonal commissioner, Bouisse had a strong revolutionary past, a large meeting hall for the primary assemblies, a 'safe and sound' place for the archives, and a tax roll of 3,700 *livres* as opposed to 500 for Lanet.

28   AN F1ᵃ 50 MI to Dept Administrations, 7 frimaire VI.

29   AN AF III 104, doss. 467 *Rapport du MI au Directoire*, fructidor VI. Some of the departmental responses are collected in AN F² I 541.

30   AN AD I 61 Council 500: *Opinion de Duplantier sur le projet de réduction des Cantons, 2 frimaire VII*; *Opinion de Delbrel contre la réduction du nombre des cantons, 2 frimaire VII*; *Opinion de Vezu . . . 2 frimaire VII*. The commissioner to Arsonval (Aube), after likewise observing that reducing the number of cantons and increasing their size would only exacerbate current difficulties, made this interesting observation: 'Les avides citadins déclament adroitement contre la circonscription actuelle, et les dépenses qu'ils exagèrent, pour envahir les communes qui les entourrent et maitriser les campagnes.' (AF III 104, doss. 467 *Observations*, vendémiaire VII.)

31   *Council 500: Réponse par Bara . . . aux objections faites contre le projet . . . 3 frimaire VII; Opinion de Mourer . . . 4 frimaire VII; Opinion de Bremontier . . . 4 frimaire VII*.

32   AN F¹ᵃ 408 prefect of Côtes-du-Nord, circular to mayors, 14 messidor VIII; prefect of Dordogne, circulars to mayors, 9 prairial and 14 messidor VIII; AN F¹ᵃ 422 prefect of Haute-Marne, circular, 9 prairial VIII.

33   For indirect but persuasive arguments about the likely negative attitude of *campagnards* towards the cantons, see P. Jones, *Politics and Rural Society: the Southern Massif Central c. 1750–1880*, Cambridge, 1985, pp. 186–203 and 244–6; and J. P. Jessenne, *Pouvoir au Village et Révolution: Artois 1760–1848*, Lille, 1987, pp. 110–21.

34   See I. Woloch, 'Napoleonic conscription: state power and civil society', *Past and Present*, 111 (1986), pp. 105–9.

Table 1 *Statistics on rural communes, by department*

	Department (population)	Total no. of communes	Rural communes	Average population of rural communes
	Ain	422	388	608
Total pop	283,809			
Agglomerated	163,479			
Dispersed	120,330			
Urban	48,000			
	Aisne	848	811	410
Total pop	430,618			
Agglomerated	369,346			
Dispersed	61,272			
Urban	98,325			
	H. Alpes	184	158	492
Total pop	118,322			
Agglomerated	70,828			
Dispersed	48,511			
Urban	41,533			
	Aube	448	410	378
Total pop	241,000			
Agglomerated	212,031			
Dispersed	28,912			
Urban	88,182			
	Aveyron	568	537	439
Total pop	315,338			
Agglomerated	154,008			
Dispersed	161,330			
Urban	79,720			
	Calvados	890	858	413
Total pop	483,108			
Agglomerated	329,925			
Dispersed	153,183			
Urban	127,986			
	Corrèze	290	250	722
Total pop	243,654			
Agglomerated	78,377			
Dispersed	165,277			
Urban	63,170			
	Côte d'Or	728	694	362
Total pop	347,642			
Agglomerated	297,312			
Dispersed	50,320			
Urban	96,621			

Table 1 *Statistics on rural communes, by department* (continued)

	Department (population)	Total no. of communes	Rural communes	Average population of rural communes
	Creuse	292	271	661
Total pop	218,422			
Agglomerated	59,921			
Dispersed	158,501			
Urban	37,318			
	Dordogne	642	612	556
Total pop	410,350			
Agglomerated	135,491			
Dispersed	275,059			
Urban	68,321			
	Doubs	601	557	271
Total pop	227,048			
Agglomerated	190,707			
Dispersed	36,341			
Urban	76,155			
	Drôme	356	340	509
Total pop	234,301			
Agglomerated	162,430			
Dispersed	71,871			
Urban	61,112			
	Eure	838	800	410
Total pop	415,574			
Agglomerated	245,132			
Dispersed	170,442			
Urban	87,688			
	Eure-et-Loire	456	439	458
Total pop	259,967			
Agglomerated	131,052			
Dispersed	128,915			
Urban	58,772			
	Finistère	282	257	1381
Total pop	474,349			
Agglomerated	169,049			
Dispersed	305,300			
Urban	119,501			
	Gard	361	323	513
Total pop	309,636			
Agglomerated	243,417			
Dispersed	66,219			
Urban	143,944			

Table 1 *Statistics on rural communes, by department* (continued)

	Department (population)	Total no. of communes	Rural communes	Average population of rural communes
	Haute-Garonne	601	570	417
Total pop	368,668			
Agglomerated	270,055			
Dispersed	98,613			
Urban	131,156			
	Ille-et-Vilaine	346	319	1083
Total pop	488,605			
Agglomerated	131,927			
Dispersed	356,678			
Urban	143,089			
	Indre	271	247	580
Total pop	207,928			
Agglomerated	81,171			
Dispersed	126,757			
Urban	64,601			
	Isère	554	522	649
Total pop	440,238			
Agglomerated	266,911			
Dispersed	173,327			
Urban	101,284			
	Jura	724	711	331
Total pop	290,081			
Agglomerated	248,036			
Dispersed	42,045			
Urban	54,648			
	Loir-et-Cher	306	281	524
Total pop	211,152			
Agglomerated	113,090			
Dispersed	98,062			
Urban	63,823			
	Loire-Inférieure	204	184	1216
Total pop	365,466			
Agglomerated	181,412			
Dispersed	184,054			
Urban	141,704			
	Lot-et-Garonne	431	411	589
Total pop	327,864			
Agglomerated	121,910			
Dispersed	205,954			
Urban	85,787			

Table 1 *Statistics on rural communes, by department* (continued)

	Department (population)	Total no. of communes	Rural communes	Average population of rural communes
	Marne	694	656	310
Total pop	310,493			
Agglomerated	282,267			
Dispersed	28,226			
Urban	107,012			
	Haute-Marne	549	520	319
Total pop	226,350			
Agglomerated	209,606			
Dispersed	16,744			
Urban	60,620			
	Meurthe	713	677	347
Total pop	342,107			
Agglomerated	325,915			
Dispersed	16,192			
Urban	107,394			
	Mont-Blanc	410	394	585
Total pop	283,106			
Agglomerated	146,845			
Dispersed	136,261			
Urban	52,613			
	Moselle	930	913	312
Total pop	353,788			
Agglomerated	335,803			
Dispersed	18,745			
Urban	67,076			
	Nord	665	635	797
Total pop	774,449			
Agglomerated	683,632			
Dispersed	90,916			
Urban	268,279			
	Oise	734	683	410
Total pop	369,094			
Agglomerated	302,805			
Dispersed	66,289			
Urban	89,090			
	Orne	623	593	506
Total pop	397,931			
Agglomerated	136,526			
Dispersed	261,385			
Urban	89,697			

Table 1 *Statistics on rural communes, by department* (continued)

	Department (population)	Total no. of communes	Rural communes	Average population of rural communes
	Pas-de-Calais	927	882	478
Total pop	567,131			
Agglomerated	485,283			
Dispersed	81,848			
Urban	145,118			
	Bas-Rhin	612	572	493
Total pop	450,159			
Agglomerated	432,953			
Dispersed	17,206			
Urban	168,129			
	Haut-Rhin	698	653	418
Total pop	382,285			
Agglomerated	350,535			
Dispersed	31,652			
Urban	108,935			
	Sarthe	409	377	795
Total pop	387,166			
Agglomerated	176,572			
Dispersed	210,594			
Urban	87,532			
	Seine-Inférieure	982	950	442
Total pop	642,773			
Agglomerated	508,472			
Dispersed	134,301			
Urban	222,838			
	Deux-Sèvres	359	334	559
Total pop	242,658			
Agglomerated	102,260			
Dispersed	140,398			
Urban	55,376			
	Tarn-et-Garonne	248	221	590
Total pop	228,330			
Agglomerated	114,719			
Dispersed	113,611			
Urban	98,023			
	Vaucluse	146	128	762
Total pop	190,180			
Agglomerated	154,468			
Dispersed	35,712			
Urban	92,619			

Table 1 *Statistics on rural communes, by department* (continued)

	Department (population)	Total no. of communes	Rural communes	Average population of rural communes
	Vendéé	321	293	590
Total pop	270,271			
Agglomerated	100,611			
Dispersed	169,660			
Urban	97,000			
	Vienne	339	299	500
Total pop	250,807			
Agglomerated	104,825			
Dispersed	145,912			
Urban	100,307			
	Haute-Vienne	221	199	895
Total pop	259,795			
Agglomerated	71,566			
Dispersed	188,229			
Urban	81,590			

Town-country and the circulation of Revolutionary energy: the cases of Bonald and Michelet

Town-country is one of those convenient binary oppositions that we use when we describe the literary and intellectual movements of the first half of the nineteenth century – along with self and world, art and nature, innocence and experience, individual and society. My argument is that it is inadequate for us to view the town-country theme in post-Revolutionary French literature and thought as a manifestation of a transhistorical patterning, simply as a further illustration of an urban-rural contrast developed by writers over the centuries and which reaches back at least as far as classical antiquity. I wish to suggest that thinking about the town-country opposition became a privileged way of articulating the conflicting meanings and values which nineteenth-century France ascribed to the Revolution. To be sure, Romanticism valorised the countryside, but this was by no means a unitary process and neither was it ideologically innocent. The various representations of the town-country relation which emerged implied contrasting assessments of the impact of the Revolution on society and offered very different perspectives on the future. For the counter-revolution it was a matter of containing and controlling the negative energies of revolution; for the republicans it was a question of reviving these self-same energies so that they might once again circulate through the body of the nation. To illustrate the first tendency I have chosen to look at Louis de Bonald (1754–1840); the second tendency will be represented by Michelet (1798–1874), who made the town-country relation a structuring opposition within his own discourse on the French Revolution.

Conservative discourse on the Revolution involved a condemnation of the Revolutionary city and a countervailing valorisation of the countryside.[1] Furthermore, conservatives used a particular view of the countryside in order to define France and Frenchness in a manner which implicitly refuted the appropriation of the countryside attempted by the Jacobins of the Year II. Louis de Bonald is representative of this tendency.[2] He pointed to the city as a dangerous dissolvent of religious belief and portrayed agrarian society as manifesting order and social discipline: the countryside provided a model for the restoration of authority. A society was not a construction of the rational will of individuals but rather the manifestation of a power which both transcended and sustained the collective entity concerned. The purpose of the social world was conservation and reproduction. The Revolution, on the other hand, was understood as a catastrophic disruption of natural processes. In Bonald's writings the urban environment – and especially Paris – was associated with moral depravity, philosophical debate and the hubris of atheistic science. Paris was the city which produced the ideas which overthrew the *ancien régime*: freedom, equality and the doctrine of popular sovereignty. In the hands of Bonald, the eighteenth century's moral and social criticism of the city became explicitly political. Viewed from the traditionalist perspective, the general movement of population from countryside to city was a matter for much regret:

> La société ne gagne pas à ce changement: les habitants des villes ont *nécessairement* des habitudes républicaines, qui naissent de leur réunion habituelle et de leur vanité. Le citadin est corrompu, parce qu'il est oisif; il a de l'esprit sans jugement, et de la politesse sans vertus. L'habitant des campagnes a des principes plus monarchiques, parce qu'il est lui-même *pouvoir* et chef de son petit Etat; il sent mieux le besoin d'une autorité tutélaire, parce qu'il est plus isolé; il est vertueux, parce qu'il est occupé, et raisonnable parce qu'il est vertueux.[3]

In Bonald's judgement this movement from country to town was an important cause of national decline. It was not, however, a phenomenon of recent date but a tendency which had been present within French culture since the reign of Francis I. At that historical moment the nobility first fell pray to the temptations of urban life and deserted the countryside in favour of residence in the towns. The process continued during the seventeenth and eighteenth centuries and had serious consequences for the well-being of the nation:

> Les villes s'embellirent par le séjour des grands propriétaires, et à mesure qu'elles devenaient plus agréables, les habitations champêtres perdaient leurs charmes. La philosophie, qui peu à peu s'introduisait en Europe, eut beaucoup de part à ce changement. La religion retient l'homme dans les campagnes, en lui inspirant le goût de la retraite, l'habitude de mœurs simples, de désirs bornés, d'une vie sobre et laborieuse; le goût du plaisir, l'orgueil du bel esprit, la curiosité, toutes les passions poussent et entassent les hommes dans les villes, en leur inspirant la démangeaison de jouir, de savoir et de parler. Les nobles acquièrent de l'urbanité aux dépens de la franchise et du bon sens. Un peuple de citadins remplaça en France une nation agricole. Les arts y gagnèrent; mais la famille, l'Etat, la religion, la société enfin y perdit.[4]

Conceding nothing to the Revolution, Bonald argued that the salvation of France lay in a return to the monarchy and the Church. In the countryside he discovered examples of the positive Christian values of order and authority which he sought to promote. Bonald held to a set of beliefs about the countryside which served to validate an authoritarian theory of society based upon the ideas of dependency and submission. The patriarchal family structure provided a model and was used to legitimise a wider system of social relations. Power, within the family or within the state was '*un*, masculin, propriétaire, perpétuel'.[5] The countryman embodied virtue born of an unquestioning acceptance of tradition. He also displayed great courage in adversity – as the Vendée had demonstrated. His relationship to nature and to the succession of the seasons inclined him to resignation not rebellion. He did not inhabit the time-world of Revolutionary modernity. Moreover, agrarian society united men, whereas industrial society isolated them: 'l'on peut dire que l'agriculture qui disperse les hommes dans les campagnes, les unit sans les rapprocher; et que le commerce qui les entasse dans les villes, les rapproche sans les unir'.[6] The city stood condemned because it was emancipatory of human consciousness. Bonald proposed a vision of the countryside which was the negation of the Revolutionary city. His idealised monarchy was in essence a unified culture of deference and submission. His assertion of the value of tradition signalled the repudiation of the very notion of positive historical change conducted by individual human agency.

Revolutionary centralisation and its attendant bureaucracy were detested by Bonald. Centralisation deprived the nation of life and

destroyed that network of local loyalties and corporations which constituted the fabric of society. But distrust of Paris did not make Bonald
an unqualified supporter of provincial autonomy. Excessive localism
might eventually come to represent a challenge to the authority of the
state: *'lorsqu'une province veut être une société, l'Etat est en révolution'*.[7] The
administration of local affairs was best served by following custom and
precedent. Cities were to be administered in the national interest but in
such a manner as to ensure that they did not represent a danger. Bonald
did concede that a central administration was required in order to meet
certain national needs – the provision of communications, for example
– but he remained suspicious of administrative bodies in general,
believing that by their very nature they tended to generate a disturb-
ingly urban sense of their own role and function:

> Le caractère particulier et le défaut des administrations collectives est de
> se laisser aller au vent des nouveautés et des systèmes, et d'être le bureau
> d'adresse de tous les faiseurs de projets. Dès que les hommes sont réunis,
> ils éprouvent le besoin d'*agir* par le sentiment qu'ils ont de leurs *forces*, et
> le besoin d'agir, lorsqu'il n'y a rien à faire, n'est que le besoin de détruire
> ce qui est fait. Or, l'administration ne consiste pas à faire, mais à con-
> server.[8]

Bonald's writings do not suggest that he responded aesthetically or
emotionally to the countryside. He seemed unaffected by the pictorial
dimensions of landscape and quite lacking in rural sensibility. Neither
did he ascribe innate goodness and moral superiority to an idealised
peasantry. In country areas religion was an essential form of social
control. The town dweller had been corrupted by the notion of individual rights, by false beliefs in political and religious freedom and by the
extension of the mechanical processes of reproduction. The countryman remained largely immune to the dangers which arose from
intellectual endeavour; but this was not because he was intrinsically
superior; nor was it because he embodied a more natural goodness, a
rural authenticity evoking the myth of a lost Golden Age. Bonald
rejected the philosophers' contention that men were degraded by the
inherently artificial experience of life in society: on the contrary, man
was irrevocably a social being. By remaining faithful to the general
truths transmitted by tradition, the rural family represented the survival
of the social and power relationships which underpinned the monarchy,
and this, in Bonald's terms, corresponded to naturality. In other words,
Bonald used the countryside to promote a politics of regression which

amounted to a containing, a disciplining of the subversive energies of the Revolution. He believed that the sickness of society could be cured by recreating a community founded on the family as opposed to the individual, and this, as we have seen, led him to valorise certain aspects of the rural experience. Bonald aspired to a culture of stasis which would endure and reproduce itself. His ideal was the rural commune – but in the form in which it had existed prior to the development of the absolute monarchy. He was not so naive as to propose a return to the countryside as a guarantee of social equilibrium. He urged a more general revival of the old values of faith and authority. The countryside was less a pivotal or organising myth and more one element in a wider politico-religious synthesis and belief system.

The second aspect of the town-country relation which I want to examine concerns the attitude of Michelet as expressed in his *Histoire de la Révolution française* (1847–53). I shall also refer to *Le Peuple* (1846), which is close in mood and content to the early volumes of the history of the Revolution.[9] In these works the town-country opposition functions as a structuring motif and is inscribed directly within national history. Michelet remained faithful to the idea of the town as intellectual and revolutionary centre (especially Paris), but at the same time he set out to reclaim the peasantry as a potentially revolutionary force. In so doing, he offered a radically different reading of the relation between the urban and the rural from that proposed by Bonald. However, Michelet did not simply reverse Bonald's polarities and ascribe value to the urban as opposed to the rural, to the dynamic energies of free thought as opposed to the unselfconscious continuities of rural life. Michelet needed to demonstrate that the countryside, too, was striving for the ideas of the Revolution. Freedom and equality were, after all, universal. Thus, while Michelet was happy to contrast the light and wisdom projected by the ideas of the *philosophes* – perceived as originating in urban culture – with the darkness of the *bocage* of the Vendée, he had to find a way of transcending this constraining opposition. His text suggests – the very real resistance of obscurantist catholic royalism notwithstanding – that the gulf between town and country was, in fact, bridgeable, at least temporarily; the two could be brought together in a world of shared revolutionary experience. My concern, therefore, lies with how in Michelet's work the terms town and country were redefined in a non-oppositional mode; how the historian's view of Revolutionary France as a dynamic unity in constant process of self-transformation allowed him implicitly to challenge the received categories of the urban and the rural.

In his history of the Revolution Michelet began very deliberately by attacking the monarchy as the enemy of the countryside. The *ancien régime* neglected the land and ignored rural poverty. The spirit of 1789, on the other hand, signalled the inception of a new relation between town and country. We see an early instance of this in Michelet's treatment of the elections to the Estates General. We are told that urban and rural areas alike benefited from a new spirit of equality. Town and country began to emerge from their mutual estrangement: '*Toutes les villes* élurent, et non pas seulement les *bonnes* villes, comme aux anciens états; *les campagnes* élurent, et non pas seulement les villes' (*Histoire de la Révolution française* [*RF*] I, p. 95). In the summer of 1789, at the time of the Great Fear, the bonds between town and country increased further: 'Dans l'été de 1789, dans la terreur des *brigands*, les habitations dispersées, les hameaux même s'effraient de leur isolement: hameaux et hameaux s'unissent, villages et villages, la ville même avec la campagne. Confédération, mutuel secours, amitié fraternelle, fraternité, voilà l'idée, le titre de ces pactes. Peu, très peu, sont écrits encore' (*RF*, I, p. 264). This new spirit of national unity took its highest form in the federations. Here the Revolution was raised to quasi-religious status. Regional diversity remained but was subsumed into something much greater, the collective life of the *patrie*. In 1790 provincial loyalties gave way and were replaced by the sense of belonging to a national community whose members were defined as 'les fils de la grande mère, de celle qui doit, dans l'égalité, enfanter les nations' (*RF*, I, p. 324). In a famous passage, Michelet likened the movement of the federations to a *farandole* moving through France. The image is indeed memorable and we should attend to its implications. It allowed diversity to be reconciled in an unfolding unity. Michelet contrasted the federations, on the one hand, with localism and federalism, on the other: 'Nulle trace dans tout cela [the federations] de l'esprit d'exclusion, d'isolement local, qu'on désigna plus tard sous le nom de fédéralisme. Ici, tout au contraire, c'est une conjuration pour l'unité de la France' (*RF*, I, p. 267). The federations brought together urban and rural France in a spirit of unity and fraternity. In this climate the attachment which the countryside still felt for the past could be overcome:

Ces fédérations de provinces regardent toutes vers le centre, toutes invoquent l'Assemblée nationale, se rattachent à elle, se donnent à elle, c'est-à-dire l'unité. Toutes remercient Paris de son appel fraternel. Telle ville lui demande secours. Telle veut être affiliée à sa garde nationale [. . .] sous la menace des états, des parlements, du clergé, les campagnes étant douteuses, tout le salut de la France semblait placé dans une ligue étroite des villes. Grâce à Dieu, les grandes fédérations résolurent mieux la difficulté. Elles entraînèrent, avec les villes, un nombre immense des habitants des campagnes. On l'a vu pour le Dauphiné, le Vivarais, le Languedoc. [*RF*, I, p. 267]

Federalism weakened the sinews of the Revolution and threatened the unity of the nation. The federations were quite different. They served the cause of genuine unity and collective self-consciousness by joining the countryside with the city, by linking the periphery with the centre. This was not to deny the indispensable role played by the city, and by the capital in particular. But what was Paris if not a concentration of French rural and provincial diversity? Paris, charged with the symbolism of the storming of the Bastille, remained the source of Revolutionary energy and the origin of the new ideas which had to be communicated to those country areas where royalism and catholicism remained influential. However, Michelet was careful not to leave all initiative with Paris. France was both town and country; both were necessary. What mattered was the new spirit of national unity, a spirit quite at odds with the mere semblance of unity offered by either royalism or federalism. Revolutionary unity valorised the centre but sought constantly to relate it to countryside. Michelet expressed this through an analogy with electricity:

La grande ville est le point électrique où tous viennent sans cesse reprendre l'étincelle, s'électriser et s'aimanter. La France doit passer là, y repasser sans cesse; et chaque fois qu'elle sort de cet heureux contact, loin de changer, elle devient elle-même de plus en plus, entre dans la vérité complète de sa nature, devient plus France encore. [*RF*, II, p. 46]

Revolutionary energy circulated through the body of France, urban and rural, but that energy was above all relayed and transformed by Paris. This was a continuous process of transformation which could be reconciled with the extremes of neither centralism nor federalism: 'Ni Robespierre ni la Gironde n'eurent le moindre sens de Paris, ne comprirent la valeur de ce creuset profond de chimie sociale où tout, hommes et idées, a sa transformation' (*RF*, II, p. 355).

However, the Revolution meant much more than the reversal of the neglect of agriculture which had characterised the *ancien régime*.

Revolutionary geography was designed to unite Frenchmen and remove the obstacles which divided them. The Revolution redefined administratively the town-country relation. At the same time it transformed the countryside through the sale of church lands to the peasantry. In Michelet's terms, this signalled that nature was emancipated along with mankind: 'La liberté n'est pas seulement la vie de l'homme, c'est celle de la nature' (RF, I, p. 73). This theme was developed in the famous opening section of Le Peuple, which was a paean of praise for the peasant who purchased his smallholding in the wake of 1789 and whose love of his land was at one with his love of France. This shift in ownership was perhaps the greatest and most durable legacy of the Revolution. The Revolution not only transformed the status of the peasantry; it established a new relation between man and nature. As a consequence of the Revolution, the land became fertile once more. In Michelet's terms, it was literally loved by its new peasant owner: '[La terre] rapporte parce qu'elle est aimée. [. . .] Le Français a épousé la France' (Le Peuple [P], p. 80). The significance of this change cannot be overestimated: 'Ce mariage de la terre et de l'homme qui cultivait la terre fut le capital de la Révolution' (RF, II, 32). The acquisition of land by the peasantry located the Revolution in the deeper continuity of the life of nature. The Revolution needed the duration of the countryside as well as the movement of the city:

> Ralentie plusieurs fois, elle [la révolution] reprend toujours, continue son mouvement. C'est qu'elle ne s'assit pas seulement sur le sol mobile des villes, qui monte et qui baisse, qui bâtit et démolit. Elle s'engagea dans la terre et dans l'homme de la terre. Là est la France durable, moins brillante et moins inquiète, mais solide, la France en soi. Nous changeons, elle ne change pas. [. . .] Cette France, dans cent ans, dans mille ans, sera toujours entière et forte; elle ira, comme aujourd'hui, songeant et labourant sa terre, lorsque depuis longtemps nous autres, population éphémère des villes, nous aurons enfoui dans l'oubli nos systèmes et nos ossements. [RF, I, p. 596]

We need to take Michelet's attitude to the relationship between man and nature very seriously for it informs the manner in which the town-country contrast operates in his text. Michelet associated nature and the countryside with the female principle.[10] In a footnote to Le Peuple, he remarked that for the Doric peoples 'la patrie' was, in fact, 'la matrie'. The historian clearly responded to the idea of the nation as female presence: 'non seulement elle nous allaite, mais nous contient en soi: In eâ movemur et sumus' (P, p. 219). A nation had its history and its traditions but it was also located in a particular environment. Michelet did not view the natural simply as resistance to the human. He represented the relationship between man and a feminised figuration of nature as dynamic and creative. '[L]'homme fait la terre', man created his environment by transforming nature (*P*, p. 84). The peasant constructed the countryside: 'il [le paysan] l'avait faite, cette terre, l'avait créée; sans lui, elle n'existait pas; c'était la lande aride, le roc et le caillou' (*RF*, II, p. 12). Michelet suggests that man is in a sense spiritualising nature by inserting it into a Revolutionary-national as opposed to a feudal-catholic order of things. The nation inscribed itself into its physical space. The peasant's attitude to the land involved not a conquering subject-object relationship, but a love-relation encompassing respect and obligation: 'il l'aime comme une personne' (*P*, p. 84). The Revolution transformed the countryside by giving the peasant property rights and by making him a soldier-citizen; it also restored the bond between the human and the natural.

For Michelet, Revolutionary freedom was the ground of collective purpose not atomistic individualism. Henceforth, Frenchmen belonged to a meaningful community; urban and rural citizens retained their identities, their distinct personalities, but ceased to live in isolation because they were participating actively in the life of the nation. They also ceased to be estranged from their natural environment. France was a religion and the countryside was the temple of the new faith: 'Un seul dôme, des Vosges aux Cévennes, et des Pyrénées aux Alpes' (*RF*, I, p. 331). Nature and man were united in a new synthesis: 'L'identité de l'homme et de la terre, ce mystère redoutable, s'accomplissant en France, faisait de cette terre une terre sacrée, inattaquable; qui l'aurait violée était sûr d'en mourir' (*RF*, II, p. 33). Or again: '[L'homme] aperçut la nature, il la ressaisit, et il la retrouva sacrée, il y sentit Dieu encore' (*RF*, I, p. 331). The Revolution, in the shape of Paris, effected a marriage of man and nature, of France with itself, a marriage which was also a union of town and country. In this context, Michelet associated the people of the countryside with the female principle and the people of the town with the male principle. The town came to represent the law, progress, the father, whereas the countryside carried a different set of meanings: nature, femininity, respect for the values of the city.[11] According to Michelet, woman was man's intellectual inferior but he was beholden to love and educate her. A similar relation obtained between town and country, between urban and rural France. The federations corresponded to a timeless moment when differences of class, age, sex and region were transcended. In the Revolution, and especially the period from 1789 to 1791, the French nation, fired with energy and ideals, seemingly realised the goal of unity, the dream of social oneness.

However, the moment of communion was transitory and the experience of fusion was fragile. What appealed to Michelet was a movement which he felt he could portray as overwhelmingly authentic and spontaneous, a movement whose strength lay in the unity of town, country and region. At that privileged moment national cohesion was such that violence did not result: 'Les grands faits nationaux, où la *France* a agi d'ensemble, se sont accomplis par des forces immenses, invincibles, et par cela même nullement violentes' (*RF*, I, p. 318). And yet, at the very moment when unity was achieved at the Champ de Mars, there commenced a falling away from the ideal, a fall into division and conflict, time and death. How secure after all was the unity of town and country? At first, the countryside seemed to be won over to the cause of the Revolution. In July 1790 'presque partout le paysan suivait, autant que les populations urbaines, l'élan de la Révolution' (*RF*, I, p. 345). Even those Michelet described as 'nos sauvages paysans du Maine et des Marches de Bretagne' appeared to have been converted (*RF*, I, p. 344). However, the countryside remained vulnerable to the propaganda of those reactionary forces which presented themselves as the guardians of the values of the past. Soon the negative energies of rural France were mobilised and the countryside was in revolt against the city. National unity was lost: 'On put, d'après 92, prévoir 93. Il n'était que trop sûr que les villes, petites et faiblement peuplées dans ce pays [la Vendée], ne pourraient, quelle que fût leur énergie, contenir les campagnes' (*RF*, II, p. 28). The countryside came under the influence of the Church and rebelled against the legitimate authority of the city. Henceforth, the energy of the countryside took the form of a fanatical resistance to the Revolution. At the same time, the city fell into the hands of the bourgeoisie and the spirit of the federations was replaced by that of Marat. The vital link which the Revolution had forged between town and country was broken.

In post-Revolutionary France the basic concepts of town and country retained their traditional meanings and associations but ceased to be self-contained. Bonald enlisted a certain idea of the countryside in order to endorse a vision of social stasis. By so doing, he hoped to contain the dangerous revolutionary forces which had their source in urban reality. Michelet, on the other hand, writing from the standpoint of a critic on the Left, sought to aid the cause of national unity and revive the republican cause by bringing town and country together within a totalising interpretation of the Revolution and its history. The concepts of town and country could thus be aligned so as to express contrasting sets of values while remaining grounded in a common reality. However, while the town-country opposition did not have a fixed signification, the meanings attributed to it inevitably implied the fact of the Revolution.

Notes

1   See J. Godechot, *The Counter-Revolution. Doctrine and Action 1789–1804*, London, 1972; F. Baldensperger, *Le Mouvement des Idées dans l'émigration française (1789–1815)*, 2 vols, Paris, 1924.

2   On Bonald, see H. Moulinié, *De Bonald*, Paris, 1916; L. Barclay, 'Louis de Bonald, prophet of the past?', *Studies on Voltaire and the Eighteenth Century*, LV (1967), Geneva, Institut Voltaire, pp. 167–204; A. Koyré, 'Louis de Bonald', *Journal of the History of Ideas*, VII (1946), pp. 56–71; R. A. Nisbet, 'De Bonald and the concept of the social group', *Journal of the History of Ideas*, V (1944), pp. 315–31; W. Jay Reedy, 'Language, counter-revolution and the "two cultures": Bonald's traditionalist scientism', *Journal of the History of Ideas*, XLIV (1983), pp. 579–97.

3   *Théorie de l'éducation sociale et de l'administration publique*, *Œuvres*, II, Paris, 1854, p. 442.

4   *Traité du ministère public*, *Œuvres*, VI, Paris, 1854, p. 309.

5   *Législation primitive considérée dans les derniers temps par les seules lumières de la raison*, *Œuvres*, VI, Paris, 1854, p. 171.

6   *De la famille agricole, de la famille industrielle et du droit d'aînesse*, Paris, 1826, p. 5.

7   *Théorie de l'éducation sociale*, p. 445.

8   *Ibid.*, p. 450.

9   See the essential study by P. Viallaneix, *La Voie royale. Essai sur l'idée de peuple dans l'œuvre de Michelet*, Paris, 1959, revised ed., 1971. For surveys of Michelet's thought see J.-L. Cornuz, *Jules Michelet. Un Aspect de la pensée religieuse au XIXe siècle*, Geneva, 1955; O. A. Haac, *Jules Michelet*, Boston, 1982; J. Gaulmier, *Michelet*, Paris, 1968; S. A. Kippur, *Jules Michelet. A Study of Mind and Sensibility*, Albany, NY, 1981. References cited in the body of the text are to *Histoire de la Revolution française*, 2 vols, Paris, 1979; and *Le Peuple*, edited by P. Viallaneix, Paris, 1974.

10   For an examination of Michelet's thematics and rhetoric, see R. Barthes, *Michelet par lui-même*, Paris, 1954;. L. Gossman, 'The go-between: Jules Michelet, 1798–1874', *Modern Language Notes*, LXXXIX (1974), pp. 503–41; G. Poulet, 'Michelet et le moment d'Eros', *Nouvelle revue française*, CLXXVIII (1967), pp. 610–35.

11   See T. Moreau, *Le Sang de l'histoire. Michelet, l'histoire et l'idée de la femme au XIXe siècle*, Paris, 1982, p. 206. See also J. Calo, *La Création de la Femme chez Michelet*, Paris, 1975.

Index